DHANURVEDA

(The Vedic Military Science)

by

Dr. Ravi Prakash Arya

AMAZON BOOKS, USA

In Association with

INDIAN FOUNDATION FOR VEDIC SCIENCE

H.O.1051, Sector-1, Rohtak, Haryana, India Ph. 01262-292580

Delhi Contact Ph. Nos.: 09313033917; 09650183260

Emails: vedicscience@rediffmail.com; vedicscience@hotmail.com

Website: www.vedicscience.net

Second Edition

Kali era: 5116 (c. 2014)
Kalpa era: 1,97,29,49,116
Brahma era: 15,50,21,97,9,49,116

ISBN No. 81-87710-82-9

Foundation's Publications

1. *New Discoveries About Vedic Sarasvati*
2. *Dhanurveda: The Vedic Military Science*
3. *Vedic Concordance (Four Vols.)*
4. *Vedic and Classical Sanskrit - A Contrastive Analysis of Phonological and Morphological Features*
5. *Vedic Meteorology: The Ancient Indian Science of Rainmaking*
6. *Vedic Theory of Origin of Speech*
7. *Researches into Vedic and Linguistic Studies.*
8. *Bhāratīya Kālagaṇanā Kā Vaijñānika evaṁ Vaiśvika Svarūpa*
9. *Jesus, the Christ was a Hindu*
10. *History and Origin of Mathematics*
11. *Indian Origin of Greece and Ancient world*
12. *India the Civiliser of the World*
13. *Yuga yugin Trigarta (Trigarta through Ages)*
14. *Vedic Microbiology*
15. *Revisiting the Roots of Judeo-Christianity*
16. *Tributes to Renaissance Rishi*
17. *Rishi Dayananda in the Eyes of the West*
18. *Yogavāsiṭha Mahārāmāyaṇa,* edited with English translation: 8 vols.
19. *Vālmīki Rāmāyaṇa,* edited with English Translation: 4 vols.
20. *Ṛgveda,* edited with English Translation: 4 vols.
21. *Sāmaveda*, edited with English Translation
22. *Yajurveda*, edited with English Translation
23. *Nature of Vedic Science and Technology*
24. *Science of Vedic Meters and Musical notes*
25. *Science and Technology in Mahabharata*
26. *Reviving the Age-old Historical Tradition of India*
27. *Vedic Farming*
28. *Psychology in Yoga Darshan*
29. *Rainmaking With the help of Yajna*
30. *Stepping into the 52nd Century*
31. *Weather Forecast in Vedic Times*
32. *Sanskrit the Original Source of English*
33. *An Introduction to Bhāratīya Kālagaṇanā*
34. *Somayāga: Vedic Process of Rainformation*
35. *Agniṣomīya Paśuyāga: Vedic Operation for Rainmaking.*
36. *Concordance of Vedic Mantras as per Ṛṣis and Devatās.* (Two vols.)
37. *Concordance of Vedic Mantras as per Devatas and Risis.* (Two vols.)
38. *Vedic Concordance* of a quarter part of a mantra (The revised,

redited, and updated Devanāgarī version of Bloomfield's Vedic Concordance) 4 Vols

39. ***Concordance of Vedic Rishis and Devatas***
40. ***Concordance of Vedic Devatā and Ṛṣis***
41. ***Indian Chronology to Indian History***
42. ***7000 years old Calendar of various Indian Eras***
43. ***7000 years' Calendar of Lunar Phases (8 Vols)***
44. ***Śrimad Bhagvad Gītā: A Vedic Scientific Scripture of Liberation***
45. ***Bible in India: Indian Origin of Hebrew and Christian Revelations***
46. ***Introduction to the Vedas***
47. ***The Ṛgveda Saṁhitā: A Spiritual, Scientific and Socio-political Commentary. Vol. 1***
48. ***Signatures of Time: A Collection of 231 Letters of Swami Dayanand Sarasvati writtn in 19th Century India***
49. **Vedika Svāsthya Vijñāna**
50. **Indic Studies and Western Hermeuneutics**
51. **Lost Scientific Literature of Bharat**
52. **Incredible India**
53. **Vedic Prayers: Vedic Yajña Vidhi**
54. **Divinizing of A Human being: Means and Methods According to Yogavāsiṣṭha**
55. **Satyarth Prakash : True Face of Hinduism and An Agenda for Reformation of World Religions**
56. **Energy in the Vedas**
57. **Contrastive Study into Phonology of Vedic and Classical Sanskrit**
58. **Vedic Value System: A Key to Modern World Crisis**
59. **Life and Culture in Ancient Indian Aśramas and Hermmitages**
60. **Origin and Development of Calendars in the World**
61. **Jesus Christ: A Misnomer of Lord Krishna of India**
62. **Psychological Concepts and Psychotherapy in Yoga Darśana**
63. **India The Cradle of Wolrd Civilizations**
64. **Swami Dayanand Sarasvati as Viewed by the West**

Vedic Science

A Quarterly Journal of Indian Foundation for Vedic Science dedicated to the Vedic Sciences and Scientific Interpretation of Vedas and Allied Literature

World Vedic Calendar

World Vedic Calendar is a *Sāyaṇa Pañcāṅga* (updated according to precession). First time in the history of Indian calendars the details of Vedic solar months and lunar months have been given. This calendar cites Indian Festivals as astronomical according to Sāyaṇa Pañcāṅga and as historical according to *Niryaṇa Pañcānga.*

Abbreviations

AV.	*Atharvaveda*
Go.Br.	*Gopatha Brāhmaṇa*
JB.	*Jaiminiya Brāhmaṇa*
JD	*Jāmadagnya Dhanurveda*
Kau. Br.	*Kauṣitaki Brāhmaṇa*
Kāt. S	*Kāṭhaka Saṁhitā*
Kāṇ. Ś. Br.	*Kāṇva Śatapatha Brāhmaṇa*
KPS.	*Kapiṣṭhala Saṁhitā*
K.S.	*Kaṭha Saṁhitā*
M.S.	*Maitrāyaṇī Saṁhitā*
Nir.	*Nirukta*
RV.	*Ṛgveda*
Ś.Br.	*Śatapatha Brāhmaṇa*
SD.	*Sadāśiva Dhanurveda*
SV.	*Sāmaveda*
TĀ.	*Taittirīya Saṁhitā*
TU.	*Taittirīya Upaniṣad*
Tāṇ. Br.	*Tāṇḍya Brāhmaṇa*
TB.	*Taittirīya Brāhmaṇa*
TS.	*Taittirīya Saṁhitā*
VD	Vāsiṣṭha Dhanurveda
VS.	*Vājasaneyī Saṁhitā*

Contents

Introduction	13
Defence Planning	18
General National Service	19
War Tactics	20
War when to be Fought	21
Constitution of Defence forces	23
Armed Force	23
Air Force	24
Naval force	25
Selection of Defence personnel	27
Qualifications of a Commander	27
Qualifications of a Warrior	28
Special Honour for Brave Warriors	29
Military Training	32
Periods Suitable for Military Training:	32
Classification of Preceptors (Trainers)	32
The Method of imparting training	33
Military Arrays	34
Divisions of Fighting	48
Equipment for the Army	49
Classification of weapons	51
Mantra Mukta (Mantra operated weapons)	53
Yantra Mukta (Machine operated weapons)	62
Hasta Mukta (Manually operated weapons)	79

Difference between Training weapons and service weapons 82

Text of Sadāśiva Dhanurveda 84

Selection for Military Training 85

Types of Fighting 85

Classification of Preceptors (Trainers) 86

Shooting Techniques 88

The Type and Size of a Bow 89

Prohibited Bows 91

The characteristics of a bowstring 93

The characteristics of Arrowheads 94

Arrowhead Types 94

Functions of various Arrowheads 96

The Feathers of Arrows 97

Types of Arrows 97

The Methods of Tempering Arrow-heads 98

Types of Rounds 100

Shooter's Standing Positions, Grips, and Modes of Shooting 100

Grips or Position of Release 107

Methods of Drawing the Bow 109

Drawing of the Bowstring 111

Types of Targets 114

Aiming or Shooting of Rounds 117

Intermissions (*Anādhyaya*) in shooting 119

Shooting Practice 120

Breath control in shooting 121

Perfect Shooting 122
Fast Shooting 123
Rules for various Shooting Ranges 123
Movement of Arrows 124
Missed Targets or Deflection of arrows 125
The Successful Targets or Correct Trajectory of Arrows 126
Characteristic of the Best Warrior 127
Four tough targets 127
Citravidhi (Technical Fight/Camouflaging) 128
Classification of Shooter/Archers 129
Hitting the Moving Targets 130
Shoot at Sound 130
Military Exercise 131
Medication 133
Count of Akṣauhiṇī Army 135
Battle Formations 137
War Ethics 140
Signs of Victory 140
Text of Vasiṣṭha's Dhanurveda 142
(Rights of teaching and learning Dhanurveda) 143
Selection for Military Training 144
Types of Fighting 144
Classification of Preceptors (Trainers) 145
Shooting Techniques 147
The Type and Size of a Bow 148
Prohibited Bows 149

The Material for Bow-making	151
The characteristics of a bowstring	152
Qualities of Arrow	153
The Feathers of Arrows	154
Types of Arrows	155
Arrowhead Types	156
Functions of Various Arrow- heads	157
The Methods of Tempering of Arrow-heads	159
Types of rounds	160
Shooter's Positions, Grips and Modes of Shooting	161
Grips or Position of Release	166
Methods of Drawing the Bow	168
Drawing of the Bowstring	170
Types of Targets	173
Target Practice	175
Aiming or Shooting of Rounds	176
Intermissions in shooting	178
Shooting Practice	179
Breath control in shooting	180
Perfect Shooting	181
Fast Shooting	182
Rules for various Shooting Ranges	183
Movement of Arrows	183
Missed Targets or Deflection of arrows	184
The Successful Targets or Correct Trajectory of Arrows	185
Characteristic of the Best Warrior	186

Four tough Targets 186
Citravidhi (Technical Fight/Coumuflage War) 188
Classification of Shooter/Archer 188
Hitting the Moving Targets 189
Method of Shooting 190
Shooting at Sound 191
Military Exercise 192
Missiles 193
Māntrika Operation of Missiles 194
Pāśupatāstra 196
Medication 198
Battle Formations 200
War Ethics 201
Symptoms of Victory 202
Military Arrays 203
Staff Array 203
Ant Array 204
Commandments to the Army 205
Infantry 205
Training of Horses 208
Training of Elephants 208
Chariots 208
Selection of Commander in Chief 209
Training and Education 209
The Ethics of the War 210
Select Bibliography 211

Introduction

War, as an art as well as science, was equally well understood in ancient India. The nation which overran nearly the whole of the habitable globe and produced Rāma, Kṛṣṇa, Arjuna, Sagar and Bali could scarcely be considered less advanced in her proficiency in military science.

Dhanurveda, the standard work on Vedic military science being lost, the dissertations on the science found in the *Mahābhārata*, the *Agni Purāṇa*, *Ākāśa Bhairava Tantra, Kauṭalya Arthaśāstra, Manusmṛti, Matsya Purāṇa, Mahābhārata, Mānasollāsa, Yukti Kalpa Taru, Viṣṇudharmottara Purāṇa, Vīramitrodaya, Samarāṅgaṇa Sūtradhāra, Śukranīti,* and other small works on *Dhanurveda* like *Auśanas Dhanurveda, Vāsiṣṭ ha Dhanurveda, Sadāśiva Dhanurveda* and *Nīti Prakāśikā* are the only source of information on the subject left to us. Dr. Sir W. Hunter says, "There was no want of a theory of regular movements and arrangements for the march, array, encampments, and supply of troops. They are all repeatedly described in the *Mahābhārata.*"[1]

Mr. Ward says, "The Hindu did not permit even the military art to remain unexamined. It is very certain that the Hindu kings led their armies to the combat, and that they were prepared for this important employment by a military education; nor is it less certain that many of these monarchs were distinguished for the highest valour and military skill."[2]

When a nation is well protected through arms only

---

[1] *Indian Gazetteer*, 'India' p. 223

[2] See the *Theosophist* for March 1881, p. 124

then can all forms of knowledge and science flourish. During the period when the Muslims ruled, dominated India, knowledge and education ceased to flourish in the North. Nalanda, like many others, was one of the most renowned places of education, which was destroyed by the Muslim invaders. The effects are felt to this day. The South is ahead of the North in terms of dance, music, culture, educational institutions and is at the forefront of India's knowledge-based industries, Information Technology and Biotechnology.

For the defence of a country, there are abundant references in the Vedas, to maintain a regular armed force. It is also enjoined therein, that the immediate control of this defence force should be under the command of a chief, who has been described by various names, like Rudra (*AV.* 4.30.5) Arbudi and Nyarbudi etc. (See Sukta 9 of *Atharvaveda*). In respect of policy matter, relating to defence, a committee of experts, known as (*Samiti / Sabhā / Surā* (*AV.* 15.8.9; 4.30.2; and *RV.* 10.125.3) is constituted. These committees are appointed by the King (*Ṛgveda,* 10.125). This whole hymn deals with advisory bodies. The king has essentially to keep three advisory bodies, for properly governing the country. One of the three Councils is to advise the king on matters of defence. (*RV.* 3.38.6)

Dhanurveda deals with the science of warfare or military science. It is considered to be an *Upaveda* or sub-branch of *Yajurveda* by learning which one can be proficient in fighting, in the use of arms, weapons, missiles, in the application of battle arrays and formations. *Śukranīti*[1] (4.278), *Kodaṇḍamaṇḍana*[2] (1.3) and *Nītiprakāśikā*[3] (p.5), Swami Madhusūdana

---

[1] युद्धशास्त्रास्त्रकुशलोरचनााकुशलो भवेत् ।यजुर्वेदोपवेदोऽयं धनुर्वेदस्तु येन च ।।

[2] यजुर्वेदोपवेदोऽयं धनुर्वेदो निगद्यते ।।

(*Prasthānabheda*, p.7)[1] accepts *Dhanurveda* as the sub-branch of *Yajurveda*. However, *Dhanurveda* taught by Vasiṣṭha[2] considers it as the sub-branch of both the *Yajurveda* and *Atharvaveda*. Generally, it is thought that *Dhanurveda* deals with the science of bows and arrows, but this is the wrong concept. All types of fighting weapons and fighting techniques are the subject matter of *Dhanurveda*. *Dhanurveda* describes different types of weapons and missiles, the process of manufacturing and procuring them, different steps in the practice of their training and application, adoption of witchcraft for winning the battle, application of herbs, charms as a preventive measure in the war, the formation of *vyūhas* (arrays), duties of kings and army commanders, training of elephants and heroes.

Presently we find a number of works on *Dhanurveda*, published and unpublished so far. For example, *Dhanurveda* of Vasiṣṭha, *Dhanurveda* of Viśvāmitra (mss. belongs to Tirupati Library No. 7493b), *Dhanurveda* of Jamadagni, *Dhanurveda* of Auśanaśa, *Dhanurveda* of Vaiśampāyana- all unpublished. *Vīracintāmaṇi* of Sāraṅgadhara (printed in *Sāraṅgadhara paddhati*). *Dhanurveda* attributed to Sadāśiva belongs to Darbar Library Nepal mss. no. 557), *Dhanurveda Prakarṇam* (Vīreśvarīyam) of Vikramāditya available in manuscript form in Darbar Library of Nepal vide mss. no. 2 (82). *Kodaṇḍamaṇḍana* available in manuscript form in the Bombay Branch of Royal Asiatic Society. *Kodaṇḍaśāstra* of Dilīpabhūbhṛta can be located in mss.

---

3 यजुर्वेदस्योपवेदो धनुर्वेद उदाहृतः। ऋचोपवेदः आयुः स्यात्। साम्नो गान्धर्व उच्यते।
अथर्वणस्य भरतमिति वेदोपवेदकाः। खड्गविद्यादिकं यत्तु यजुर्वेदांग हि तत्।।

1 तथाहि ऋग्वेदो यजुर्वेदः सामवेदोऽथर्ववेद इति वेदाश्चत्वारः।
अर्थवेद चतुष्ट्यस्य क्रमेण चत्वार उपवेदाः।। (प्रस्थानभेद, पृ. 7)

2 गो–ब्राह्मण–साधु–वेदसंरक्षणाय च यजुर्वेदाथर्वसम्मितां संहिताम्।

form to Deccan College Research Institute's collection and Oriental Library Baroda. *Dhanurvidyādipīkā*, *Dhanurvidyārambha Prayoga*, *Dhanurveda Cintāmaṇi* of Narsiṅha Bahṭṭa, *Iśānasaṅhitā*, *Kodaṇḍa-caturbhuja*, *Sāra-saṅgraha*, *Saṅgrāma-vidhi* - all these are available in Darbar Library Nepal. These all treatises on *Dhanurveda* are too small to represent the actual *Dhanurveda*. In addition to the above treatises, some other works on *Dhanurveda* have also been referred to here and there, but their existence is not known. For example, Swami Dayananda Sarasvati[1] makes a mention of *Dhanurveda* of Aṅgirā. Similarly, Ācārya Dviendranātha Śāstri mentions '*Dhanuṣ-pradīpikā*' attributed to Droṇācārya which contained 7000 *ślokas*. *Dhanuṣcandrodaya* attributed to Paraśurāma is said to have contained 60,000 thousand *ślokas*.

According to *Nītiprakāśikā* (1.20-28) of Vaiśampāyana, Brahmā was the first propagator of *Dhanurveda* who taught *Dhanurveda* consisting of 1,00,000 *ślokas* to Pṛthu son of Vena. The same was abbreviated into 50,000 *ślokas* by Rudra which was further abbreviated into 12000 *ślokas* by Indra and 6000 and 3000 *ślokas* by Precatas and Bṛhaspati respectively. Śukrācārya abridged the same further into 1000 *ślokas*, Bharadvāja into 700, Gaiśira into 500 and Vedavyāsa into 300. Vaiśampāyana abridged it into 8 chapters.

In addition to the above history of origin and development of *Dhanurveda* or Military science in ancient India, we come across several traditions of *Dhanurveda*. According to *Vīracintāmaṇi*, (p.2) *Dhanurveda* taught by Brahmā, Rudra, Prajāpati and Viśvāmitra was learnt by Paraśurāma, Droṇa and

---

1 *Satyarth Prakash* : 3rd *Samullāsa*;
Sanskāra Vidhi : *Vedārambha Sanskāra*

Bhiṣma.

There were round six to seven traditions of *Dhanurveda* in ancient India. *Tāntrika* fighting has been described in *Vāsiṣṭha Dhanurveda*, missile fighting has been described in detail in *Jāmadgeya Dhanurveda* (authored by Paraśurāma of Jamadgni). The revival of deads has been dealt with in detail by Śukrācārya in the *Dhanurveda* of Ūśanā. Electric weapons were discovered by Maharṣi Bhārdvāja. Different types of weapons have been described by Vaiśampāyana.

The present work takes into account all the data available to the present author in fragment form or manuscript form or the published form of various treatises of *Dhanurveda*, so that a factual and actual picture of military science or the science of warfare in ancient India may be drawn for the modern-day readers and researchers.

Here it may not be odd to mention that the entire *Dhanurveda* has been divided into four sections:

1. The first section is known as '*Dikṣā*'. It deals with instructions on all principles.
2. The second section is called '*Saṅgraha*'. It deals with the rules for procuring of weapons.
3. The third section is known as '*Siddhaprayoga*'. It described how to hit the targets.
4. The fourth section is known as '*Prayogavidhi*'. It talks about the techniques of operating various weapons.

Defence Planning

Vedic scholars were well aware that 'armies can signify little unless there is a council or a wise management at home'. The efficiency of an army is thus very much dependent on the efficiency of the ministry of defence. There should be defence planners. No war is to be declared without the consent and clear directive of the Ministry of Defence. In ancient India, the defence was clearly divided into fighters and planners very much like operations and strategy. Today things are different, however. The Armed Forces consist of fighters and planners supplemented recently with the National Security Advisory Board. At the Present-day it seems, that the Ministry of Defence in India plays mainly a supervisory role, one of controlling the armed forces, as the purpose, and to play supercop. Today in India, bureaucrat's run the ministry, not military planners. This was not the case in ancient India.

(*AV.* 7.12.2) recommends the formation of an advisory Samiti that could chalk out the plan and decide the strategy to fight out the war. The members of such a *Samiti* are called Nariṣṭa (whose orders are bound to be obeyed). People shall obey their orders. All the members of this council have to work collectively.

In *AV.* (4.30.5) Rudra refers to the commander-in-chief and *Samiti* issues instructions to him to fight out the enemy who is out to disturb peace in the country.

General National Service

The Vedas support the idea of General National Service, as envisaged in the Indian constitution (Part IV-A). The security of a country is the responsibility of every citizen. He must give a few years of his life for service to the Nation. In the Vedic age, brahmacharis (Scholars) were given military training in *Aśramas. RV.* (5.53.10 and 5.58.1) indicates this fact by the use of the words which means the general public. New recruits of the same age are to be posted in different places and in different cantonments. National service, which in times of emergency can be developed into a nation in arms. Nationalism and National service grow hand in hand.

War Tactics

Following Vedic *mantras* also makes a mention of army tactics as follows. *RV.* (1.39.2), 'May your arms, namely your cannons, rifles, bow and arrows, swords, spears and all other war weapons be strong and firmly wielded by you to repel the wicked foe, bent upon injuring you as well as for opposing and setting at nought the force of his machinations against you. May your army, the strength of the nation, be worthy of praise'.

AV. (11.10.17) : 'O Commanding-chief! if the enemy makes a stronghold of the physical forces (against us) and through science produces effective means of shelter (trenches, forts etc.) taking all steps for the shelter of their persons, conquer him and take necessary steps to defeat him'.

AV. (4.22.6) : 'Cut off supplies, including the food of the enemy's army. *Kāṇḍa* sixth and *Maṇḍal* 65th and 66th of *Atharvaveda* deal with the subject of defeating the enemy's army by taking away or destroying his arms and ammunition'.

AV. (4.31.3) : 'O Commander! You make the enemy sick by use of gas or poison'.

AV. (8.8.9) : 'By creating weakness, misfortune, pain, fatigue, languor, drowsiness, I defeat the enemy'.

AV. (11.9.19): 'Let the wings with tongues of fire and crest of smokes go conquering the foe'.

AV. (8.8.16): 'O enemy, there are spread the trap of death or the fatal missiles, of which you can never escape, and this complicated device would smite and slay thousands of your soldiers'.

AV. (8.8.18) : 'O Foe! get your share of the flame

of death, hunger, exhaustion, slaughter and fear. Let the electricity and fire destroy you with snares and nets prepared specifically for the job'.

AV. (11.10.7) : 'Let the army of the foe of the ground be troubled in the eyes with smoke and gases and let them cry'.

AV. (11.9.5) : 'O brave and winner commander! you rise with your army, breaking the nests of the enemy and surround him as snake surrounds the prey with its winding coils'.

In the case of need use of chemicals for destroying the enemy is allowed in Vedas. For example:

AV. (5.31.1) recommends mixing the deadly poison in the food or the milk, or in the fruits, etc. of the enemy.

To kill the enemy, there are instructions in *AV.* (1.16.2) that the powder glass is administered orally in a bomb etc.

War when to be Fought

RV. (5.54.14) and AV. (11.10.1), instructs the brave warriors to rise with their banners and prepare themselves for (battle) to protect the territorial boundaries of the country. Further, it is said, 'O snake-like swift warriors, O demons like men and other people, chase the enemy who attempts to attack'.

RV. (5.54.7) clearly, points out, 'O warriors, you cannot be conquered by anyone, you can not be killed or subdued by anyone, but you do not trouble anyone nor plunder any area. You are assigned to protect the Kingdom'.

Thus according to Vedas, war with an enemy is normally to be started when he first attacks or intends to attack. It is not to be fought out simply to acquire the territory of any other country. At times of internal disturbances, the army is also required to suppress revolt etc. The Army is intended for the help of the King under the eventualities.

Now, this is very interesting. It says that a King will only attack to defend himself and not to conquer the territory of another country. Now compare this with Islam and Christianity. Both these religions have attacked the world like none other while India has never invaded any other country ever. While there are many reasons for India not having done so, the Vedas, the oldest schools of Indian thought pronounce a defensive approach. Since 1947, Bharat has fought 4 wars with Pakistan and not once did we start it. Even during the recently held Agra Summit, it was the Pakis who were attacking the Indians by saying that Kashmir must be a part of Pakistan, it was only after the Pakis attacked us then did we respond. During the Summit, we did not hear India challenge the Pakistani position on the Accession of Jammu and Kashmir to India or non-adherence by Pakistan of the 1948 UN Resolution that Pakistan has been harping on for nearly 50 years.

Constitution of Defence forces

In ancient India, defence forces were constituted of Land Army, Navy- and Airforce.

Armed Force

In the land army, the Indians had, besides the infantry and the cavalry, elephants and chariots also. The elephants, "the living battering rams" as Macaulay calls them, were a source of great strength when properly managed and skilfully supported by other arms. Of the elephants given by Chandragupta to Seleucus, Professor Max Dunker says, "These animals a few years later decided the day of Ipsus in Phrygia against Antogonus, a victory which secured to Seleucus the territory of Syria, Asia Minor, etc." According to Ctesias, Cyrus was defeated and killed by the enemy, only because of the strong support the latter received from the Indian elephants.[1]

Air Force

---

[1] 'The proficiency of the Indians in this art (management of elephants) early attracted the attention of Alexander's successors; and natives of India were so long exclusively employed in this service, that the term Indian was applied to every elephant-driver, to whatever country he might belong." Wilson's *Theatre of the Hindus*, Vol. I, p.15.

'In war, the King of India was preceded by 10,000 elephants and 3,000 of the strongest and the bravest followed him." Max Dunker's *History of Antiquity*.

'Sixty years after the death of the Enlightened, the Indians assisted the Persian King, the successor of Darius in the invasion of Greece, when they trod the soil of Hellas and wintered in Thessaly. They defeated the Greeks and saw the temple of Athens in flames. Max Dunker's *History of Antiquity*, Vol. IV, p. 384

During Vedic times Airforce was one of the major forces in the nation. Following quotes from Vedas prove the existence of Air Force. For instance,

Those warriors (airmen) who come by aeroplanes are free from the effect of dust (*RV.*1.168.4).

O, warrior! You come through the shining sky. (*RV.*1.6.9.)

Warriors! Your enemy cannot trace you out in the space. (*RV.* 1.39.4)

We bow to you, O soldier, who flying in the outer space protects those living beings there. (*AV.* 11.2.4.)

Thus besides land Army, another remarkable and astonishing feature of the Indian science of war, which would prove that the ancient Indians cultivated every science to perfection, was that the Indians could fight battles in the air. Air raids were carried out in the name of divine attacks or Māyāvī attacks. Camouflaging was also a prevalent technique in the war. Camouflaging was done even in the case of airplanes, so that enemies cannot detect planes. Thus, the ancient Indians "could navigate the air, and not only navigate it but also fight battles in it, like so many war-eagles combating for the dominion of the clouds. To be so perfect in aeronautics, they must have known all the arts and sciences relating to the science of war, including the strata and currents of the atmosphere, the relative temperature, humidity and density and the specific gravity of the various gases."[1]

Vimāna Vidyā was a science which was not even talked about before 1902 AD. In 1873, many years

---

[1] Colonel Olcott's lecture at Allahabad in 1881. See the Theosophist for March 1881.

before 1902, facts concerning this science found in ancient Indian records[1] were rejected as absurd and impossible belief. But now of the advancement of science and technology has proved the existence of such sciences in ancient India. Now the time has come when not only the ancient Indian inventions in this area of science will be recognised, but the results achieved by Indians will again be achieved by men to mark their rise to the level of the ancient Indians.

Naval force

Vedas make also a mention of Naval forces. Accordingly, the ships (sea horse) carry away necessary wealth, ration etc. for those soldiers who are stationed beyond the sea. (*RV.*1.167.2)

In one of the *mantras* of the *RV.* (5.52.9), a warrior is described as a bird who travels in the sea underwater. This indicates the existence of submarines in the Vedic age through which soldiers go under the sea.

About Indians naval warfare skill, Colonel Tod says, "The Hindus of remote ages possessed great naval power."[2]

Being the greatest commercial nation in the ancient world, and enjoying sea trade with nearly every part of the world (see *India the Pioneer of the World*

---

[1] A Sanskrit manuscript on the science of aeronautics was discovered in India in the middle of 19th century. Swami Dayananda Sarasvati of Arya Samaj in one of his lectures delivered in Poona in 1883 makes a mention of having come across a manuscript on '*Vimānas*'. Later on the same book it was edited and published with English and Hindi Translations in the name of '*Bṛhadvimānaśāstra*'.

[2] Tod's *Rajasthan*, Vol. II, p. 218

Civilisation, edited by the same author), they were compelled to look to their navy to guard their trade and to make it sufficiently strong to ensure their position as the "mistress of the sea." Their position in the ancient world was unrivalled so far as maritime affairs were concerned, their navy, too was equally eminent and powerful. Manu mentions navigation to have existed among the Indians from time immemorial. Strabo mentions a naval department in addition to the others in the Indian army.

Selection of Defence personnel

The military personnel were not selected at random or whoever wanted to offer his services in the military. But a proper procedure was followed to select the suitable soldiers. It has been prescribed in *Śaiva Dhanurveda* (SD) (Dhaurveda belonging to the tradition of Śiva) (Verse, 6) that a preceptor should give the training of military science or select a person for military services after properly examining him. The qualities of a good trainee are said not to be greedy, cunning, ungrateful or foolish.

The recruitment of the soldiers was also done according to their constellations of birth. A person born on Moon's sojourn in particular constellations were considered to be fit for recruiting in the military (SD: 10). For instance, if a person is born on Moon's sojourn in the Constellation of Hasta, Punarvasu, Puṣ ya, Rohiṇī, three Uttaras (i.e. Uttaraṣāḍhā, Uttaraphalguni, and Uttarabhādrapada), Anurādhā, Aśvinī, Revatī and also on the tenth lunar day i.e. Daśamī tithi are fit to be recruited in the military. On the other hand, people born in the third, sixth, seventh, tenth or eleventh day of the lunar fortnight was supposed to be fit for conducting all types of work (SD: 11).

Qualifications of a Commander

In Vedas, the Commander-in-chief is mostly addressed as *Rudra* or *Maruta.* Both these words indicate his quality. Rudra means fearless and Maruta means swift in action. He is to be a man of strong will, sturdy and of impressive physique, should be able to command and protect the country from internal as well as from external invasions.

According to *Vājasaneyī Saṁhitā* (16.1), the commander-in-chief should be able to deal with the wicked persons. He should possess the capacity and power to annihilate the enemy. He should be equipped with requisite weapons and should be respected by everyone.

Some of the qualities required for a chief of an army are dealt with in detail in the *RV.* (2.33) and *AV.* (11.2). Only a few of them are noted below:

Kavi: Fully conversant with the art of fighting a war (*RV.*1.114.4).

Śvitice: Possessing an exemplary character. (*RV.* 2.33.8)

Vajrabāhu: Whose arms are like that of a thunderbolt. (*RV.* 2.33.3)

Purūrupa: Capable of handling all sorts of situations. (*RV.* 2.33.9)

Sahasrākṣa:Equipped with a spying system. (*YV.*)

Aveviraḥ: Outstanding warrior. (*AV.* 19-12-2)

Qualifications of a Warrior

The foremost qualification of the warrior is that he must be deeply in love with his motherland. It is only then, that he can put his whole soul to save his motherland from all sorts of troubles.

A good warrior has almost the same qualities, which are possessed by the army commander. He is named as *urga* (*RV.*1.19.4), one who is swift to take action, one who has the indomitable courage (*RV.*1.19.4), one who is fearless (*RV.*1.19.5), one who is bright (*RV.*1.37.2) and the one who is prepared to die for his cause. (*RV.*1.37.1)

The warrior should be brave, an expert in the use of weapons, capable of defeating the enemy, should be an expert (in driving and riding etc.) and in full knowledge of army rules and affairs.

Valiant women are also to be recruited in the army who are bodily fit like men.

Yajurveda (7.44) talks about to raise a battalion of women in the army. Accordingly, the Queen has been advised to organize the band of the army of women the slayer of foes, that may bewilder the hearts of the forces of the enemy, remain aloof from sin, and burn down the foes.

We cannot forget the heroic deeds of Kaikeyī in the period of Rāmāyaṇa and of the Rani of Jhansi or Ahilyabai Holkar in the present age.

Special Honour for Brave Warriors

Vedas lay down that special respect, honour should be accorded to defence personnel, as they are the protectors of the country.

Respect for the warrior, respect to the commander, respect for all the ranks. Every essential item needed, should be offered to those who are in the vehicles and also to those who drive these vehicles. Full honour should be bestowed on all those who fight the enemy either on land, in the air or in the sea. According to *Yajurveda* (16.26), not mere honour, but all kinds of facilities are to be provided to army men. A special type of clothing, proper nursing, food, living accommodation, clubs, playground, hospitals, places of the prayers and educational facilities are to be provided to them.

As regards to the soldierly qualities of the Indians even of the present day, Sir Charles Napier, one of the highest authorities on the subject, says, "Better soldiers or braver men I never saw, superior in sobriety, equal in courage, and only inferior in muscular strength to our countrymen. This appears to me, as far as 1 can judge, the true character of the Indian army in the three Presidencies, and 1 have had men of each pressidencies under my command."[1]

The chivalrous conduct of the Indian sepoys on the occasion of the defence of Arcot by Clive, and when, towards the close of the war with Tipu in 1782, the whole of the force under General Mathews were made prisoners is well known. The sepoys magnanimously and spontaneously contrived with great personal risk to send every pie of their petty savings to their imprisoned officers, saying, "We can live upon anything, but you require mutton and beef." The conduct of the Indian sepoys shown on such occasions sheds lustre on the whole profession. General Wolseley, in a paper on "Courage," contributed to a journal, highly eulogised the bravery of the Indian sepoys. "During the siege of Lucknow," he said, "the sepoys performed wonderful feats of valour."

Mr. Elphinstone says, "The Hindus display bravery not surpassed by the most warlike nations and will throw away their lives for any considerations of religion or honour. Hindu sepoys, in our pay, have in two instances advanced after troops of the king's service have been beaten off; and on one of these occasions, they were opposed to French soldiers. The sequel of this history will show instances of whole bodies of troops rushing forward to certain death."[2]

---

[1] *The Indian Review* (Calcutta) for November, 1885, p. 181

[2] Elphinstone's *History of India*, p. 198

Clive, Lawrance, Smith, Coote, Haliburton and many others speak of the sepoys in the highest terms.

Military Training

Periods Suitable for Military Training:

The third, fifth, seventh, tenth, twelfth and thirteenth day of the lunar fortnight were accepted as suitable for Military training (SD:12). Sundays, Fridays and Thursdays were taken to be very suitable for starting any work relating to Military Training (SD: 13). The training should be started with the performance of a *Yajña* (SD: 14).

It has been further (SD: 7) clarified, that the training in operation of weapons of the mass destruction, i.e. of the class of missiles (or bow and arrow) should be given to a soldier who is of a Brāhmaṇa personality type. The training of operation of weapons of the class of sword, should be given to a person who is endowed with the personality of Kṣ atriya. The training of weapons of the class of spear or lance should be given to a person who is of Vaiśya personality type. The training of weapons of the class of Gadā (or mace) should be given to the persons who are attributed with the personality of Śudra.

Classification of Preceptors (Trainers)

Dhanurveda classifies trainers or preceptors into four types of fighting. A preceptor excelling in different types of fighting has been designated differently. For instance, if a preceptor excels in all seven types of fighting, he is called as *Saptayodhā*. He is called as a '*Bhārgava*' if he is well-versed in four types of fighting. An expert in two forms of fighting is known as '*yodhā*' and if one is versed in only one type of fighting, he is known as '*Gaṇaka*' (SD: 9).

The Method of imparting training

According to the experts of *Dhanurveda*, the trainee should be allowed to practice from easier to more complex arrows. For example, first of all, an archer should learn to pierce a flower with an arrow devoid of Arrowhead, and then he will pierce a fish with an arrow equipped with the arrowhead. Then the disciple is made to pierce the upper skin of an animal etc. (*mānsavedha*) without harming lower skin or bones. These are the three types of piercing. By practising shooting of arrows gradually at targets in such manner the soldier will achieve the skill to pierce his targets more effectively and efficiently (SD: 16-17; VD, 17-18).

Military Arrays

Vyuha means an arrangement of the army in the battlefield in a particular style. An arranged army is more powerful than the non-arranged army on the battlefield. The first indication of the battle array is found in *Atharvaveda.* There we find a mention of protecting one's army from the alien army arranged in a serpent array.[1]

Śri Rama invaded Sri Laṅkā with his army arranged in the Garuḍa style array.[2]

It is said that the Vedic people divided their army in the following manner: (1) *Uras* or centre (breast), (2) *Kakṣas* or the flanks, (3) *Pakṣas* or wings, (4) *Praligraha* or the reserves, (5) *Koṭi* or vanguards, (6) *Madhya* or centre behind the breast, (7) *Pṛṣṭha* or back a third line between the *madhya* and the reserve[1].

Vedic people were experts in arranging different types of an array of forces or formations of armies in action which generally termed as *vyūha.*

Some *vyūhas* are named from their object. Thus: (1) *Madhyabhedī* = one which breaks the centre, (2) *Antarbhedi* = that which penetrates between its division. More commonly, however, they are named from their resemblance to various objects. For instance (1) *Makaravyūha*, or the army was drawn up like the *Makara*, a mire monster (2) *Syenavyūha*, or the army in the form of a hawk or eagle with wings spread out. (3) *Śakaṭa-vyūha*, or the army in the shape of a waggon.

---

[1] उत्तिष्ठ त्वं देवजनार्बुदे सेनया सह। भंजन्नमित्राणां सेनां भोगेभिः परिवारय
AV. 11.9.5

[2] गरुडं व्यूहमास्थाय सर्वतो हरिभिर्वृतः। मां विसृज्य महातेजा लंकामेवाभिवर्तते।
रामा. युद्धकाण्ड 21.12, भण्डारकर संस्करण।

(4) *Ardhacandra*, or half-moon. (5) *Sarvatobhadra*, or hollow square (6) *Gomutrikā*, or echelon (7) *Daṇḍa* or staff, (8) *Bhoja* or column; (9) *Maṇḍala* or hollow circle, (10) *Asaṅhata* or detached arrangements of the different parts of the forces, the elephants, cavalry, infantry severally by themselves. Each of these *vyūhas* has subdivisions; there are seventeen varieties of the *Daṇḍa*, five of the *Bhoja* and several of both the *Maṇḍala* and *Asaṅhata*.[1]

In the *Mahābhārata* (Vol. VI., pp. 699-729), Yudhiṣṭhira suggests Arjuna the adoption of the form of *Sūcimukha*, or the needle-point array (similar to the phalanx of the Macedonians), while Arjuna recommends the *vajra* or thunderbolt array for the same reason. Duryodhana, in consequence, suggests *Abhedya*, or the impenetrable.

According to the *Śaiva Dhanurveda*, an emperor desirous of victory should organize his army comprising four divisions ('*Caturaṅga*', i.e. the charioteers, soldiers mounted on an elephant, cavalry and infantry) into a formation or battle array (*vyūha*) to encircle the enemy deploying valiant heroes in front of it.

According to *Vāsiṣṭha Dhanurveda* (217), If the young soldiers are kept in the middle of the Army, they would fight the war and win. The king should keep two groups of armies on each side and one group at the

---

[1] See *Agni Purāṇa*. "The most important part of Hindu battles is now a cannonade. In this they greatly excel, and have occasioned heavy losses to us in all our battles with them. Their mode is to charge the front and the flanks at once, and the manner in which they perform this maneuver has sometimes called forth the admiration of European antagonists. Elphinstone's *History of India*, p. 82.

back. One group of the army should remain outside of battle and move here and there (mainly for vigilance)[1].

The technique of making a formation (*vyūha*) in a battle is as follows - the charioteers should be placed in front, followed by the elephants followed by the infantry. The cavalry should be placed on both sides[2].

The battle array may be formed in the shape of an *Ardhacandra* (half-moon), or as a *Chakra* (circle) or a *Śakaṭa* (carriage), *Makara* (a fish), *Kamala* (a lotus), (*Śreṇikā*) (simply by making rows) or in the shape of a *Gulma* (bush)[3].

According to *Vāsiṣtha Dhanurveda* (218), there are several types of military formations. These are *Daṇḍa* (staff array), *Śakaṭa* (or car-shaped array), *Varāha* or boar shaped array, *Matsya* or fish-shaped array, *Makara* or crocodile shaped array, *Padma* (lotus) shaped array, *Sūcimukha* or needle-shaped array and *Garuḍa* or eagle-shaped array[4].

Vāsiṣtha Dhanurveda has described various types of military arrays to combat different situations. If the army is surrounded by the enemy, then *Daṇḍa vyūha* or staff array is prescribed[5].

---

[1] युवास्वरे मध्यसेना युद्धं कुर्य्यादतन्द्रिता।
द्वेसेने पार्श्वयाश्चैका पृष्ठतो रक्षयेत् सदा।।
एकां विकटसेनान्तु दूरस्थां भ्रामयेद् युधि।।

[2] मुखे रथा गजाः पृष्ठे तत्पृष्ठे च पदातयः।
पार्श्वयोश्च हयाः कार्या व्यूहस्यायं विधिः स्मृतः।। SD. 175

[3] अर्धचन्द्रं चक्रंच शकटं मकरं तथा।
कमलं श्रेणिकां गुल्मं व्यूहानेवं प्रकल्पयेत्।। *SD.* 176

[4] दण्डव्यूहश्च शकटो वराहो मकरस्तथा।
सूचीव्यूहोऽथ गरुडः पद्मव्यूहादयो मताः।। 218।।

[5] सर्वतो भये दण्डव्यूहस्य रचनाकार्य्या।। VD 220।।

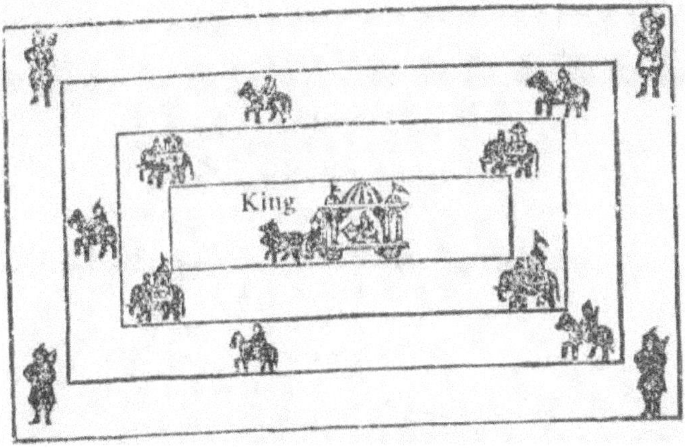

Daṇḍa vyūha or staff array

If there is the apprehension of danger at the back, then *Śakaṭa* or the waggon shaped array is prescribed[1].

If there is the apprehension of danger on sides, then *Varāha* (boar) or *Gaja* (elephant) shaped array is prescribed[2].

If there is the apprehension of danger on the right and left sides, then the *Varāha* (boar) or *Garuḍa* (eagle) shaped array should be created[3].

---

[1] पश्चाद्देशे भये समुत्पन्ने शकटाकारेण व्यूहं रचयेत्।। VD. 221

[2] पार्श्वाभये वराहव्यूहो गजव्यूहो वा विधेयः।। VD.222

[3] दक्षिणावामपार्श्वयोर्भये उपस्थिते।
वराहव्यूहो गरूडव्यूहो वा कार्य्यः।। VD. 223

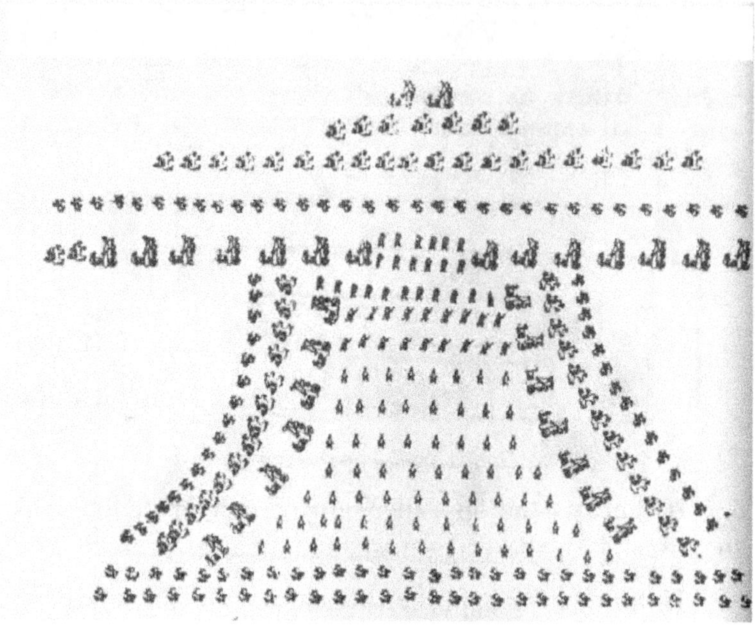

Śakaṭa or waggon shaped array

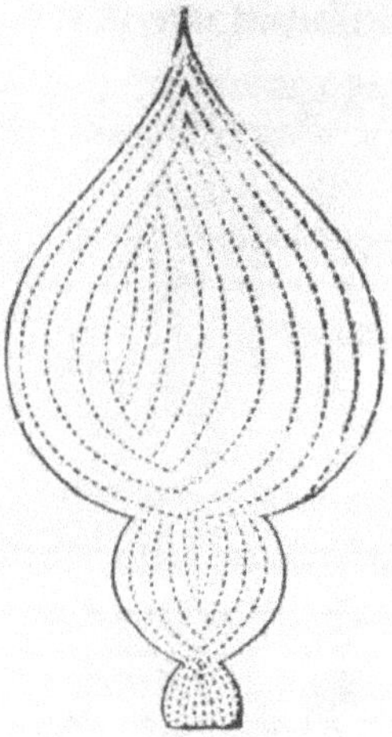

Varāha (boar) shaped array

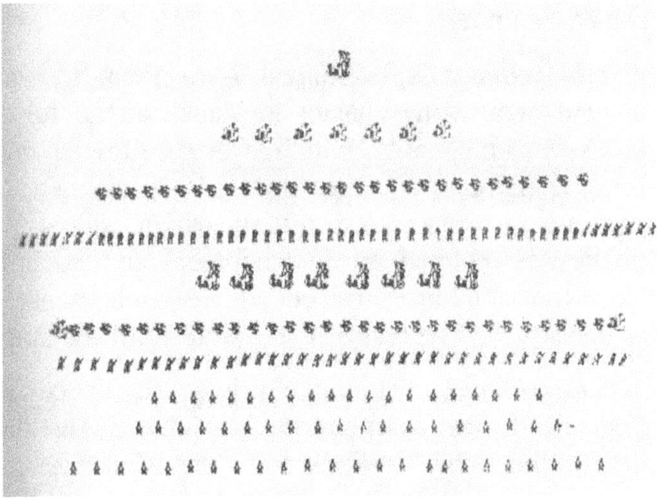

Garuḍa (eagle) shaped array

If there is the apprehension of danger of an enemy on the front side, *Pippīlikā* or ant array is prescribed[1].

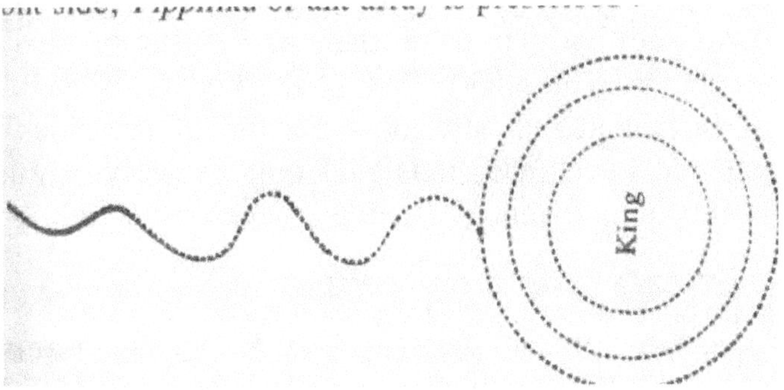

Pippīlikā or ant array

Thus in ancient India the army was placed in various battle arrays to ensure the victory over the enemy. Some of the famous battle arrays can be

[1] सन्मुखे शत्रुभये जाते पिपीलिका पंक्तिरूपः व्यूहविन्यासः कार्यः। VD. 224

described as under:

1. ***Śyenavyūha***: (Eagle shaped Array): In the eagle-shaped array, one chariot is placed ahead followed by seven elephants which were followed by 30 horses guarded by one hundred swordsmen. Side portions are protected by spearmen. The middle portion is manned by 8 charioteers and 30 horses. Both the sides are covered with two elephants each at each side. The rest of the warriors follow suit.[1]

2. ***Krauñca vyūha***: If two chariots are placed ahead instead of one as mentioned in the Eagle shaped array, the array is known as the *Krauñca* shaped array[2].

3. ***Śakaṭa Vyūha* (Car shaped array)**: In a car-shaped array, two chariots are placed ahead and are followed by seven elephants, which were followed by twenty elephants and 50 horsemen. Both the side portions are guarded by seven chariots each backed up by two elephants. The same number of chariots form the body part of the car, is surrounded by elephants. The middle part of the body is manned by infantry and the outermost portion of the sides are manned by horses. It is said that an army arranged in this array cannot be defeated even by Gods[3].

---

[1] एको रथोऽग्रे कर्तव्यः पश्चाद् द्विरदसप्तकम्। त्रिंशदश्वाः खड्गशतं पार्श्वे कुन्तधरास्तथा। मध्येष्टौ रथिनस्त्रिंशदश्वाः पार्श्वे गजद्वयम्। ततश्चपृष्ठतः सर्वश्येनव्यूहः स उच्यते। (वीरमित्रोदय, राजचक्रलक्षण)

[2] अग्रे द्वौ पृष्ठगाश्चान्ये क्रौंचप्यूह स उच्यते।। (वीरमित्रोदय, राजविजय, 5)

[3] अग्रे रथद्वयं पश्चाद् गजाः सप्त व्यवस्थिताः।। 6।।
तत्पृष्ठे विंशतिरिभाः पंचाशद्वजिवाहकाः।
सप्त सप्त रथाः पार्श्वे गजौ द्वौ द्वौ ततः स्थितौ। 7।।
तत् प्रमाणैर्रथैर्वेदी बहिस्तत्तद् गजाः स्थिताः।
मध्येपदातयश्चान्ते पार्श्वयोश्च तुरंगमाः।। 8।।

4. ***Siṅhavyūha* (Lion shaped array)**: Three chariots are placed in front to be backed up by elephants placed in the shape of an elephant. Side portions are guarded by five chariots each and sixty bowmen. Sixty warriors stay in the middle. The chariots and elephants form the tail part of the array. This array is formed in order to defeat the army arranged in the Śakaṭa (car) array. This array can be combated with the help of an army arranged in the *Sūcīmukha* (needle array). The lotus array is combated with the lion array and the needle array is combated with the crow shaped array[1].

5. ***Cakravyūha* (Wheel shaped array):** First of all 16 elephants are placed in a circular shape followed by chariots, then spearmen, then bowmen, then swordsmen backed up by three lines of horsemen. The rest of the army is also to be placed in the alike manner. It is said that the army arranged in the wheel-shaped array cannot be defeated even by Gods[2].

विज्ञेयः शकटव्यूहो न भेद्यस्त्रिदशैरपि। (वीरमित्रोदय, राजविजय–6,7,8)

[1] अग्रे रथत्रयं पृष्ठे गजाकारो गजव्रजः।। 9।।
स्यन्दनाः पंचपंचैव अथो षष्टिर्धनुष्मताम्।
मध्ये पदातयः षष्टिः पार्श्वयो रथिनो गजाः।।10।।
पृष्ठे तू सकला सेना सिंहव्यूहः प्रजायते।
शकटव्यूहे कालेऽयं सूचीव्यूेन भिद्यते।। 11।।
पद्यमव्यूहस्तु सिंहेन सूची काकेन भिद्यते।।(वीरमित्रोदय, राजविजय–9,10,11)

[2] गजषोडशकं मध्ये वृत्ताकारेण कल्पयेत् ।। (वीरमित्रोदय, राजविजय, 12)
बाह्यतो रथिभिर्वेष्ट्यं तद् बाह्ये कुन्तधारकैः।। (वीरमित्रोदय, राजविजय, 13)
शरचापधरा बाह्ये खड्गचर्मधरास्ततः।
बाह्यतोऽश्वैः समावेष्ट्यं पंक्तित्रितयतः क्रमात्।।(वीरमित्रोदय, राजविजय, 14)
पुनः पुनः प्रकुर्वीत् यावद् भवति वाहिनी।
चक्रव्यूहः स विज्ञेयो दुर्भेद्यस्त्रिदशैरपि।। (वीरमित्रोदय, राजविजय,15)

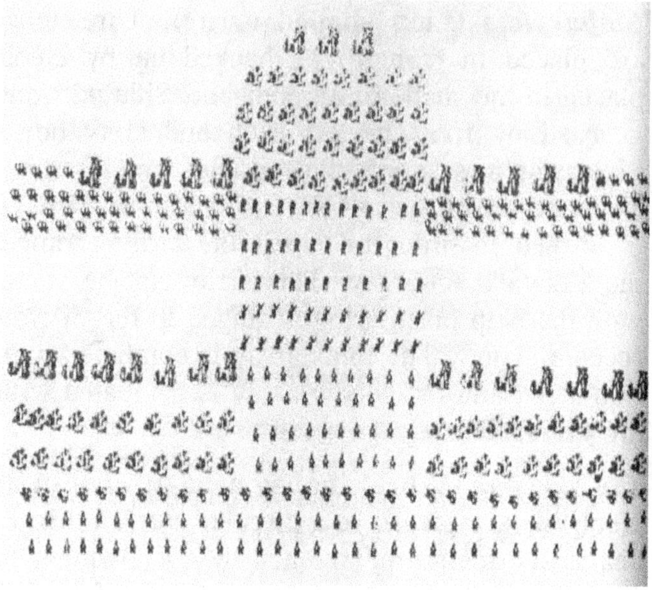

Sinhavyūha (Lion shaped array)

अथवा चक्रवद् व्यूहं कारयेन्नृपतिः प्रिये।
चक्राकारं भटैः कुर्यात् प्राकारं प्रथमं ततः।
द्वितीयमश्वैर्मातंगैस्तृतीयं स्यन्दनैस्ततः। तुरीयमेवं निर्माय चक्रव्यूहं तदन्तरे।।
स्वयमाप्तजनैः साकं युद्धे बद्धस्पृहो भवेत्।। (आकाश भैरव पटल, 137)

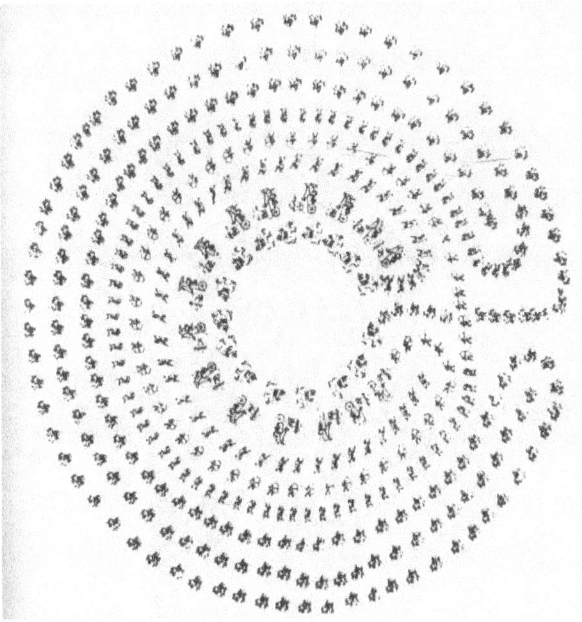

Cakravyūha (Wheel shaped array)

6. ***Padma vyūha* (Lotus shaped array):** One chariot each is to be placed in a circle at 8 different places, followed by 5 elephants and 9 horsemen preceding 15 soldiers of infantry in each petal of the lotus. 7 chariots and 13 elephants are to follow 15 infantry soldiers. Afterwards, 19 horses and 28 infantry soldiers should be stationed. In the middle portion of the lotus array, where the pollen is located, elephants and chariots are stationed. In the centre, the King should stay mounted on the elephant back. Its petal portion is formed by the presence of three chariots, elephants and horses each at each petal of the lotus array and thirty soldiers from infantry. Since this array is shaped like a lotus, it is called a lotus-shaped array[1].

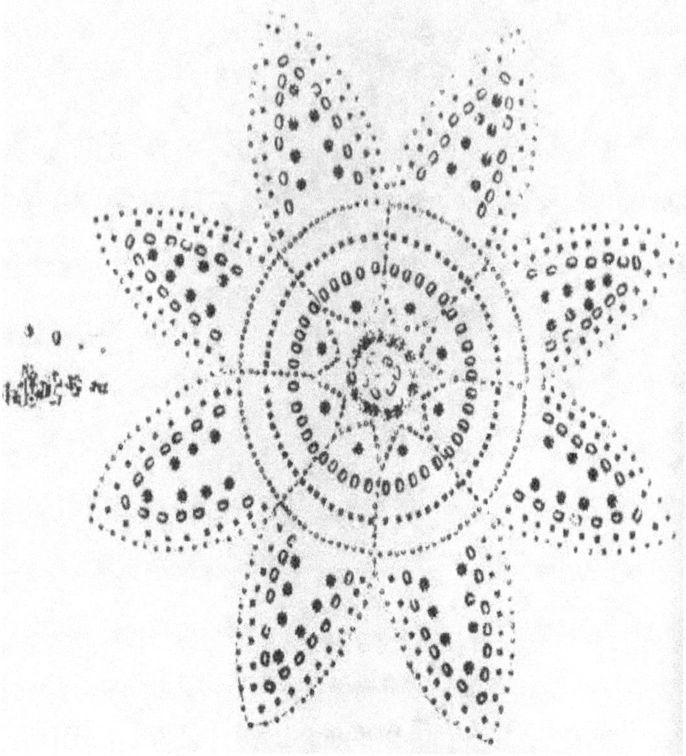

Padma vyūha (Lotus shaped array)

7. ***Sarpavyūha* (Serpent array):** Two chariots each in all the four directions followed by 10 elephants 24 horses, 30 swordsmen preceding 30 bowmen, 30 shieldmen, 30 spearmen each. They should be followed by 30 lancermen, 30 spearmen and machines are stationed behind them. Since this array

[1] अन्तरे रथमेकैकं स्थानेष्वटसु कल्पयेत्। तदन्तरे गजान् पंच नवाश्वान् स्थापयेत् ततः। ततः पत्तीन् पंचदश पत्रे पत्रे प्रकल्पयेत्। तन्मध्ये स्यन्दनान् सप्त गजांश्चैव त्रयोदश।। एकोनविंशति हयान् पदातीनष्टविंशतिम्। गजैः रथैः पूरणीया पद्ममध्यस्य कर्णिका।। तन्मध्ये गजमारूढश्चमूपो वा नृपऽथ वा। अन्तरे द्राणिकायां तु रथा द्विरदवाजिनः।। त्रयस्त्रयश्च सर्वत्र त्रयत्रिंशत् पदातयः। पद्मव्यूहः स विज्ञेयः पद्माकारः कृतो यतः।।

वीरमित्रोदय, राजविजय 16–20

is formed with the help of chariots, elephants, horses and infantry soldiers placed in a serpent-like shape, this array is called a serpent array. The army arranged in this array leads to the devastation of the enemy in the war like Yama, the God of death[1].

8. ***Agnivyūha* (Fire array):** Chariots, Elephants, horses and infantry soldiers - all in seven numbers each are placed in seven lines. The number of chariots, elephants, horses and infantry soldiers will increase seven times each with every second phase of placement. The entire army is to be arranged like this. This array is known as Agni array. Just as fire increases with the increase of flames, similarly the number of army increases in fire array with the increase of lines. The army arranged in this array destroys enemies just like fire[2].

---

[1] चतुर्दिक्षु रथौ द्वौ तत् पृष्ठे तु द्विरदा दश।
चतुर्विंशतिरश्वाश्च त्रिंशत खडगध्रास्ततः।
शरचापधराश्चैव खेटपट्टिशधरिणः। तेषां पृष्ठे कुन्तधराः यन्त्रधरास्तथैव च।।
सर्पाकारं रथेभाश्वैः पूरयेत् सैनिकैरपि।
सर्पव्यूहः स विज्ञेयः कृतान्तो युद्धकर्मणि।। वीरमित्रोदय, राजविजय, 22–24

[2] सप्तधा स्युः सप्त रथा गजवाजिपदातयः।
रथेभाश्वाः पत्तयश्च सप्त–सप्तगुणाः क्रमात्।।
अधोऽधः कल्पयेदेवमाग्निव्यूहः स उच्यते।। (वीरमित्रोदय, राजविजय, 25)
सर्वोत्तमोऽयं व्यमहानामग्निवन्नाशकारकः।। राजविजय, 25

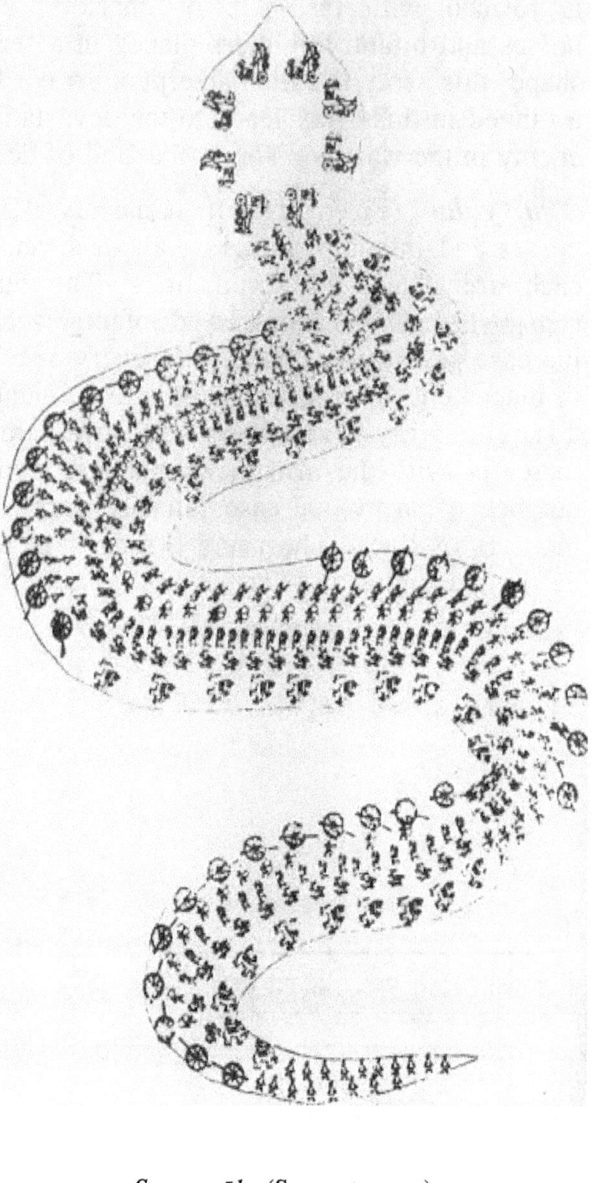

Sarpavyūha (Serpent array)

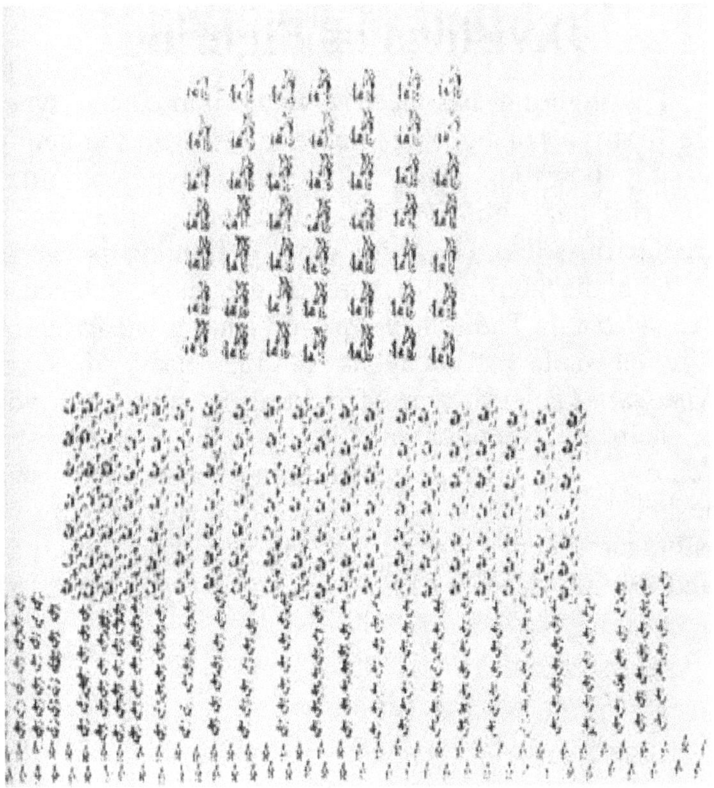

Agnivyūha (Fire array)

Divisions of Fighting

The fighting has been divided into seven types. The first type of fighting is carried out with the help of missiles, bows and arrows. The second type of fighting is carried out with *Chakras* or weapons of the class of circular missiles. The third type of fighting is carried out with the help of weapons of the class of lance or spear (*Kunta*). The fourth type of fighting is carried out with the help of weapons of the class of sword (*Khadga*). The fifth type of fighting is carried out with the help of weapons of the class of bayonet type (*Churikā*). The sixth type of fighting is carried out with the help of weapons of the class of mace (*Gadā*) and lastly, the seventh type of fighting is carried out with a hand to hand fighting (*Sadāśiva Dhanurveda*: Verse, 8).

Equipment for the Army

Based on fighting divisions, various equipment for the army was invented. *Yajurveda* (16.10), emphasizes the production of good quality of arms and ammunitions. It warns the ordnance factories and the suppliers of the arms to vouchsafe, that the arms that are being supplied are in good condition and shall never fail while in use by the Warriors who are wholly and perfectly devoted to defending their mother-land.

We know that unless the army is fully equipped with in all respects, it is not possible to win the war. Soldiers are, therefore, to be provided with all the necessary weapons, quick transport, medical facilities, the requisite number of tanks and other carriers, aeroplanes, ships, etc. and above all, the proper and adequate ration for the front. Weapons and carriers are to be manufactured in ordnance factories and supplied from other supply depots. India's failure in the year 1962, the war with China was solely due to Indian leadership being overtaken by the Gandhian concept of non-violence. Nehru and his comrades like Acharya Kriplani neglected the defence needs of the country.

A brief list of army weapons, referred to in Vedas, is given below:

(1). *Yajurveda* (33.46): Makes a mention of a weapon that was equivalent to the modern bomb.

(2). *Yajurveda* (10.21;10.22): Weapons emitted rays to destroy the enemy.

(3). *Yajurveda* (16.11): Makes a mention of a weapon that was not thrown like a bomb but used in fighting.

(4). *Yajurveda* (15.16): Makes a mention of a

weapon that was very strong.

(5). Atharvaveda (11.10.2): It consists of three joints almost like a rocket.

(6). *Atharvaveda* (11.10.3): Makes a mention of a weapon in which small pieces of iron were attached.

(7). *A V.* (11.10.3): Makes a mention of a weapon that has a pin like a nail at the mouth.

(8). *A V.* (11.10.1): Makes a mention of a weapon that spreads smoke.

(9). *A V.* (11.10.7): Mentions a weapon that makes the enemy senseless.

(10). *A V.* (11.9.7): makes a mention of a weapon that emits tear gas.

(11). *A V.* (11.9.19): Mentions a weapon that emits fire.

Besides the above-referred ones, there are various kinds of (traps) mentioned in the Vedas, which are to be used to capture the enemy. To name a few of them *Jaiapāśa* (*A V.*11.10.25), *Kavaca Pāśa* (*A V.*11.10.25), *Nāga Pāśa, Chakra Pāśa, Padma Pāśa.*

Yajurveda (16.53) makes a mention of hundred kinds of weapons and *pāśas.* The *mantra* reads like this, 'O the effluent commander, you with your hundred kinds of weapons and *pāśas* can push the enemy back'.

One more *Yajurveda* (16.53) *mantra* makes a mention of a thousand kinds of weapons and *pāśas.* The *mantra* reads like this, 'O commander-in-chief, the thousands of weapons and traps that you possess can tear off the enemy'.

Now as regards the weapons used by the Indians, Professor Wilson is assured that the Indians cultivated archery most assiduously, and were masters in the use of the bow on a horseback. Their skill in archery was wonderful. "Part of the archery practice of the Hindus consisted of shooting several arrows at once, from four to nine at one time." Arjuna's feats in archery at the tournament before Draupadi's marriage, and again on the deathbed of Bhishma, must excite universal admiration.

Classification of weapons

In Ancient India, weapons were divided into two types: *Astras* and *Śastras.* Astras were those weapons whose operation depended upon a *mantra* (click of a particular idea in the mind) or a machine (*yantra*) or by firing the Agnichūrṇa (gunpowder).[1] The rest of weapons were called as *Śastras.*

Again *Astras* were divided into two types. *Māntrika* and Tubular. In *Śukranīti* it has been advised that if a king does not have *māntrika* weapons, he should use tubular ones to ensure his victory along with other *Śastras.*[2]

Tubular weapons have been further divided into two types according to the small and large sizes of the operating machines.[3] Small-sized barrelled machines were having a barrel with an oblique (horizontal) and a straight (perpendicular) hole at the origin (breech). It had the length of five vitastis (45 inches), a sharp point both at the forefront (muzzle) and at the origin, which

---

[1] अस्यते क्षिप्यते यत्तु मन्त्र–यन्त्राग्निभिश्च तत्।
अस्त्रं तदन्यतः शस्त्रमसिकुन्तादिकं च।। शुक्रनीति– 4.7.191

[2] अस्त्रं तं द्विविधं ज्ञेयं नालिकं मान्त्रिकं तथा।
यदा तु मान्त्रिकं नास्ति नालिकं तत्र धारयेत्।।
सह शस्त्रेण नृपतिर्विजयार्थं तु सर्वदा। शुक्रनीति– 4.7.192

[3] नालिकं द्विविधं ज्ञेयं बृहत्क्षुद्रविभेदतः। शुक्रनीति– 4.7.194

can be used in aiming at the objective, which has fire produced by the pressure of a machine, contains balls made of stones or iron and powder. In the original form it has a good wooden handle at the top (Butt), and has an inside hole of the breadth of the middle finger, holds gunpowder in the interior and has a strong rod.[1] This small-sized weapon was nothing but the modern gun. The striking range of the tubular weapons increases with the increase in the width of the hole of the barrel and an increase in the length and width of the ball.[2]

The Large-sized tubular weapon was like that of a modern cannon. According to the description of *Śukranīti*, the large-sized tubular weapon is that which has post or wedge at the origin or breach, and according to its movements, can be pointed towards the aim has a wooden frame and drawn on a carriage.[3]

According to *Śukranīti*, a war which was fought with tubular weapons is said to be an Āsura or Māyika (wizardly) war.[4] The war fought with the *māntrika* weapons (operated at the click of a particular idea in the mind) is said to be a divine war.

The following fivefold classification of Indian weapons is exhaustive: (1) Missiles were thrown with an instrument or engine called *yantramukta*; (2) that operated mannualy were called as *hastamukta*; (3) Weapons which may or may not be thrown, e.g.

---

[1] लघुदीर्घाकारधारभेदैः शस्त्रास्त्रनामकम्।
प्रथयन्ति नवं भिन्नं व्यवहाराय तद्विदः।। शुक्रनीति– 4.7.193

[2] यथा दीर्घं बृहद्गोलं दूरभेदि तथा तथा। शुक्रनीति– 4.7.198

[3] मूलकीलभ्रमाल्लक्ष्यसमसन्धानभाजि यत्।
बृहन्नालिकसंज्ञं तत् काष्ठबुध्नविनिर्मितम्।। शुक्रनीति– 4.7.199

[4] अस्त्रं तु द्विविधं ज्ञेयं नालिकं मान्त्रिकं तथा। शुक्रनीति – 4.7.192
मन्त्रस्त्रैर्दैविकयुद्धं नालास्त्रैस्तथासुरम्। शुक्रनीति – 4.105.3

muktāmukta, like javelins, tridents, etc.; (4) Which are not thrown, like swords, maces, etc.; (5) Natural weapons, as fists, etc.

Broadly weapons were divided into three categories: 1. *Mantra Mukta* (operated by mantra), 2. *Yantra mukta* (operated by machine) and 3. *Hasta mukta* (operated manually). Now we give here a detailed description of weapons categorised in the above three categories.

Mantra Mukta (Mantra operated weapons)

(Weapons of Mass Destruction or Atomic weapons)

We find that different types of offensive and defensive weapons of mass destruction were also used in ancient India. Their operation was *māntrika* and was fully under the control of the operator. The operator was equipped with such capabilities as could withdraw and operate weapon in the time of need. The missiles generally returned to their point of operation after successfully hitting the target. *Māntrika* operation was generally preferred instead of Yāntrika or mechanical operation. Nowadays we have not been able to develop *Māntrika* science and technology as it was in ancient India. We are depending upon the mechanical operation or at the most computerized electronic operation of the weapons. Mechanically or electrically controlled weapons can be operated by any person. They may even fall into wrong hands leading to the disaster of humankind. But weapons controlled through mental waves of the operators cannot be handled by unwanted persons. They can more safely be preserved.

Here it may be known that *mantra* operated weapons were known as *Divyāstras* or Divine weapons. The following are the Divine weapons.

1. ***Pāśupatāstra***: It was an extremely powerful missile

that was capable of destroying the three worlds i.e. the entire earth including equatorial and polar regions. It was irresistible and could resist all missiles simultaneously. It was the discovery of Śiva. Arjuna received its technical know-how from Śiva himself.

2. ***Brahmāstra:*** It was a discovery of Brahmā. It was a missile that was specially designed to carry the nuclear warhead. Brahmāstra is repeatedly mentioned in Sanskrit works. For its use see Śri Bhāgvat describing the fight between the son of Droṇa and Arjuna with the Brahmāstra. The Rev. KCM. Banerjee in his work, "The Encyclopaedia Bengalensis," says that the Brahmāstra was probably a piece of musketry not unlike the modern matchlocks." Madame Blavatsky, in her Isis Unveiled, also shows that "fire arms were used by the Indians in ancient times."[1] Brahmāstra, in fact, was an atomic weapon invented by Brahmā." Now when the nuclear weapons have been discovered and techniques of measuring radiation levels were explored, we have become able to say that nuclear wars are also the discovery of Vedic period. This fact was confirmed by Dr. S.K. Trikhā, Head of the Physics Dept. of Delhi University in his research paper read by him in a seminar organised by Rashtriya Sanskrit Sansthan from 11th October 1995 to 15th Oct. 1995 to celebrate its Silver Jubilee function. Dr. Trikhā proved in his paper that nuclear weapons were used in the great war of Mahābhārata. In support of his contention, he located some such spots around Kurukshetra where the radiation level is 2.5 times higher than the normal level even at this time when 5100 years have elapsed after the occurrence of war. This level of radiation is said to be equal to the level of radiation at the spot of Hiroshima and Nagasaki

---

[1] *Encyclo. Bengal,* Vol. III, p. 21

in Japan where the American forces dropped the atomic bomb during the second world war in 1944. Thus it became a proved fact that Mahābhārata war was a nuclear war that took place in Kurukshetra. The power of nuclear weapons can be imagined by the radiation level which even after 5000 years equals to the radiation level of Hiroshima and Nagasaki of Japan 60 years ago when the atom bomb was dropped there by Americans.

3. ***Āgneyāstra:*** It was developed by Bṛhaspati who first taught its operation to Bhardvāja, who passed it over to Agnivesh. Agnivesh handed it over to Droṇa, who ultimately taught it to Arjuna. It was extremely dreadful and frightful (Mahābhārata - 5.140.6). It espoused fire all around. It was counteracted with Vāruṇāstra.

4. ***Vāruṇāstra:*** It was used to shower rains upon the enemy.

5. ***Vāyvāstra:*** Dust storms were created by the use of this weapon.

6. ***Parjnyāstra***: It was used to make the weather cloudy.

7. ***Antardhānāstra:*** Its use could make one invisible instantaneously.

8. ***Nāgāstra or Nāgapāśa:*** This weapon was developed by Varuṇa. Arjuna learnt its use from Varuṇa only. It was used to punish the sinners. It was combated with Garuḍāstra.

9. ***Mahendrāstra:*** It was used by Arjuna upon Karṇa, who combated it with Bhārgavāstra.

10. ***Akṣisammārjanāstra:*** The use of this missile caused the enemy to die or made him insane or sometimes

made him sleep or on certain occasions made him laugh incessantly. (Mbh. 5.94.38-40)

11. ***Ayojāla:*** This divine weapon when used 'created a net of iron'.

12. ***Atharvanāstra:*** This missile was popularly known as the killer of enemies. It was, in fact, a combat weapon for Āgneyāstra.

13. ***Asurāstra:*** It was a prominent missile generally used by Asuras. Ghaṭotkaca (son of Bhima) knew its operation perfectly.

14. ***Isikāstra:*** It was considered as the most powerful missile (paramāstra), unparalleled producing huge flames and surrounded by a circle. Its effect could be pacified only by Brahmāstra. When Aśvatthāmā used it to destroy the Pāṇḍvas, Arjuna had to employ Brahmāstra.

15. ***Gandharvāstra:*** It was a missile developed by Gandharvas. Arjuna got it from Tumburu and other Gandharvas.

16. ***Nārāyaṇāstra:*** It was a missile developed by Nārāyaṇa. Droṇācārya learnt its know-how from Nārāyaṇa himself. Only Droṇa and Aśvatthāmā knew its operation. Surprisingly enough, even Krishna and Arjuna did not know its operation. It never returned without hitting the target. Owing to its invincibility and irresistibility, it could be employed only once. Only Pāsupatāstra was superior to this.

17. ***Pramohanāstra:*** It was also a māntrika missile. Its use rendered the enemy unconscious. In the period of Rāmāyaṇa also this missile was in currency.

18. ***Prajñāstra:*** It was a combat weapon for

Pramohanāstra. It was used to bring to consciousness those rendered unconscious by the use of Pramohanāstra.

19. ***Other Divyāstras:*** The Following were also enumerated as divyāstras. Sthunākarṇa, Indrajāla (witchcraft), Saura and Saumya.

20. ***Combat Weapons:*** During the Vedic period military science was so advanced, that divine combat weapons were also developed to neutralize the effect of certain Divine weapons, e.g.

21. ***Nāgāstra*** was counteracted with the help of Garudāstra.

22. ***Bhargvāstra*** was used to counteract the Mahendrāstra.

23. ***Aharavaṇāstra*** could be counteracted with Āgneyāstra.

24. ***Īṣikāstra*** was combated with the help of Brahmāstra.

25. ***Effect of Pramohanāstra*** was neutralized with the help of Prajñāstra.

1. Āganeyāstra was combated with the help of Varuṇāstra.

2. Māntrika Technology: In the Vedic period, all three types of science and technology were in use. We come across references to war vehicles including airplanes as operated by mantra (mental power of the user) in addition to manually operated war vehicles.

Based on the foregoing discussion, it can unhesitatingly be maintained that during the time of Vedas, Nuclear science and technology was far more advanced than it is today. Military science also witnessed the culmination of its advancement. This is the reason why a great annihilation of mankind and its knowledge took place. Apart from the above, we find other sciences also fully developed at the time of Mahābhārata.

Missiles: Missiles were a weapon that was operated both by *mantra* and machine. Mr. H. H. Elliot, Foreign Secretary to the Government of India (1845), after discussing the question of the use of fire-arms in ancient India, says: "On the whole, then, we may conclude that fire-arms of some kind were used in early stages of Indian history, that the missiles were explosive, and that the time and mode of ignition was dependent on the pleasure of the operator; that projectiles were used which were made to adhere to gates and buildings, and machines setting fire to them from a considerable distance; that it is probable that saltpeter, the principal ingredient of gunpowder, and the cause of its detonation, entered into the composition, because the earth of Gangetic India is richly impregnated with it in a natural state of preparation, and it may be extracted from it by lixiviation and crystallization without the aid of fire, and that sulphur may have been mixed with it, as it is in abundant in the north-west of India."[1]

Circular Missiles: One of the seven types of wars mentioned in *Vāsiṣtha Dhanurveda* (9) was fought with weapons of the class type of circular missiles[2]. The first mention of the circular missile is attested in the *Ṛgveda*[3].

---

[1] *Bibliographical Index to the Historians of M. India*, Vol. J. p. 373.

[2] धनुष्चक्रन्तु कुन्तंच खड्गंच्छुरिकां गदाम्।
सप्तमं बाहुयुद्ध स्यादेवं युद्धानि सप्तधा।। 8।।

In Rāmāyaṇa also we come across the mention of *Chakra* (circular missile) several times[1]. Śri Krishna's *Sudarśana Chakra* is quite a famous weapon in *Mahābhārata.* When the king Sālva started a bombardment upon the city of Dwarika from fighter plane called *Saubha Vimāna*, Śri Krishna used the *Sudarśana* missile to destroy his plane. After hitting the target successfully, *Sudarśana* (named circular missile) returned it to the place of origin[2]. This missile was discovered at the time of the firing the *Khāṇḍava* named forest. *Purāṇas* have extolled the significance of this missile[3]. As per the figurative description of the *Purāṇas*, Viśvakarmā is said to be the inventor of Viṣ ṇu's *Sudarśana* missile, Rudra's Triśūla (Trident), Kuber's *Puṣpaka* aeroplane and Kārtikeya's *Śakti.* All these weapons were divine weapons or *mantra mukta* weapons. They could be operated at the click of a *mantra* in the mind of the operator. All these weapons were made of the energy of the sun, just like modern-day laser beams or laser-guided missiles.

---

3 *anāyudhāso asurā adevāñścakreṇa tā apa vapa ṛjiṣīna* (RV. 8.96.9)

1 *khadgaiśca cakrairgadābhiśca*. Rām. *Yudhakāṇḍa* 53.9. See also Yuddha. 109.17, 86.21, 96.26)

2 *Mahābhārata, Vanaparva*, 21.2

3 *Viṣṇu Purāṇa, Uttarakhaṇḍa*, Ch. 145

According to *Padmapurāṇa* (*Uttara Khaṇḍa*, Ch. 145), this missile was very fierce, emitted fierce rays all around and used to fly at the speed of light and was able to destroy all sorts of nuclear weapons of mass destruction[1].

Harivaṁśa Purāṇa (Bhavi. 55.21-22) describes it among the class of Āgneyāstras which was a sharp-edged weapon and emitted rays like that of the sun. It was able to destroy and burn down all types of soldiers: cavalry, infantry and also soldiers armed with divine weapons.

In *Nītiprakāśikā*, although generally a *Chakra* (Disc-shaped missile) has been enumerated in the category of *Mukta* weapons (which were operated either manually, or by machine and mantra), but certain types of *Chakras* like *Daṇḍacakra*, *Dharmacakra* were counted in the category of *Muktāmukta* weapons, meaning weapons that could be recalled by the operator to their place of origin after hitting or without hitting the target. *Muktāmukta* weapons were under the full control of the operator. *Sudarśana chakra* was, in fact, a *Paramāstra* which could not be combated by any other combat weapon.

Auśanasa Dhanurveda has divided circular missiles into uttama (best), *madhyam* (middle) and *adhama* (third) category types in view of a different number of spokes, sizes and weight.

***Uttama chakra* (the best type of disc missile):** First class *chakras* should have 8 spokes. 30 *pala* (34.92 kg.)[2] is considered to be the best weight of *chakra* used

[1] अथ विष्णुमुखा देवाः स्वतेजांसि ददुस्तथा। तेनाकरोन्महादेवः ....
चक्रंसुदर्शन नाम ज्वालामालातिभीषणम्

[2] **Note :** In the measurement of heavy weights 1 *pala* was taken

by adult warriors, whereas in case of young warriors the weight of a *chakra* should not go beyond 12 *palas* (13.96 kg.).

Similarly, the measurement (diameter) of a first-class *chakra* should be 16 *aṅgulas* [1] (12 inches) in the case of adults and 8 *aṅgulas* in the case of young ones. Rim of the first-class *chakra* should be around 3 *aṅgulas*, round, ornamented and heavy-duty rims are considered to be the best for disc missiles.

According to *Śukranīti*, the perimeter of a disc missile should be six hands (9 feet) with its diameter of 2.8 feet.

***Divine Wars*:** In addition to the above mantra operated weaponry in war, a more astonishing thing about the wars in ancient India was, that they were also fought in a mysterious and wizardly way. Most often than not, 'In case of war, divine missiles were used very often to matrialise such wars. This divine weaponry was called *Astra Vidyā*, the most important and scientific part of the art of war in ancient India, which is not known to the soldiers of our age till recently. It consisted in annihilating the hostile army by involving and suffocating it in different layers and masses of atmospheric air, charged and impregnated with different substances. The army would find itself plunged in a fiery, electric and watery element, in total thick darkness, or surrounded by a poisonous, smoky, pestilential atmosphere, full sometimes of savage and terror-striking animal forms (snakes and tigers, etc.)

---

to be 100 *tulā* and 1 *tulā* was equal to 11.640 grams).

[1] Twelve *aṅgulas* is equal to one *vitasti* or a span and 24 *aṅgulas* is equal to one *hasta* or cubit. One vitasti is equal to 9 inches.

and frightful noises. Thus they used to destroy their enemies.[1] The party thus assailed counteracted those effects by arts and means known to them, and in their turn assaulted the enemy by means of some other secrets of the *Astra Vidyā.* Col. Olcott 'also says, "*Astra Vidyā,* a science of which our, modern professors have not even an inkling, enabled its proficient use to completely destroy an invading army, by enveloping it in an atmosphere of poisonous gases, filled with awe-striking shadowy shapes and with awful sounds." This fact is proved by innumerable instances in which it was practised. For example, the *Rāmāyaṇa* mentions it. Jalandhar had recourse to it when he was attacked by his father, Mahādeva (Śiva), as related in the *Kārtika Mahātmya.*

Yantra Mukta (Machine operated weapons)

Apart from the above Divyāstras (*mantra*-operated weapons), many other machine-operated defensive weapons were in use in ancient period, e.g.

Śataghnī: It was a small rocket capable of killing 100 or 1000 persons at a time. It was operated from the walls or the gates of the forts.

In Vedas, we do not find the direct mention of *Śataghnī,* but there are references to the words like *Sahasraghnī*[2] and *Śatavadha* that gives the meaning of - *śataghnī. AV.* (1.16.44)[3] directs the killer of a cow to be shot with the help of bullet made of lead. Similarly, a gunshot or bullet has also been referred to in *AV.*[4]

---

[1] *Theosophist,* March 1881, p. 124

[2] धनुबिभर्षि हरितं हिरण्ययं सहस्रघ्नि शतवधम्। अथर्व. 11.2.12

[3] तं त्वा सीसेन विध्यामो यथानोऽसौ अवीरहा।

[4] जिह्वा ज्या भवति कुडमलं वाङ् नालिका दन्तास्तपसाभिदग्धाः।

(5.18.8). In *Ṛgveda*[1] (8.69.12), *Śataghnī* has been quoted as *Sūrmī.* In *Taittirīya Saṁhitā*[2] (1.5.7) and Sāyaṇa's *Bhāṣya*[3] *Sūrmī* has been used in the form of cannon or gun-like weapon. *VD* (67) specifically points out the existence of *Śataghnī* and *Rañjaka* (gun-powder). Accordingly, for the protection of the throne of the king, cannons must be installed on the fort and a lot of gunpowder should also be stored. The Cannon in ancient India was known by the name of *Śataghnī.*

In *Rāmāyaṇa*[4] (5.11) also we find the mention of śataghnī. In *Bālakāṇḍa, Ayodhyā* has been described as a city consisting of high towers and flags equipped with hundreds of *Śataghnīs*, which shows that cannons or machines of some kind or other were used in those days to fortify and protect citadels.

The *Rāmāyaṇa*, while describing the fortifications, says "As a woman is richly decorated with ornaments, so are the towers with big destructive machines."[5] This shows, that cannons or big instruments of war like cannons, which discharged destructive missiles at a great distance, were in use at that time.

In descriptions of fortresses and battles, *Śataghnis* are often mentioned. *Śataghni* literally means "that which kill hundreds at once." In Sanskrit dictionaries, *Śataghni* is defined as a machine which shoots out a piece of iron and other things to kill a large number of

---

[1] अनुक्षरन्ति काकुदं सूर्म्यं सुषिरामिव।

[2] एषा वै सूर्मी कर्णिकावती। एतया ह स्म देवा असुरान् शततर्हास्तृहन्ति। य एतया समिधमादधाति वज्रमेषैतच्छतघ्नीं यजमानो भ्रातृव्याय प्रहरति।

[3] ज्वलन्ति लोहमयी स्थूणा सूर्मी। सा च कर्णिकावती छिद्रवती। अतएव ज्वलन्तीत्यर्थः। एकेन प्रहारेण शतसंख्याकान् मारयन्तः शूराः शततर्हाः।

[4] उच्चाट्टालध्वजवतीं शतघ्नीशतसंकुलाम्।

[5] *Rāmāyaṇa*, *Sundara Kāṇḍa*, Third Chapter, 18th verse.

men. Its other name is *Bṛścī Kālī* बृश्चीकाली[1]

Śataghnis and similar other machines are mentioned in the following *ślokas* of the *Rāmāyaṇa*:

Canto	3	--- --- ---	*Ślokas* 12, 13, 16 and 17
"	4	--- --- ---	23
"	21	--- --- ---	last *śloka*
"	39	--- --- ---	36
"	60	--- --- ---	54
"	61	--- --- ---	32
"	76	--- --- ---	32
"	76	--- --- ---	68
"	86	--- --- ---	22

The *Rāmāyaṇa* says that the *Śataghnī* was made of iron. In the *Sundara Kāṇḍa,* it is compared in size with big broken trees or their huge offshoots, and in appearance it is said to 'resemble the trunks of trees." "They were not only mounted on forts but were carried to the battle-fields, and they made a noise like thunder." What else could they, therefore, be but cannons?

Besides the *Rāmāyaṇa*, the *Purāṇas* make frequent mention of *Śataghni* being placed on forts and used in times of emergency. The name used in *Matsya Purāṇa* is *Sahasraghani* (शत and सहस्र mean hundreds and thousands or innumerable)[2] guns and cannons are

[1] See Raja Sir Rādhā Kant Deva's *Śabdakalpadruma.*

[2] *Śataghnī* differed widely from *Matvāla* in that the *Matvāla* were roiled down from maintains, while *Śataghnī* was an instrument from which stones and iron balls were discharged. *Jamera* was another machine that did fatal injury to the enemy

mentioned as existing in Laṅkā, under Rāvaṇa. They were called *Nhulat Yantras.*

Commenting on the passage in the Code of Gentoo (Hindu) Laws that "the magistrate shall not make war with any deceitful machine or with poisoned weapons, or with cannons and guns, or any kind of fire-arms," Halhed says, "The reader will probably from hence renew the suspicion which has long been deemed absurd, that Alexander the Great did absolutely meet with some weapons of that kind in India, as a passage in Quintus Curtius seems to ascertain. Gunpowder has been known in China, as well as India, far beyond all periods of investigation. The word fire-arms is literally the Sanskrit *Āgneyāstara*, a weapon of fire; they describe the first species of it have been a kind of dart or arrow tip with fire and discharged upon the enemy from a bamboo. Among several extraordinary properties of this weapon, one was, that after it had taken its flight, it divided into several separate streams of flames, each of which took effect, and which, when once kindled, could not be extinguished: but this kind of Āgneyāstra is now lost."[1] He adds "A cannon is called '*Śataghnī*, or the weapon that kills one hundred men at once,' and, that the *Purāṇas* ascribe the invention of these destructive engines to Viśvakarmā, the Vulcan of the Hindus."

In Mahābhārata also we find the mention of a war weapon like *Śataghnī.* In *Mahābhārata, Śataghnī* has been described as *aśmaguḍā* (pelting stone balls) or *ayoguḍā* (pelting iron balls).[2] They have also been

by means of stones. See accounts of battles with Mohamed Kasim.

[1] Halhed's *Code of Gentoo Laws, Introduction*, p. 52. See also *Amarakoṣa* and *Śabda Kalpadrum*, Vol. I, p. 16

described carried by two wheels and sometimes on four wheels[1].

But the western scholars think that the first time cannon in India was used by the Babars. The time of the Babar is 1526 AD. As such according to western scholars, the cannon was not found in India before 1526 AD.

Arrows: Arrows were machine (bow)-operated weapons. There were various types of arrows like *nārāca*, *nālīka*, *varāhakarṇa*, *kṣura*, *añjlika*, *ardhacandra*, and *vaitastika*.

Vāsiṣṭha Dhanurveda (45-48), gives the characteristics of the good arrow. Accordingly, an arrow should neither be too thick nor too thin. It should also be either made out of the unripe wood material product of the vile land. The arrow should have strong welded joints. It should be made of ripe wood and should have to shine. It should not have weak joints and be free of any cracks. The time of preparation of wood arrows has also been narrated. The appropriate time for preparation of reed arrows is autumn.

VD. (45-47) has prescribed the quality of reed for arrows. The reed which has a round and hard stem and which has been grown in favourable (sunny and fertile) place can be used for making arrows. The measurement of the arrow should be two hands excluding the measurement of a fist, i.e. 30 inches. (One hand is 18

---

[2] (क) परिगृह्य शतघ्नीश्च सचक्रा सगुडोपलाः। वनपर्व. 284.31
(ख) शूलाभुशुण्ड्योश्मगुडाः शतघ्न्यः। द्रोणपर्व. 179.37
(ग) प्रादुरासन् महाराज कार्ष्णायसमया गुडाः। चतुश्चक्रा द्विचक्राश्च शतघ्न्यो बहुला गदा। द्रोणपर्व. 199.18–19

[1] प्रादुरासन् महाराज कार्ष्णायसमया गुडाः। चतुश्चक्रा द्विचक्राश्च शतघ्न्यो बहुला गदा। द्रोणपर्व. 199.18–19

inches. If the measurement of a fist is excluded it will be around 15 inches). The thickness of an arrow has been prescribed equally to that of the smallest finger of the hands. The tail end of the arrow should be shaped like the feathers of a crow, swan, brown hawk, crane, peacock, vulture, osprey. SD (51) also adds the shapes of cātaka (an extinct species of a cuckoo which lived upon the drops of rain), heron, vulture and cock or feathers made of small bells. The gap between the two feathers should be six aṅgulas or five inches. But the gap between two feathers in the case of Śāraṅga bow has been recommended to be 10 aṅgulas or 8 inches. These feathers should be joined strongly or tied with sinew at the rate of four features per reed arrow.

The Types of arrows

VD (53-54) and SD (46-47) have divided arrows in three categories: female, male, and impotent. The one heavier towards the point is female, the one heavier towards the end is male and the one equal throughout is termed as impotent. The impotent type is helpful in the practice of archery, the female type is a fast runner and the male type is able to pierce an object placed at a long distance.

The Manufacturing, Types and Functions of Arrowheads :

According to SD (45), the arrow-head should be made purified iron, be sharp and pointed. They should be painted with a hardening substance according to their feathers.

Various types of arrow-heads have been described in VD (53,54) and SD (46,47). The shape of arrow-heads differs from country to country. The arrow-heads can be of awl type, razor blade type, like that of a cow's tail, crescent moon shaped, needle-pointed, spear-headed, teeth of calf shaped, two-pronged type, pear-shaped, the beak of crow and many other types.

The various types of arrow-heads have various types of functions. For instance, the *ārāmukha* or an arrowhead like an awl can cut through the skin, arrowhead-like a razor blade (*kṣurapra*) is used to combat the arrows of the enemy or to cut up the hand of the enemy. Gopuccha (an arrow-like the cow's tail) is good for hitting a target in general. The arrow-shaped like the crescent moon is used to sever the enemy's head, neck, and bow. The needle pointed arrows were used to pierce the armour of an enemy. The spear-headed arrow was used to pierce the chest of an enemy, while two-pronged arrows were used to counteract the arrows of the enemy. Calf's teeth shaped arrows were used to cut the bowstrings of the enemy. *Kārṇika* (flower petal-shaped) arrows were used to counter the metallic arrows of the enemy. Crow's beak-shaped arrows were used to pierce any pierceable object (VD 55-57; SD 48-50).

In addition to the above arrowheads, a special *gopuccha* type (shaped like cow's tail) arrow-head has been prescribed in VD (58) and SD (48). According to VD, this arrow-head is made of sapless wood and has got a metallic nail of three *aṅgula* lengths fixed at its tip. On the other hand, SD describes it to be made of a pure bell metal. According to another view of VD (59), a *gopuccha* can be made by replacing the head by an iron nail. This Gopuccha arrow-head was used for practices in aiming for targets and archery.

The arrows made completely of metals were called as *nārāca*. Some *nārācas* had five broad wings and they were able to make anybody successful in his target (VD 65; SD 60). Gun-shots or bullets were known as small arrows. They were fired by a machine fitted with a barrel (just like a modern-day gun). Those small arrows or bullets were useful in shooting a target placed at very high or distant places or in war taking place in a fort (VD 66; SD 61). Thus in ancient times, the guns were also used in fighting.

The Methods of Tempering Arrow-heads:

In ancient times various methods were applied for the tempering of arrow-heads, to enhance their devastating power. The arrow-heads thus tempered like this, were able to pierce even the unbreakable armours just like a leaf of a tree (VD 62; SD 56). Long pepper (*pippalī*), *saindhava* (rock-salt), *kuṣṭha* (a medical plant named Costus Speciosus or arabicus, used as a remedy for the disease called *takman*, in Hindi this plant is called as *kūṭha*) should be ground and pounded by mixing urine of a cow to prepare a paste. That paste should be smeared over the arrow-head or a weapon and then it should be heated on fire till it becomes blue like the peacock's neck. When it absorbs the entire paste, it must be quenched in water. Such weapons will become the best weapons (VD 63-54; SD 57). According to SD (58) and *Jāmadgneya Dhanurveda* (JD. p.117), the paste prepared out of five types of salt-soaked in honey and mustard oil is also very good for tempering. It is also indicated in VD 60-61, that when the colour of white reed plant turns yellow after receiving rainwater on *Svāti Nakṣatra* day, its root becomes poisonous. This root if anointed on the arrow-head (tip of weapon) act as a fatal addition. The best way to recognise the plant is, that it trembles always even in the absence of wind.

***Bows*:** Bows were missile- operating machines. Some famous bows were Gaṇḍīva of Arjuna, Pināka of Śiva and Vijaya of Karṇa.

In *Dhanurveda*, bows have been classified differently according to their sizes, measurements, and joints.

The first class of bows is called *Divya* or Divine bows. Their measurement was prescribed five hands and a half, i.e. 99 inches. The bow with the same measurement was invented by Śaṅkara in ancient times. Paraśurāma also used the bow with the same measurement. After Paraśurāma, it was used by Ācārya Droṇa. From Droṇa, its use was made by Arjuna and after Arjuna, Sātyaki started using it. Thus in *Satyayuga* Mahādeva invented it, in *Tretā,* Śri Rāma used it and in *Dvāpara,* Droṇa became its operator. The second type of classification of bows was done as *Mānuṣa* bows or human bows. A bow measuring four hands, i.e 72 inches is called *Mānuṣa* bow. The length of one hand is equal to the length of 24 fingers or 18 inches. A good quality bow either have three, five, seven or nine joints. A bow with nine joints was called as '*Kodaṇḍa*', which was considered squarely an auspicious one. A bow with four, six or eight joints were considered as an inauspicious one (*Sadāśiva Dhanurveda*: verse, 21-27).

Among the categories of *Divya* or Divine bows, one was called as Śārṅga bow. It was used by Viṣṇu and considered to be the best one. This bow measured seven vitasti i.e. 63 inches. (Note: One *vitasti* is a distance between the long thumb and a little finger or between the wrist and the tip of the finger and is said to be equal to 12 Aṅgulas or about 9 inches). It was made by Viśvakarmā. This bow could not be handled by anybody either in the North (Note: the northern hemisphere was called as *Svarga loka* and the southern hemisphere was called as *Pātāla* or *asura loka.* Equatorial regions were known as *Mānuṣa loka*). It was handled by Viṣṇu only. In addition to the *Divya* category, The *Śārṅga* bow was also available in *Mānuṣa* or human category. It was said that it was developed with great efforts over many years. It also served all purposes. According to *Sadāśiva Dhanurveda* (45) its measure was seven vistasti or 63 inches, but according to *Vāsiṣṭha Dhanurveda* (46) it measured six *vistati* and half i.e 59 inches. This bow could be easily used by all category of soldiers like soldiers of cavalry, infantry, soldiers on elephant's back and charioteers. The *Mānuṣ a* category of *Śārṅga* bow was made of bamboo. (SD 34-37; VD 35).

According to *Vāsiṣṭha Dhanurveda* (48) three types of materials were used in manufacturing bows in ancient times. It was metals, horns, and wood.

Among metals gold, silver, copper, and steel were used to manufacture bows. Among horns, horns of the buffalo, Śarabha (Śarabha was an octopod antelope that possess big horns and almost looks like a camel found in Kashmir. It was considered more powerful even than the elephant and lion. Now, this species of antelope has become extinct. This shows the long tradition of *Dhanurveda* in India. The animals mentioned in these books have become extinct) and Rohit (a stag) were used to develop bows. The wood which is useful in manufacturing bows were described as sandal, cane, *śāla* (Vatica Robusta, a valuable timber tree), *sādhāvana* (a kind of hedyserum), *kakubha* (Pentaptera Arjuna), *śālmali* (silk cotton plant), segaun (teak wood), *vanśa* (bamboo) and *Añjana* tree. (VD.38).

The characteristics of a bowstring: The strings were be made of three round threads which were free from any joints, pure, fine, very soft, and polished so that these threads could withstand an attack in a war.

For want of silk thread, the string can be made with intestines of a deer or with the intestines of a she-buffalo or a cow. Fine strings are to be made with the skin of a goat or Gokarṇa (another variety of animals). The hair on the skin should be removed thoroughly.

Sometimes strings are prepared with the bark (outer skin) of mature bamboos (plants) and those strings are tied with silken threads for making strings that withstand adverse situations in war.

At the advent of the month of *Bhādra* (September) the bark of the *Arka* tree becomes commendable for making strings and hence hard and sacred strings were made with it.

The threads which were obtained from the barks of the *Arka* tree are eighteen cubits in length and these should be made in triple-ply to make a proper string (for the bow).

Firearms: The chief distinction of the modern military science is the extensive employment of firearms, their invention being attributed to the Europeans, and it was supposed that fire-arms were unknown in ancient India. Nothing, however, is farther from the truth. Though the Indian masterpieces on the science of war are all lost, yet there is sufficient material available in the great epics and the *Purāṇas* to prove that firearms were not only known and used on all occasions by the Indians, but that this branch of their armoury had received extraordinary development. In mediaeval India, of course, guns and cannons were commonly used. In the twelfth century, we find pieces of the ordinance being taken to battle-fields in the armies of Prithviraj. In the 25th stanza of *Prithvirāja Raso* it is said, "The cavillers and cannons made a loud report when they were fired off, and the noise which issued from the ball was heard at a distance of ten *kosa.*"

नृप पंग नयर छूटे अराब।
कोटह कंगूर चढि–चढि सिताब।।
जंबूर तोप छूटहि झंनकि।
दश कोश जाय गोला मनकि।।
सिरदार भार बाराह रोह।
लंगी अभंग बर हनै कोह।।

An Indian historian, Raja Kundan Lall, who lived in the court of the king of Oudh, says that there was a big gun named lichmā in the possession of His Majesty the King (of Oudh) which had been originally in the artillery of Mahārājā Prithviraj of Ajmer. The author speaks of a regular science of war, of the postal department, and of public or common roads. See *Muntakhab Tafsee-ul-Akhbar*, pp. 149, 50.

"Maffei says that the Indians far excelled the Portuguese in their skill in the use of fire-arms."[1]

Another author quoted by Bohlen speaks of a certain Indian king being in 'the habit of placing several pieces of brass ordnance in front of his army.[2]

Bullets: Bullets were made of iron with other substances inside or without any such substance. For smaller guns, the bullets were made of lead or any other metal.[3]

Bullets were fired by firing the gunpowder in the barrel.[4]

Guns: Here it may also be pointed out that guns,

---

[1] Hist. *Indica*, p. 25

[2] *Das Alte Indien*, Vol. II, p. 63

[3] सीसस्य लघुनालार्थे ह्यन्यधातुप्रभवोऽपि वा। शुक्रनीति– 4.7.204

[4] कर्णचूर्णाग्निदानेन गोलं लक्ष्ये निपातयेत् । शुक्रनीति– 4.7.211

cannons, and gun-powders were also in vogue in warfare in ancient India.

Guns were made of iron or some other metal. They were rubbed and cleaned daily and covered by armed men. According to Śukranīti (4.7.209-210), before use, the instrument has to be cleaned first, then gunpowder has to be put in, then it is to be placed lightly at the origin of the instrument by means of the rod. Then the bullet has to be introduced followed by gunpowder at the ear, then the fire was given to it, and the bullet is projected to the objective.

"Faria-e Souza speaks of a Gujrat vessel in 1500 AD. which fired several guns at the Portuguese[1], and of the Indians at Calicut using fire vessels in 1502 AD., and of the Zamorin's fleet carrying in the next year 380 guns."[2]

Cannons: In the description of Ayodhyā it is mentioned that the *yantras*[3] were mounted on the walls of the fort, which shows that cannons or machines of some kind or other were used in those days to fortify and protect citadels.

The *Rāmāyaṇa*, while describing the fortifications, says "As a woman is richly decorated with ornaments, so are the towers with big destructive machines."[4] This shows that cannons or big instruments of war like cannons, which discharged destructive missiles at a great distance, were in use at that time.

Rockets: "Rockets," says Professor Wilson,

---

[1] Asia Portuguesa, Tom I, Part I, Chapter 5.

[2] *Ibid*, Chapter 7

[3] *Yantra* means 'machine with which weapons were operated.'

[4] *Rāmāyaṇa*, *Sundara Kāṇda*, Third Chapter, 18th verse.

"appear to be an Indian invention, and had long been used in their native armies when Europeans came first in contact with them."

Col. Tod says, "Jud Bhan (the name of a grandson of Vajra, the grandson of Krishna), 'the rocket of the Yadus,' would imply a knowledge of gun-powder at a very remote period."

Rockets were unknown in Europe until the last century (1906 AD.). "We are informed by the best authorities that rockets were first used in warfare at the siege of Copenhagen in 1807."[1] Mr. Elliot says, "It is strange that they (Rockets) should now be regarded in Europe as the most recent invention of artillery."[2]

Machine throwing liquids: There were in ancient India machines which, besides throwing balls of iron and other solid missiles, also threw particular kind of destructive liquids at great distances. The ingredients of these liquids are unknown: their effects, however, are astonishing.

Ctesias[3], Elian[4] and Philostratus[5] all speak of an oil manufactured by Indians and used by them in warfare in destroying the walls and battlements of towns that no "battering rams or other polioretic machines can resist it," and that "it is inextinguishable and insatiable, burning both arms and fighting men."

Lassen says, "That the Hindus had something like 'Greek fire' is also rendered probable by Ctesias, who

---

[1] Tod's *Rajasthan*, Vo. II, p. 220

[2] *Penny Encyclopaedia*, V, 'Rocket.'

[3] Ctesie, *Indica Exerpta*, XXVII (ed. Baer), p. 356

[4] *De Natura Animal*, *Lib.* V., cap. 3

[5] *Philostrati Vita Apollonu*, Lib. III, cap. 1

describes their employing a particular kind of inflammable oil for the purpose of setting hostile towns and forts on fire."[1]

Eusebe Salverte, in his Occult Sciences, says "The fire which burns and crackles on the bosom of the waves denotes that the Greek fire was anciently known in Hindustan under the name of *baḍavā.*"[2]

Gunpowder: It has also been noticed that gun-powders were also in vogue in warfare in ancient India along with cannons and guns. VD (67) specifically points out the existence of *Rañjaka* (gun-powder). Accordingly, for the protection of the throne of the king, lot of gunpowder should also be stored. Gunpowder in ancient India was known by the name of *Rañjaka.* In *Jāmadagneya Dhanurveda* gun powder has been called as *Cūrṇa.* In *Śukranīti*, the same has been described as *Agnicūrṇa* or *Agni.*

In *Śukranīti*, the method and chemical composition for the preparation of gunpowder has been given. Accordingly, five *palas* (582.5 milligrams) *suvarci* salt, one *pala* (11.5 milligrams) of sulphur and one *pala* (11.5 milligrams) each of the charcoal received from the wood of *arka* (swallow wart or asclepias gigantia), *snuhi* and aṅgāra plants by the Ayurvedic process of *Sadhūma Puṭapāka* where a drug, which is prepared in a closed vessel placed in a pit. The above-mentioned salts and charcoals should be purified, powdered, and mixed together. This mixture should then be soaked into the juices of *snuhi*, *arka,* and garlic. It should be dried up in the sun and finally powdered like sugar, the substance will be gunpowder.[3]

---

[1] Lassen's *Ind. Alt.* II, p. 641

[2] English Translation, Vol. II, p. 223

In another type of preparation, the substances are the same, but the quantity of *survarci* salt is changed into six or four parts quantity of sulphur and charcoal remain the same.[1]

Experts also made gunpowder in various other ways of white and other hues of their choice according to the relative quantities of constituents like *Aṅgāra*, shulphur, *survarci* salt, *śilājit*, *haritāla*, left out the lead after being purified, hiṅgula, iron filings, camphor, *jatu*, indigo, and juice of *sarala* tree, etc.[2]

Professor Wilson says, "Amongst ordinary weapons one is named *vajra*, the thunderbolt, and the specification seems to denote the employment of some explosive projectile, which could not have been in use except by the agency of something like gunpowder in its properties."[3]

As regards "gunpowder," the learned Professor

---

[3] स्नुह्यर्काणां रसोतस्य शोषयेदातपेन च।
पिष्ट्वा शर्करवच्चैतदग्निचूर्णं भवेत् खलु।। शुक्रनीति– 4.7.202

[1] सुवर्चिलवणाद्भागाः षड् वा चत्वार एव वा ।
नालास्त्रार्थाग्निचूर्णे तु गन्धांगारौ तु पूर्ववत्।। शुक्रनीति– 4.7.203

[2] अंगारस्यैव गन्धस्य सुवर्चिलवणस्य च
शिलाया हरितालस्य तथा सीसमलस्य च।
हिंगुलस्य तथा कान्तारजसः कर्पूरस्य च।
जतोर्नील्याश्च सरलनिर्यासस्य तथैव च। शुक्रनीति– 4.7.194

[3] Wilson's Essays, Vol. II, p. 302. The Indians are from time immemorial remarkable for their skill in fireworks. The display of fire works has been from olden days a feature of the Dassehra festival. Mr. Elphinstone says, 'In the Dassehra ceremony the combat ends in the destruction of Laṅkā amidst a blaze of fireworks which, would excite admiration in any part of the world. And the procession of the native prince on this occasion presents one of the most animating and gorgeous spectacles ever seen.' Elphinstone's *History of India*, p. 178.

says, "The Indians, as we find from their medical writings, were perfectly well acquainted with the constituents of gunpowder sulphur, charcoal, saltpetre, and had them all at hand in great abundance. It is very unlikely that they should not have discovered their inflammability, either singly or in combination. To this inference, *a priori* may be added that drawn from positive proofs, that the use of fire as a weapon of combat was a familiar idea, as it is constantly described in the heroic poems."[1]

The testimony of ancient Greek writers, who, being themselves ignorant of firearms used by Indians, give peculiar descriptions of the mode of Indian warfare is significant. "The mistius mentions the Brāhmaṇa fighting at a distance with lightning and thunder."[2]

Alexander, in a letter to Aristotle, mentions "the terrific flashes of flame which he beheld showered on his army in India." See also Dante's Inferno, XIV,31-7.

Speaking of the Indians who opposed Alexander the Great, Mr. Elphinstone says, "Their arms, with the exception of firearms, were the same as at present."[3]

Philostratus thus speaks of Alexander's invasion of the Punjab "Had Alexander passed the Hyphasis he could never have made himself master of the fortified habitations of these sages. Should an enemy make war upon them, they drive him off by means of tempests and thunders as if sent down from Heaven. The Egyptian Hercules and Bacchus made a joint attack on them, and by means of various military engines

---

[1] Essays, Vol. II, p. 303

[2] Orat, XXVII, p. 337. See Ap. Duten's *Origin of the discoveries attributed to the Moderns*, p. 196.

[3] Elphinstone's *History of India*, p. 241

attempted to take that place. The sages remained unconcerned spectators until the assault was made when it was repulsed by fiery whirlwinds and thunders which, being hurled from above, brought destruction to the invaders."[1]

The western scholars think that the gunpowder was invented for the first time in Europe in the 14th century AD. First of all, the name of German monk Barthold Schwarz who dabbled in the black art of alchemy is quoted behind the invention of gun-powder. But later in the *Encyclopaedia Britannica* (P.5), it was stated that gun powder was either discovered in China or India. According to *Encyclopedia Columbia* (p.896), gun powder was invented in China. The knowledge of gun powder reached Europe through the Arabs. But nobody tried to know how the Arabs received this knowledge. India is the source of all knowledge and science that reached the Arabs.

Hasta Mukta (Manually operated weapons)

The following are hand-operated (manually operated) weapons used for a close range of fighting.

1. Paṭṭiśa
2. Śakti, Vyjanti, etc.
3. Mugdar
4. Bhuśuṇḍī
5. Aśni
6. Daṇḍa
11. Tomar
12. Parigh
13. Musala
14. Kaṁpana
15. Karaṇī
16. Vārāhakarṇa

---

[1] Philostrati Vit: Apollon, *Lib* II, C. 33

7. Akṣurapri	17. Bhindipala
8. Ṛṣṭi	18. Silimukh
9. Vatsadanta	19. Vipāṭa
10. Asi	20. Aṅkuśa

A more detailed description of some of the manually operated weapons is given below:

Daggers: Warlike weapons and splendid daggers were presented at the International Exhibitions of 1851 and 1862, and a critic speaking of them, says, "Beautiful as the jewelled arms of India are, it is still for the intrinsic merit of their steel that they are most highly prized."[1]

Swords: That the ancient Indians were celebrated for their sword fight is evident from the Persian phrase, "to give an Indian answer," meaning "a cut with an Indian sword." The Indian swordsmen were celebrated all over the world. In an Arabic poem of a great celebrity, known as *Sabaa Moalaqa*, there occurs the passage, "The oppression of near relations is more severe than the wound caused by a Hindu swordsman."[2]

Ctesias mentions that the Indian swords were the best in the world.[3]

Explosives: In addition to the above weapons, ancient Indians also used explosive weapons. Commenting on the stratagem adopted by King Hal in the battle against the king of Kashmir, in making a clay elephant which exploded, Mr. Elliot says, "Here we have not only the

---

[1] Manning's *Ancient and Mediaeval India*, Vol. II, p. 365

[2] The Tafsir Azizi says: *Teghi-i-Hindi va Khanjar-i-roomi-Na Kunad aanki intiazar Kunad.*

[3] Max Dunker's *History of Antiquity*, Vol. IV, p. 436

simple act of explosion but something very much like a fuse, to enable the explosion to occur at a particular period."[1]

Viśvāmitra, when giving different kinds of weapons to Rāma, speaks (in the *Rāmāyaṇa*) of one as *Āgneya*, another as *Śikhara.*

आग्नेयमस्त्रन्दयितं शिखरन्नाम नामतः ।

"Carey and Marshman render *Śikhara* as a combustible weapon."[2]

In the *Mahābhārata* we read of "a flying ball emitting the sound of a thunder-cloud which is expressed in referring to artillery."[3]

The *Harivaṁśa* thus speaks of the fiery weapon:

आग्नेयमस्त्रं लब्ध्वा च भार्ग्गवात्सगरो नृपः ।
जिगाय पृथिवीं हत्वा तालजङ्घान्सहैहयान् ।।

"King Sagara having received fire-arms from Bhargava conquered the world, after slaying the Tāljaṅghas and the Haihayas."

M. Langlois says that "these fire-arms appear to have belonged to the Bhargavas, the family of Bhṛgu."[4] Again,

---

[1] Elliot's *Historians of India*, Vol.I, p. 365

[2] Various kinds of weapons are mentioned, some of which are extraordinary. As it is not known how they were made, what they were like, and how they were used, people think they are only poetic phantasies. Mr. Elliot says, "Some of these weapons mentioned above were imaginary, as for instance, the *vāyava* or airy." But who would not have called the gramaphone, the cinematograph and wireless telegraphy imaginary only 50 years ago.

[3] Bohlen, *Das Alte Indien*, II, 66

[4] *Harivañśa*, p. 68

उर्ध्वस्तु जातकर्म्मादि तस्य कृत्वा महात्मनः ।।
अध्याप्य वेदानखिलांस्ततोऽस्त्रम्प्रत्यपादयत् ।

आग्नेयन्तु महाबाहुरमरैरपि दुस्सहम् ।।
स तेनास्त्र बलेनाजी बलेन च समन्वितः ।

"Aurva having performed the usual ceremonies on the birth of the great-minded (Prince), and having taught him the Vedas instructed him in the use of arms; the great-armed (Aurva presented him the fiery weapon, which even the immortals could not stand."

Difference between Training weapons and service weapons

According to *Dhanurveda*, there should be a difference between training weapons and service weapons. The service weapons should be powerful with less weight and length than the arms of the soldier. A soldier who is overburdened by the weight of the weapon can never be successful in hitting the target. A weapon which can be operated easily by the soldier was considered to be auspicious and good for the soldier (*Sadāśiva Dhanurveda*: verse, 21-27).

Appendix - 1

(Text of Sadāśiva Dhanurveda)

(Sadāśiva Dhanurveda belongs to the tradition of Śiva. Śiva taught it to Paraśurāma.)

ईश्वरोक्ताद्धनुर्वेदाद् व्यासस्यापि सुभाषितात्।
पदान्याकृष्य रचितो ग्रन्थः संक्षेपतो मया।। 1।।

1. I have composed this work in brief by extracting the excellent utterances from the *Dhanurveda* of Iśvara (Śiva) and wise instructions of (Sage) Vyāsa.

विना शार्ंगधरं नान्यो धनुर्व्वेदस्य पारगः।
अतः स्वपने निशि प्राप्ते शिवतत्त्वविचारणम्।। 2।।

2. Nobody but Sārṅgadhara is considered to be an expert in *Dhanurveda*, because he learned this science in a dream at night from Śiva Himself.

अतः सन्देहदोलायां रोपणीयं न मानसम्।
ग्रन्थऽस्मिन् चापचतुरैर्वीरचिन्तामणौ क्वचित्।। 3।।

3. So, one should not harbour any doubt about this book just because some of its contents appear elsewhere in other works by others, excelling in this science, like *Vīra Cintāmaṇi.*

यस्याभ्यास प्रसादेन निष्पद्यन्ते धनुर्द्धराः।
जेतारः परसैन्यानां तस्याभ्यासो विधीयताम्।। 4।।

4. Archers (and warriors) should practise and sharpen their skill (weapon training) in such a way, that they are able to perform their duties and conquer the enemy.

एकोऽपि यत्र नगरे प्रसिद्धः स्याद्धनुर्द्धरः।
ततो यान्त्यरयो दूरं मृगाः सिंहगृहादिव।। 5।।

5. If just one famous Archer lives in a city, then the enemies will prefer distance just as animals maintain distance from the den of a lion.

अथ धनुर्दानविधिः
Selection for Military Training

आचार्य्येण धनुर्देयं ब्राह्मणेन परीक्षिते।
शठे धूर्त्ते कृतघ्ने च मन्दबुद्धे न दीयते।। 6।।

6. A preceptor should give the training of military science or select a person for military services after properly examining him who is not greedy, cunning, ungrateful or foolish.

ब्राह्मणाय धनुर्देयं खड्गं वै क्षत्रियाय च।
वैश्याय दापयेत् कुन्तं गदां शूद्राय दापयेत्।। 7।।

7. A person of *Brahmaṇa* personality should be selected for the training of weapons of mass destruction like missiles etc. A person of *Kṣatriya* personality should be selected for the training of weapons of the class of sword and falchion, etc. A person of *Vaiśya* personality is perfect for the training of weapon of the category of lance or spear. *Śudra* personality types of persons are fit to be trained into operations of weapon like (*Gadā*) mace.

अथ युद्धप्रकाराः
Types of Fighting

धनुष्चक्रन्तु कुन्तं च खड्गंच्छुरिकां गदाम्।
सप्तमं बाहुयुद्धं स्यादेवं युद्धानि सप्तधा।। 8।।

8. The fighting has been divided into seven types. The first type of fighting is carried out with the help of missiles, bows and arrows. The second type of fighting is carried out with *chakras* or weapons of the class of circular missiles. The third type of fighting is carried out with the help of weapons of the class of lance or spear (*kunta*). The fourth type of fighting is carried out with the help of weapons of the class of sword (*khaḍga*). The fifth type of fighting is carried out with the help of weapons of the class of bayonet type (*churikā*). The sixth type of fighting is carried out with the help of weapons of the class of mace (*Gadā*) and lastly, the seventh type of fighting is carried out with hand to hand.

अथाचार्यलक्षणम्

Classification of Preceptors (Trainers)

आचार्य्यः सप्तयुद्धैः स्याच्चतुर्भिर्भार्गवस्तथा।
द्वाभ्यांचैव भवेद्योद्धा एकेन गणको भवेत्।। 9।।

9. *Dhanurveda* classifies trainers or preceptors into four types according to the types of fighting. A preceptor excelling in different types of fighting has been designated differently. For instance, if a preceptor excels in all sevens types of fighting, he is called as *Saptayodhā*; he is called as '*Bhārgava*' if he is well-versed in four types of fighting. An expert in two forms of fighting is known as '*yodhā*' and if one is versed only in one type of fighting, he is known as '*Gaṇaka*'

हस्तः पुनर्व्वसुः पुष्यो रोहिणी चोत्तरात्रयम्।
अनुराधाश्विनी चैव रेवती दशमौ तथा।। 10।।

10. A person born on Moon's sojourn in particular constellations were considered to be fit for recruiting in the military. For instance, if a person is born on Moon's sojourn in the Constellation of *Hasta*, *Punarvasu*, *Puṣya*, *Rohiṇī*, three *Uttaras* (i.e. *Uttaraṣ āḍhā*, *Uttaraphalguni*, and *Uttarabhādrapada*), *Anurādhā*, *Aśvinī*, *Revatī* and also on the tenth lunar day i.e. *Daśamī tithi* are fit to be recruited in the military.

जन्मस्थे च तृतीये च षष्ठे वै सप्तमे तथा।
दशमैकादशे चन्द्रे सर्व्वकर्माणि कारयेत्।। 11।।

11. On the other hand, people born in the third, sixth, seventh, tenth, or eleventh day of the lunar fortnight was supposed to be fit for conducting all types of work.

तृतीया पंचमी चैव सप्तमी नवमी तथा।
त्रयोदशी द्वादशी च तिथयश्च शुभा मताः।। 12।।

12. The third, fifth, seventh, ninth, twelfth, and thirteenth day of the lunar fortnight is accepted to be auspicious for military training.

सूर्य्यवारः शुक्रवारो गुरूवारस्तथैव च।
एतद् वारत्रयं धन्यं प्रारम्भे शस्त्रकर्म्मणि।। 13।।

13. Sundays, Fridays, and Thursdays are taken to be very suitable for commencing any work relating to military training or weapon training.

एभिर्द्दिनैश्च शिष्याय गुरूः शस्त्राणि दापयेत्।
सन्तर्प्यदानहोमाभ्यां सुरान् शास्त्रविधानतः।। 14।।

14. On these days the preceptor should give training and hand over weapons to his disciples after paying due homage to the scholars through donations and *homa* as per the injunction of the *Śāstras*.

शिष्याय मानुषं चापं धनुर्व्वेदाभिमन्त्रितम्।
काण्डात्काण्डेति मन्त्रेण दद्याद्वेदविधानतः।। 15।।

15. The preceptor should hand over after proper training a *Mānuṣa* bow to his disciple with the chanting of Yajurvedic *Mantra* (13.20) '*kāṇḍāt kāṇḍāt prarohanti...*'[1].

---

[1] *kāṇḍāt kāṇḍāt prarohantī paruṣaspari*

अथ वेधविधिः
Shooting Techniques

प्रथमं पुष्पवेधंच फलहीनेन पत्रिणा।
ततः फलयुतेनैव मत्स्यवेधंच कारयेत्।। 16।।

16. The above verse deals with the method of shooting a target. Accordingly, a trainee should be allowed to practice first with arrows devoid of their heads, then with arrows equipped with their heads. First of all, a trainee should try to hit the target with arrows devoid of their heads or say with blunt arrow-heads, then he should try to hit the targets with arrows equipped with their heads. By this method, a trainee will be able to hit the target exactly.

मांसवेधन्ततः कुर्य्यादेवं वेधो भवेत्त्रिधा।
पुर्व्ववेधैः कृताः पुंसा शराः स्मः सर्व्वसाधकाः।। 17।।

17. Afterwards, the disciple is made to pierce the upper skin of an animal, etc. (*mānsavedha*) without harming the lower skin or bones. These are the three types of piercing. By practicing shooting of arrows gradually at targets in such manner the soldier will achieve the skill to shoot his targets more effectively and efficiently.

एवं वेधत्रयं कृत्वा शंखदुन्दुभि निस्वनैः।
ततः प्रणम्य गुरवे धनुर्बाणान्निवेदयेत्।। 18।।

18. The above mentioned three types of shooting should be done accompanied by the sound of a conch-shell and drum, and then the trainee should entrust his bow and arrow to his preceptor by bowing down to him and offering his obeisance.

---

evā no dūrve pra tanu sahasreṇa śatena.

अथ चापप्रमाणम्

The Type and Size of a Bow

प्रथमं पौरुषं चापं युद्धचापं द्वितीयकम्।
निजबाहुबलोन्मानं किंचदूनं शुभं भवेत्।। 19।।

19. The first form of the bow is a practice bow (mainly used for practice). The second one is a bow that is used in fighting (battle). A bow that is inferior to the archer as compared to his physical power and weight is regarded as the best one.

वरं प्राणाधिको धन्वी न तु प्राणाधिकं धनुः।
धनुषा पीड्यमानस्तु धन्वी लक्ष्यं न पश्यति।। 20।।

20. The life of an archer is more precious than that of a bow. An archer, who is overburdened by his bow, never hits the target.

अतोनिजबलोन्मानं धनुः स्याच्छुभकारकम्।
देवानामुत्तमं चापं ततोन्यूनं च मानवम्।। 21।।

21. So a bow that is compatible with the physical power and weight of an archer is considered to be the best one. The *Deva* type of bow is said to be the best one followed by a *Mānuṣa* bow.

सार्द्धपंचमहस्तन्तु श्रेष्ठं चापं प्रकीर्त्तितम्।
तद्विज्ञेयं धनुर्दिव्यं शंकरेण धृतं पुरा।। 22।।

22. A bow measuring five hands[1] and a half (99 inches) is considered to be the best one and that type is called a '*Divya* bow', held by Saṅkara in ancient days.

तस्मात् परशुरामेण ततोद्रोणेन धीमता।
द्रोणाद्गृहीतं पार्थेन ततः सात्यकिना धृतम्।। 23।।

---

[1] **Note** : The length of one hand is equal to the length of 24 fingers or 18 inches)

23. From Śaṅkara, the bow was taken by Paraśurāma and from him, it came to Droṇa and then it was received by Pārtha (Arjuna) from Drona, and thereafter it was taken by Sātyaki.

कृतयुगे महादेवः त्रेतायांचैव राघवः।
द्वापरे द्रोणविप्रश्च दैवं चापमधारयत्।। 24।।

24. During *Satyayuga*, the Daiva (divine) type of bow was held by Mahādeva. In the Tretā yuga, it was held by Rāghava. During the Dvāpara yuga, it was handled by Dronācārya.

चर्तुविंशागुंलो हस्त चतुर्हस्तं धनुर्भवेत्।
तद्भवेन्मानुषं चापं सर्व्वलक्षणसंयुतम्।। 25।।

25. The length of a hand is equal to the length of twenty-four fingers of the hand i.e. 18 inches, and a bow which measures four hands (72 inches) in length is called as *Mānava* or *Mānuṣa* bow attributed with all qualities.

त्रिपर्व्वं पंचपर्वंच सप्तपर्व्वंच कीर्त्तितम्।
नव पर्वंच कोदण्डं चतुर्द्धा शुभदायकम्।। 26।।

26. A good quality bow either has three, five, seven, or nine joints. A bow with nine joints was called as '*Kodaṇḍa*' which was considered squarely the best one.

चर्तु पंचपर्वंच षट्पर्व्वमष्टपर्व्वंच वर्जयेत् ।
केषाचिच भवेच्चाप वितस्तिनव सम्मितम्।। 27।।

27. A bow having four, six, or even eight joints should be discarded. But there are some bows which measure 9 *vitastis*[1] i.e. 81 inches in size.

---

[1] Note : One *vitasti* is a distance between the long thumb and a little finger or between the wrist and the tip of the finger and said to be equal to 12 *Aṅgulas* or about 9 inches)

अथ वर्जितधनुः
Prohibited Bows

अति जीर्णमपक्वंच ज्ञातिधृष्टन्तथैव च।
दग्धं छिन्नं न कर्त्तव्यं बाह्याभ्यन्तरहस्तकम्।। 28।।

28. A bow that is extremely old, or made of unripe materials, or used by one's kinsmen, or burnt or perforated one, should be discarded.

गुणहीनं गुणाक्रान्तं काण्डदोषसमन्वितम्।
गलग्रन्थि तलग्रन्थि न कर्त्तव्यं सदा बुधैः।। 29।।

29. A bow without a string or a bow overwhelmed by string should be avoided. A bow with a defect in the stem, or a bow having joints at the neck (upper portion) and also at the bottom should not be used by a wise warrior.

अपक्वं भंगमायाति अतिजीर्णन्तु कर्कशम्।
ज्ञातिधृष्टन्तु सोद्वेगं कलहो बान्धवैः सह।। 30।।

30. A bow made of unripe material may break up easily. An old bow, or a bow made of a very old material loses its elasticity. A bow already used by one's kinsmen may always be an object of anxiety or dispute among friends and relatives.

दग्धेन दह्यते वैश्मच्छिद्रं युद्धविनाशनम्।
बाह्ये लक्ष्यं न लभ्यते तथैवाभ्यन्तरऽपि च।। 31।।

31. A burnt or perforated bow may cause a fire and bring defeat and destruction in war. Such a bow does not reach the target, external or internal.

हीने तु सन्धिते बाणे संग्रामे भंगकारकम्।
आक्रान्ते तु पुनर्लक्ष्ये लक्ष्यं न प्राप्यते दृढम्।। 32।।

32. If an inferior type of bow is fixed with an arrow, it may break up in war. A perfect shooting is not possible if the bow is overwhelmed by a string.

गलग्रन्थि तलग्रन्थि धनहानिकरं धनुः ।
एतैर्द्दोषैर्विनिर्मुक्तं सर्वलक्षणकारकम् ।। 33 ।।

33. A bow with a knot or joint at the neck or bottom may lead to the loss of wealth. A bow devoid of all such flaws is considered to be good for all purposes.

शार्ंगन्तु वै धनुर्दिव्यं तद्विष्णोः परमायुधम् ।
वितस्तिसप्तमं मानं निर्म्मितं विश्वकर्मणा ।। 34 ।।

34. The *Divya* (*mantra* operated) *Sāraṅga* bow is the great weapon of Viṣṇu. It was made by Viśvakarmā and measured seven *vitastis* (63 inches)

न स्वर्गे न च पाताले न भूमौ कस्यचित् करे ।
तद्धनुर्नवशं याति मुक्तैकं पुरुषोत्तमम् ।। 35 ।।

35. That bow could not be handled by anybody on the poles (north and south poles: North pole is called as *Svarga*, south pole is called a *Pātāla*) and the equator (equtorial regions are called as *Bhūmi loka*) except Viṣṇu.

पौरुषेयन्तु यत्कार्य्यं बहुयत्नेन योजितम् ।
वितस्तिभिः सप्तभिश्च मितं सर्व्वार्थसाधकम् ।। 36 ।।

36. Gradually, over many years, Viśvakarmā invented a bow which could be operated manually. It measured seven vitastis (i.e. 63 inches). The bow serves all purposes.

प्रायोज्ञेयं धनुः शार्ंगं गजारोहस्य साधनम् ।
रथिनांच पदातीनां वांशं चापं प्रकीत्तितम् ।। 37 ।।

37. A *Sāraṅga*-bow (made of horns) is usually used by the soldiers on an elephant back and the cavalry. However, a *Vāñśa* bow (made of Bamboo) is more useful for charioteers and infantry.

अथ गुणलक्षणानि

The characteristics of a bowstring

गुणानां लक्षणं वक्ष्ये यादृशं कारयेद्गुणम्।
धनुः प्रमाणं निःसन्धिः कार्य्यस्त्रिगुणतन्तुभिः।। 38।।

38. I shall narrate the characteristics of the bowstring, and these are to be applied while making a string. The length of the string should be equal to that of the bow. It should be without joints and made of twisting three strings.

वर्त्तितः स्याद्गुणः सूक्ष्मः सर्व्वकार्य्य सहो युधि।
पट्टसूत्रैः गुणः कार्य्यः कनिष्ठामानसम्मितः।। 39।।

39. The strings should be made of silken strings thinner than that of the wick of the earthen lamp. It should be twisted in the thickness of the little finger. A string thus made withstand all strains during the war.

अभावं पट्टसूत्रस्य हरिणो स्नायुरिष्यते।
गुणार्थमय संग्राह्याः स्नायवो महिषो गवाम्।। 40।।

40. For the want of a silk thread, the string can be made with sinews of a deer or a buffalo or a cow.

तत्काले हत गोकर्णचर्म्म वा छागलस्य वा।
विलोमतन्तुरूपेण कुर्य्याद्वा गुणमुत्तमम्।। 41।।

41. Fine strings are to be made with the skin of a goat or *gokarṇa* (another variety of animal extinct now) died recently. The hair on the skin should be removed thoroughly.

पक्ववंश त्वचा कार्य्यो गुणस्तु स्थविरो दृढ।
पट्टसूत्रेण संन्नद्धः सर्व्वकार्य्य सहोयुधि।। 42।।

42. The bowstrings made of bark (skin) of ripe bamboo and twisted around with a silken thread are very strong and durable. They can withstand all types of stress and strain in the war.

प्राप्ते भाद्रपदे मासे त्वगर्कस्य प्रशस्यते।
तस्यास्तत्र गुणः कार्य्यः पवित्रः स्थावरोदृढ।। 43।।

43. At the advent of the month of Bhādrapada (September) the bark of the Arka (Sun Plant) becomes commendable for making fine bowstrings and hence the best and strong strings should be made with it.

वृत्तार्कसूत्रतन्तुनां हस्ता अष्टादश स्मृताः।
तद्वृत्तं त्रिगुणं कार्य्यं प्रमाणाऽयं गुणस्य च।। 44।।

44. The threads which are obtained from the barks of the *Arka* tree are eighteen hands in length and these should be made in triple-ply to make a proper string (for the bow).

अथ फललक्षणानि

The characteristics of Arrowheads

फलन्तु शुद्धलोहस्य सधारं तीक्ष्णमस्तकम्।
योजयेद् वज्रलेपेन सारपक्षानुसारतः।। 45।।

45. The arrow-head should be made of purified iron, be sharp and pointed. They should be coated with the hardening plaster according to their feathers.

अथ फलप्रकाराः

Arrowhead Types

आरामुखं क्षुरप्रंच गोपुच्छं चार्द्धचन्द्रकम्।
सूचीमुखंच भल्लंच वत्सदन्तं सुवल्लभम्।। 46।।

46. The arrow-heads can be of the awl type, razor blade type, like that of a cow's tail, crescent moon shaped, needle-pointed, spear-headed and shaped like teeth of calf.

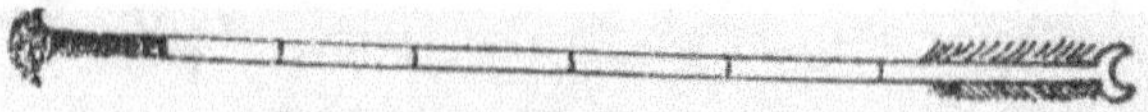

Ārāmukha (Awl type)

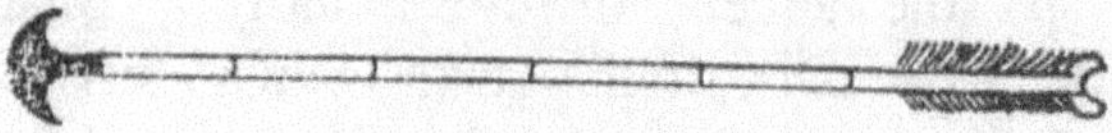

Kṣurapra (Razor Blade type)

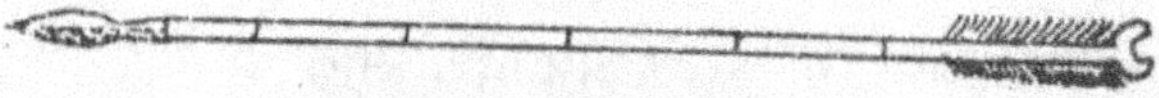

Gopuccha (Cow's tail type)

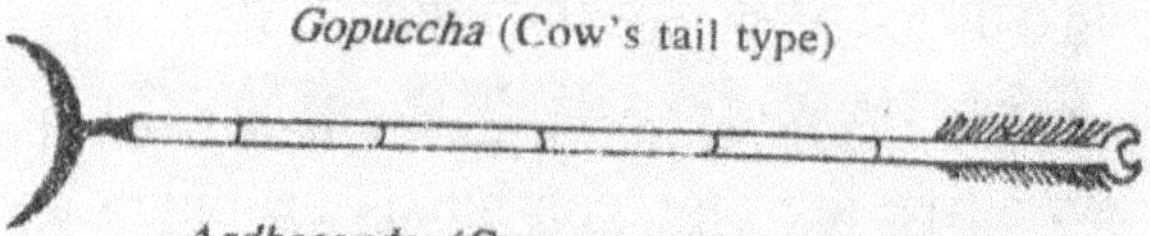

Ardhacandra (Crescent moon shaped)

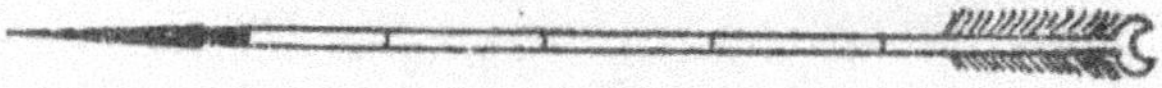

Sūcīmukha (Needle pointed)

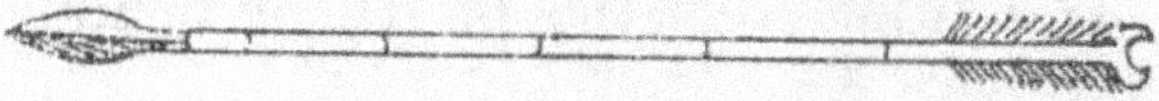

Bhalla (Spear-headed)

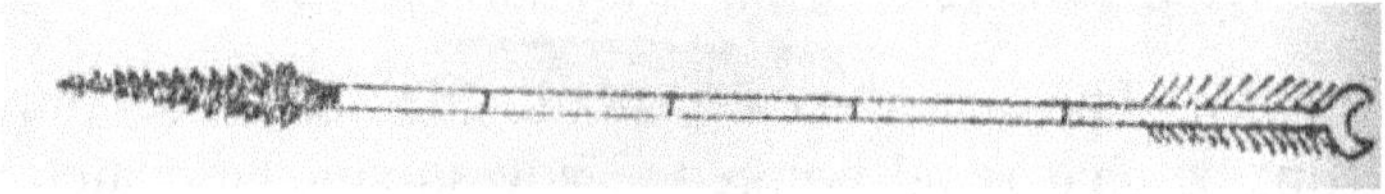

Vatsadanta (Teeth of calf shaped)

कर्णिकं काकतुण्डंच तथाचान्येऽप्यनेकशः
फलानि देशदेशेषु भवन्ति बहुरूपतः || 47 ||

47. The arrowhead may be of petal of flower type, the beak of a crow, and many other types. The shape of arrow-heads differs from country to country.

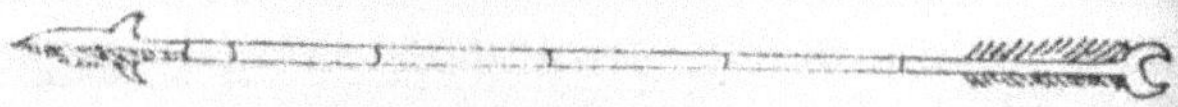

Karṇī (petal of flower type)

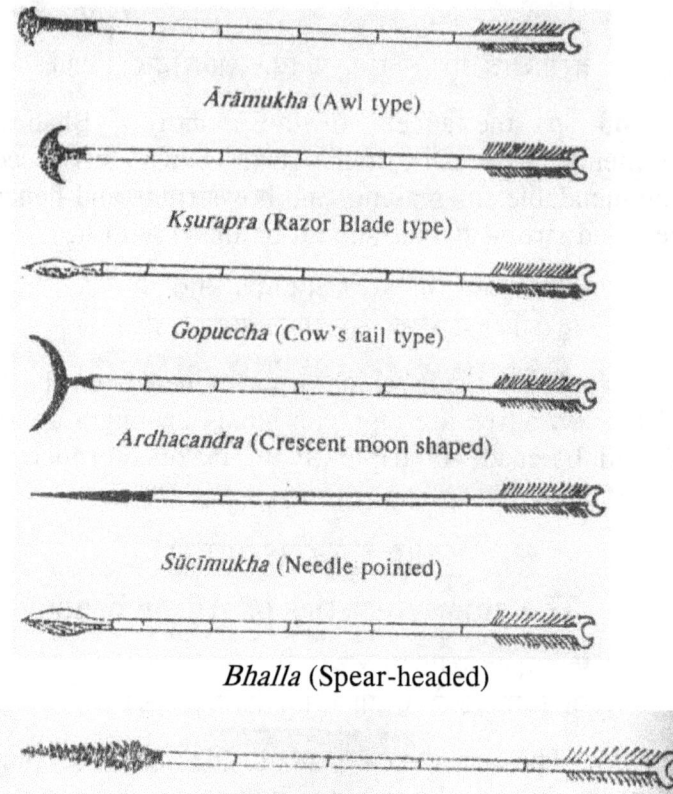

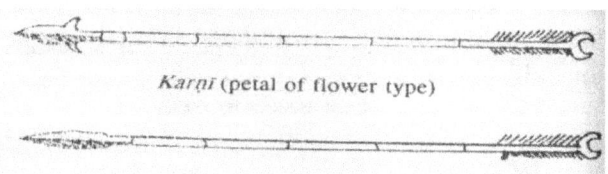

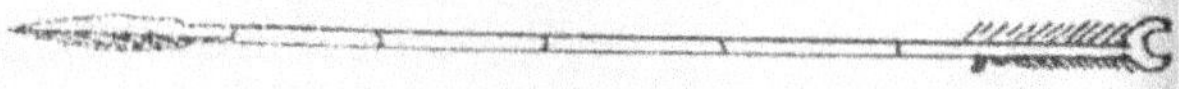

Kākatuṇḍa type (beak of crow type)

अथैतेषां कर्म्माणि

Functions of various Arrowheads

आरामुखेनवै चर्म्म क्षुरप्रेण च कार्म्मुकम्।
सूचीमुखेन कवचमर्द्धचन्द्रक मस्तकम्।। 48।।

48. The various types of arrowheads have various types of functions. For instance, the *ārāmukha* or an arrowhead like an awl can cut through the skin, an arrowhead like razor blade (*kṣurapra*) is used to combat the arrows of the enemy or to cut up the hand of the enemy. *Gopuccha* (an arrow like cow's tail) is good for hitting a target in general. The arrow-shaped like crescent moon is used to sever the enemy's head, neck, and bow. The needle pointed arrows were used to pierce the armour of an enemy.

भल्लेन हृदयं वेध्यं द्विभल्लेन तथैव च।
लोहंच काकतुण्डेन लक्ष्यं गोपुच्छकेन च।। 49।।

49. The spear-headed arrow and two-pronged arrows were used to pierce the chest of an enemy, while the arrowhead of crow's beak type and cow's tail types are used to hit (combat) the metallic weapons.

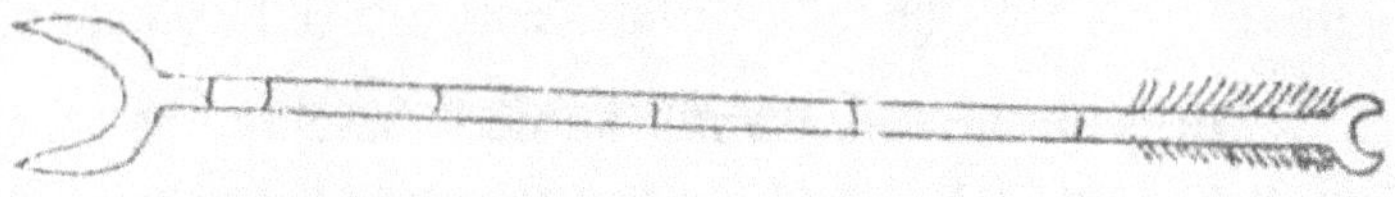

Dvibhalla (Two spear-headed)

अन्यद्गोपुच्छकं ज्ञेयं शुद्धकांस्यै विनिर्म्मितम्।
मुखेन चापि कण्ठेन वेधमगुंलिसम्मितम्।। 50।।

50. In addition to the above arrowheads, there is a special *gopuccha* type (shaped like cow's tail) arrowhead, which is made out of pure bell metal and has got a metallic nail of three *aṅgula* lengths fixed at its tip.

This *gopuccha* arrowhead was used for practices in aiming for targets and archery.

अथ शरपक्षाणि
The Feathers of Arrows

कंकहंसशशादानां मत्स्यादक्रौंचकिंकिनाम्।
गृध्रानां कुक्कुटानां च पक्षा एतेषु शोभनाः।। 51।।

51. The end of an arrow may be fletched with the feathers like that of crane (*kaṅka*), swan (*haṁsa*), *śaśāda* (a variety of bird which has become extinct now), fisher bird (*matsyāda*), heron (*krauñca*), vulture (*gṛdhra*) and cock (*kukkuṭa*) along with small bells (*kiṅkinī*).

एकैकस्य शरस्यैव चतुष्पक्षाणि योजयेत्।
षडगुंलप्रमाणेन पक्षच्छेदं च कारयेत्।। 52।।

52. Four feathers are to be attached to each arrow. The gap between two feathers should be six fingers (five inches).

दशांगुलमिताः पक्षाः शांर्गचापस्य मार्गणे।
योज्या दृढाश्चर्तुसंख्याः सन्नद्धाः स्नायुतन्तुभिः।। 53।।

53. In the bow (*Dhanu*) named *Sārṅga*, the gap between two feathers is to be ten fingers (8 inches) and the four feathers should be firmly tied with hard sinews.

अथ शराणां वर्णनम्

Types of Arrows

शराश्च त्रिविधा ज्ञेयाः स्त्री पुमांश्च नपुंसकः।
अग्रे स्थूलो भवेन्नारी पश्चात्स्थूलो भवेत्पुमान्।। 54।।

54. There are three types of arrows - male, female,

and impotent. The one heavier towards the point is female, the one heavier towards the end is male.

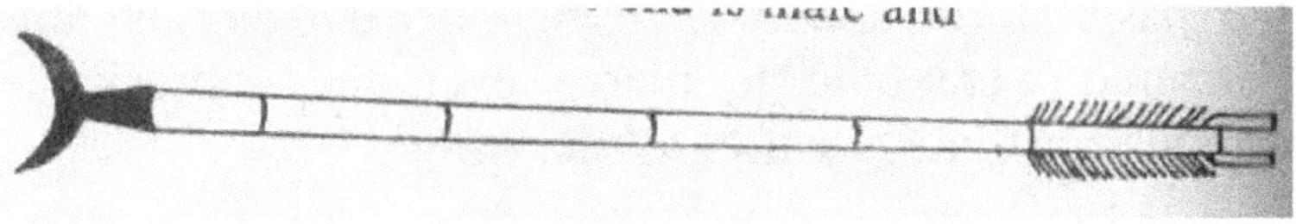

Female Arrow

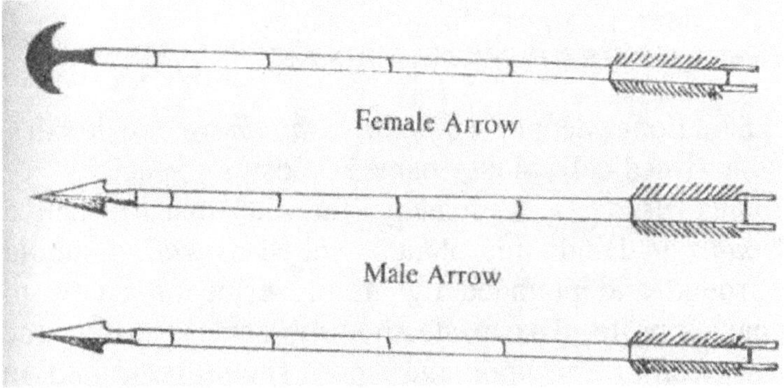

Impotent Arrow

समं नपुंसकं ज्ञेयं तल्लक्ष्यार्थं प्रशस्यते।
दूरापातं युवत्या च पुरुषो भेदयेद् दृढम।। 55।।

55. The one equal throughout is termed as impotent. The impotent type is helpful in the practice of archery, the female type is a fast runner and hit targets at long distance and the male type is able to pierce a strong and tough target.

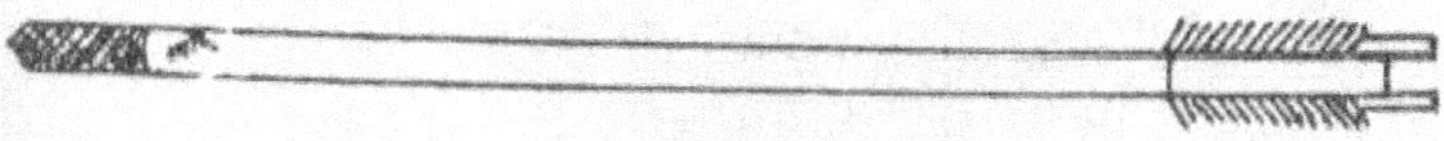

Impotent Arrow

अथ पायनम

The Methods of Tempering Arrow-heads

फलस्य पायनं वक्ष्ये दिव्यौषधि विलेपनम्।
येन दुर्व्वेध्य वर्म्माणि भेदयेत्तरुपत्रवत्।। 56।।

56. let me narrate the process of tempering arrowheads. The process starts by smearing them into the paste of certain medicines. The arrowheads thus tempered were able to pierce even the unbreakable armours just like a leaf of a tree.

पिप्पली सैन्धवं कुष्ठं गोमुत्रेण च पेषयेत्।
अनेन लेपयेच्छस्त्रं लिप्तं चाग्नौ प्रतापयेत्।।
अविष्पातं बलाविद्धं पीतमग्नौ तथौषधम्।
ततो निर्व्वापितं लोहं तत्र वेधे विशिष्यते।। 57।।

57. Long pepper (*pippalī*), *saindhava* (rock-salt), kuṣṭha (medical plant named Costus Specious or arabicus used as a remedy for the disease called *takman*, in Hindi this plant is called as *kūṭha*) should be ground and pounded by mixing urine of a cow to prepare a paste. That paste should be smeared over the arrow-head or a weapon and then it should be heated on fire till it becomes blue like peacock's neck. When it absorbs the entire paste, it must be quenched in water. Such weapons will become the best weapons.

पंचभिर्लवणैः पिष्टैर्मधुसिक्तैः ससर्षपैः।
एभिः प्रलेपयेच्छस्त्रं लिप्तं चाग्नौ प्रतापयेत्।। 58।।

58. The paste prepared out of five types of salt-soaked in honey and mustard oil is also best for tempering. The arrowhead should be besmeared with this paste and then heated over a fire.

शिखिग्रीवानुवर्णाभं तप्तपीतं तथौषधम्।
ततस्तु विगलं तोयं पाययेच्छस्त्रमुत्तमम्।। 59।।

59. When it becomes blue like peacock's neck, and the whole paste disappeares, quench it into the water. It will become the best weapon.

अथ नाराच–नालिकशतघ्नीनां वर्णनम्

Types of Rounds

सर्वलोहास्तु ये बाणा नाराचास्ते प्रकीर्त्तिताः।
पंचभिः पृथुलैः पक्षैर्युक्ता सिद्धयन्ति कस्यचित्।। 60।।

60. The missiles made completely of metals were called as *nārāca*. Some *nārācas* had five broad wings and they were able to make anybody successful in hitting his target.

Nārāca Arrow

नालीका लघवो बाणा नलयन्त्रेण चोदिताः।
अत्युच्चदूरपातेषु दुर्गयुद्धेषु ते मताः।। 61।।

61. Gun-shots or bullets were known as small arrows or *Nālikā*. They were fired by a machine fitted with a barrel (just like the modern-day gun). Those small arrows or bullets were useful in shooting a target seated at the very high place or in war taking place in a fortress. Thus in ancient times, guns were also used in fighting.

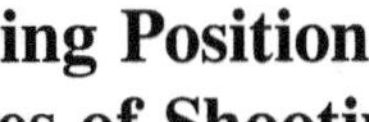

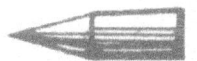

Nālika Arrow (Bullets)

अथ स्थानमुष्ट्याकर्षणलक्षणानि

Shooter's Standing Positions, Grips, and Modes of Shooting

स्थानान्यष्टौ विधेयानि योजयेद्भिन्नकर्मणा।
मुष्टयः पंच समाख्याता व्यायाः पंच प्रकीर्त्तिताः।। 62।।

62. '*Sthāna*' (the position to be taken by a warrior while shooting) is of eight types for performing different types of shooting. '*Muṣṭi*' holding the string or 'grips of string' are of five types, while the position of drawing the string is also of five types.

अग्रतो वामपादं च दक्षिणं जानुकुञ्चितम् ।
आलीढं तु प्रकर्तव्यं हस्तद्वयसविस्तरम् ।। 63 ।।

63. If during the time of the shooting, the left leg of a shooter is stretched out and the right leg is contracted at the knee, the distance between both the legs being two hand units (36 inches) apart (of the concerned shooter, such posture of a shooter is known by the term '*Ālīḍha*'.

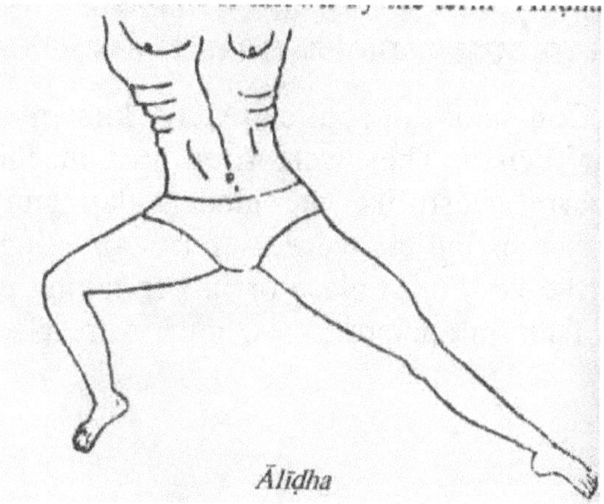

Ālīḍha

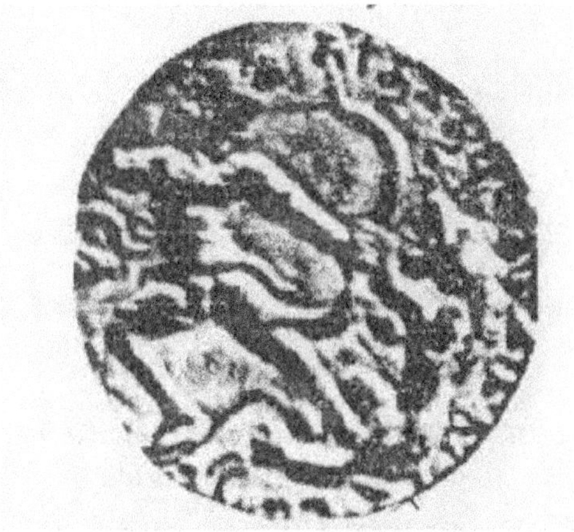

Ālīḍha posture of a bowman also depicted into the golden coins of Gupta period

प्रत्यालीढं तु कर्त्तव्यं सव्यं चेदानुकुचितम्।
दक्षिणं च पुरस्तद्वद्दूरपाते विशिष्यते।। 64।।

64. If during the time of the shooting, the right leg of a shooter is stretched out and the left leg is contracted at the knee, this position is called as *Ptatyālīḍha*'. It is extremely useful in hitting distant targets.

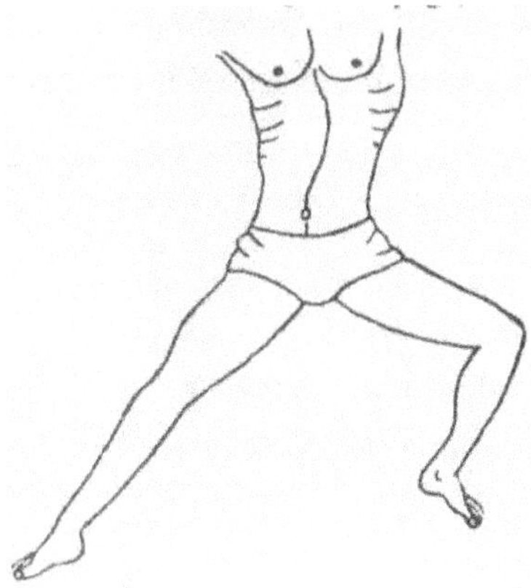

Pratyālīḍha

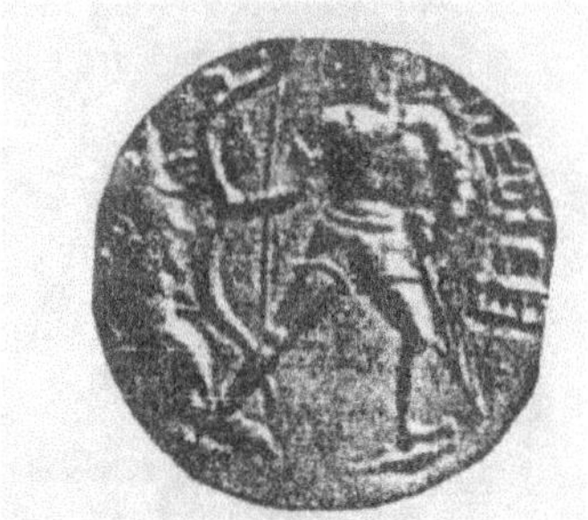

Prtyālīḍha posture of a bowman also depicted into the golden coins of the Gupta period

पादौ सुविस्तरौ कार्यौ समो हस्तप्रमाणतः।
विशाखस्थानकं ज्ञेयं कूटलक्ष्यस्य वेधने।। 65 ।।

65. If the shooter extends his legs equally and their distance is one hand (18 inches) apart, this position is known as '*viśākhasthāna*' and useful to hit the complex or invisible targets.

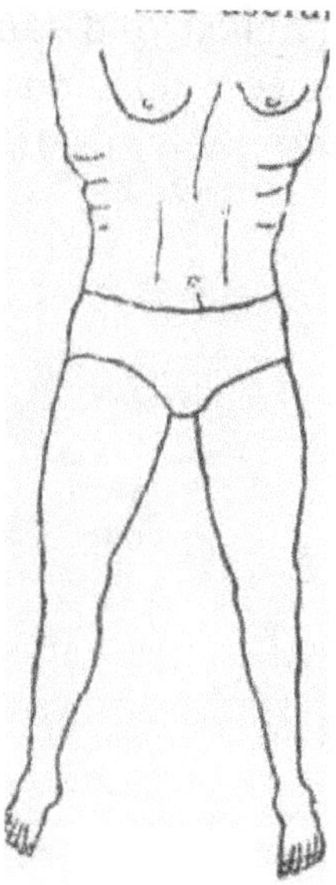

Viśākha

समपादे समौ पादौ निष्कम्पौ च सुसंगतौ।
असमे च पुरो वामे हस्तमात्रे नतं वपुः।। 66।।

66. In the *Samapāda* position, both legs are together close to each other at an equal distance, steps are firm and unsteady. In *Asamapāda* position, the left leg is placed in front with a distance of one hand (18 inches) from the right leg. The body is bent forward.

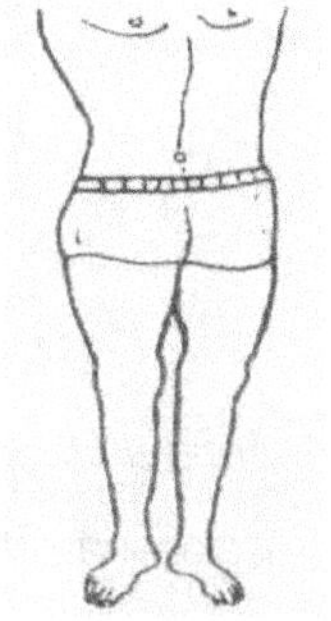

Samapāda

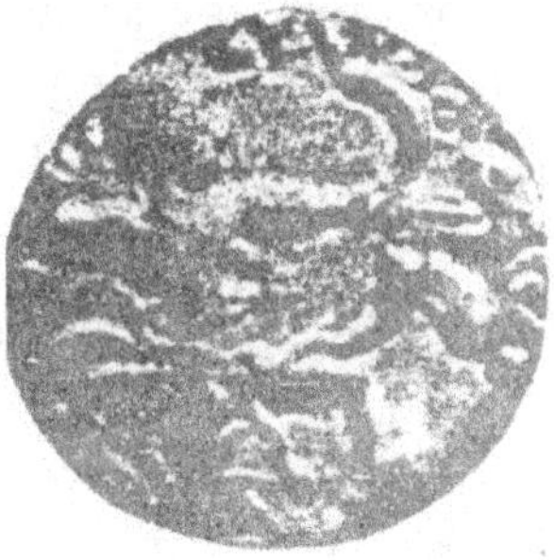

Asampāda posture of a bowman also depicted into the golden coins of the Gupta period

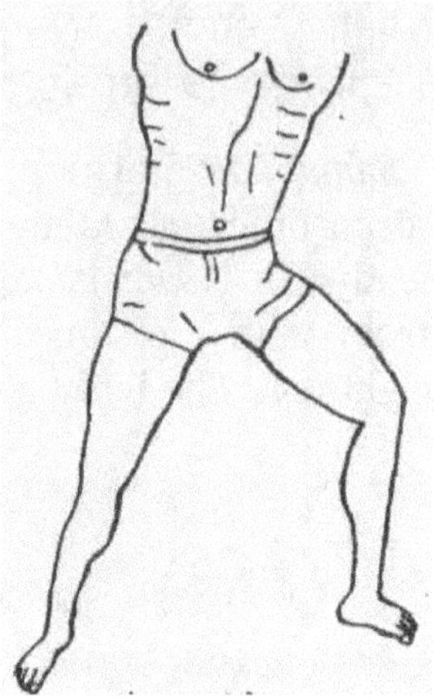

Asamapāda

आकुचितोरु द्वौ यत्र जानुभ्यां धरणिगतौ।
दर्दुरक्रममित्याहुः स्थानकं दृढभेदने।। 67।।

67. If the shooter kneels down and his thighs are contracted, his position is known by the name '*Dardurakrama*', (literally meaning 'the movement of the frog'). This position is useful for hitting a strong or difficult target.

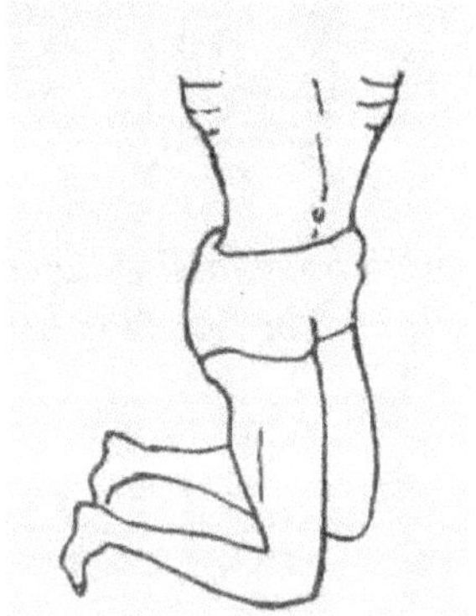

Dardurkrama

सव्यं जानुगतं भूमौ दक्षिणं च सकुचितम्।
अग्रतो यत्र दातव्यं तं विद्याद्गरुडक्रमम्।। 68।।

68. If the left knee rests on the ground while the right knee is contracted and kept in front, the position of the shooter is known as '*Garuḍakrama*'.

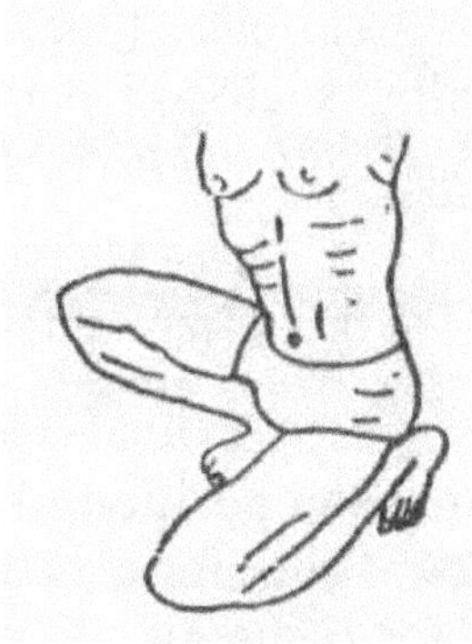

Garuḍakrama

पद्मासनं प्रसिद्धं उपविश्य यथाक्रमम्।
धन्विनां तत्तु विज्ञेयं स्थानकं शुभलक्षणम्।। 69।।

69. A shooter should sit in *Padmāsana* which is a well-known position of sitting (cross-legged). It is a very good pose for shooters also.

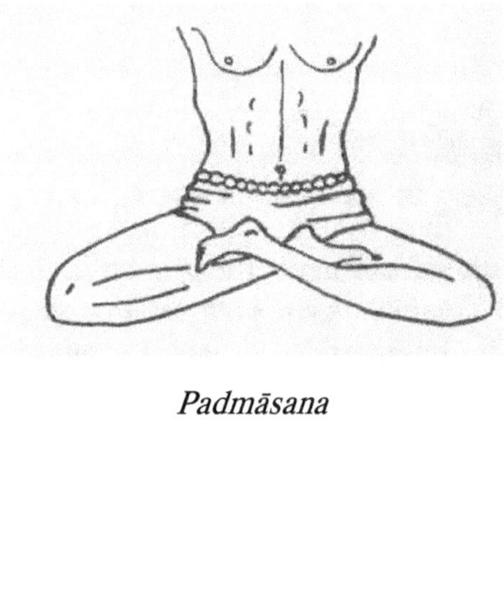

Padmāsana

अथ गुणमुष्टिः

Grips or Position of Release

पताका वज्रमुष्टिश्च सिंहकर्णी तथैव च।
मत्सरी काकतुण्डी च योजनीया यथाक्रमम्।। 70।।

70. There are various types of grips while triggering or shooting such as '*patākā*', '*vajramuṣṭi*', '*siṁhakarṇī*', '*matsarī*' and '*kākatuṇḍī*' etc.

दीर्घा तु तर्ज्जनी यत्र ह्याश्रिताऽगुंष्ठमूलकम्।
पताका सा च विज्ञेया नालिका दूरमोक्षणे।। 71।।

71. If the forefinger is extended and brought under the root of the thumb, the position of the grip is known by the name '*Patākā*'. This form of the grip is applied by a shooter for shooting *nālikās* (gunshots /rounds/small arrows) at a distant target.

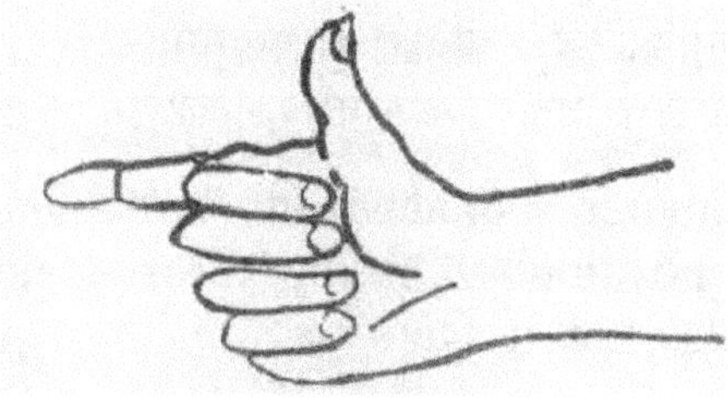

Patākā

तर्ज्जनी मध्यमा मध्यमगुंष्ठो विशते यदि।
वज्रमुष्टिस्तु सा ज्ञेया स्थूले नाराचमोक्षणे।। 72।।

72. If the thumb enters the gap between the middle finger and the forefinger then such a grip is called '*Vajramuṣṭi*'. Such a grip is used in releasing nārācās (missiles/metallic arrows) at distant targets.

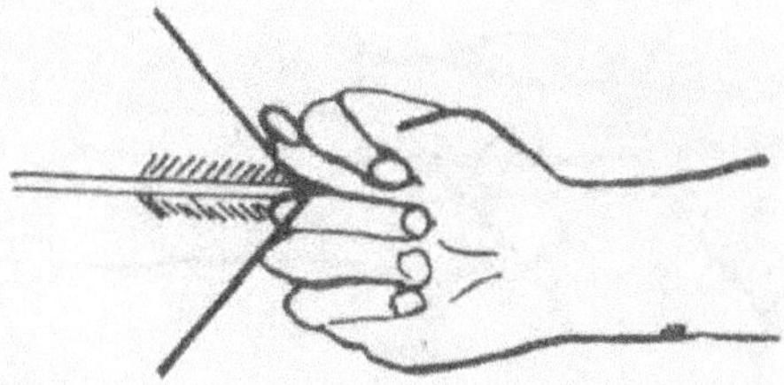

Vajramuṣṭī

अगुंष्ठनखमूले तू तर्ज्जन्यग्रं सुसंस्थितम्।
मत्सरी सा च विज्ञेया चित्रलक्ष्यस्य वेधने।। 73।।

73. If the tip of the forefinger is placed squarely on the nail of the thumb, such a grip is known by the name '*Matsarī*'. This grip is used in hitting *citra* (camouflaged) targets.

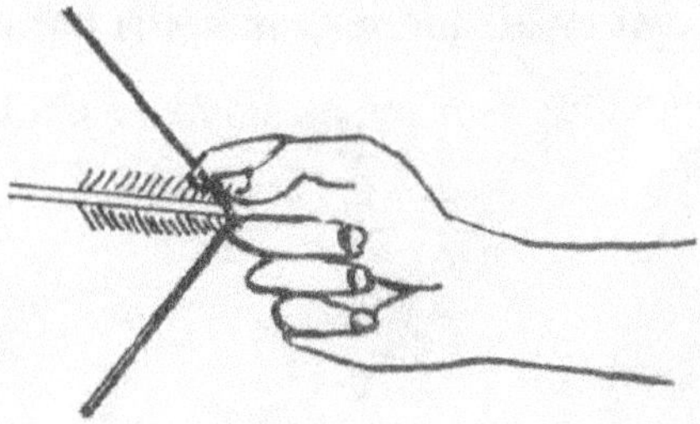

Matsarī

अगुंष्ठाग्रे तु तर्ज्जन्या मुखं यत्र निवेशितम्।
काकतुण्डी च विज्ञेया सूक्ष्मलक्ष्येषु योजिता।। 74।।

74. A grip is known by the name '*Kākatuṇḍī*' (like the beak of a crow) if the top portion of the thumb is placed on the tip of the forefinger. Such a grip is useful to hit the minute target.

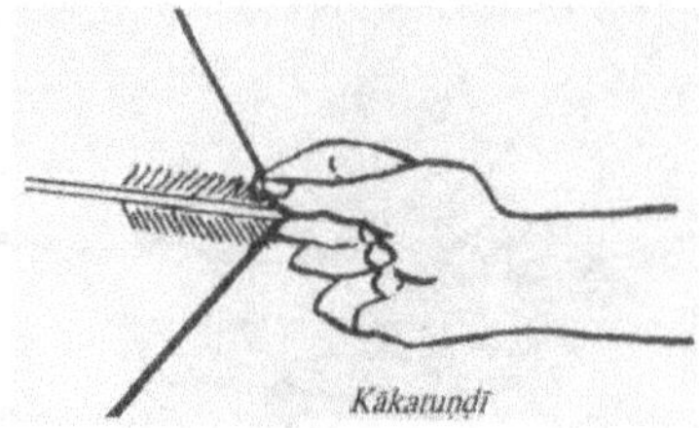

Kākatuṇḍī

अथ धनुर्मुष्टिसन्धानम्
Methods of Drawing the Bow

संधानं त्रिविधं प्रोक्तमधमूर्ध्वं समं तथा।
योजयेत्त्रिप्रकारं हि कार्येष्वपि यथाक्रमम्।। 75।।

75. There are three methods of drawing the bow, namely (i) lower; (ii) higher, and (iii) parallel.

i. In the lower draw, a stave is kept lower to the body.

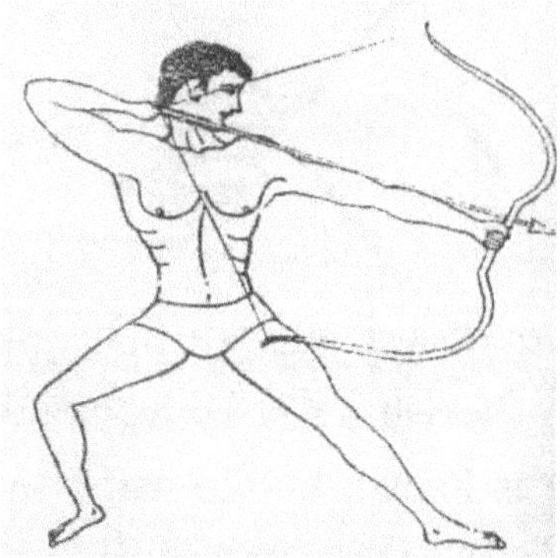

Adhaḥsandhāna (Lower Draw)

ii. In the higher draw, the stave is kept higher than the body.

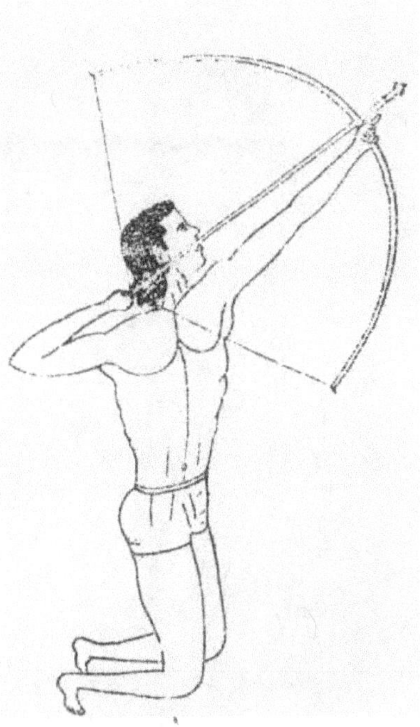

Ūrdhvasandhāna (Higher Draw)

iii. In the parallel draw, the stave is kept parallel to the body.

अधश्च दूरपातित्वं समे लक्ष्यं सुनिश्चितम् ।
दृढस्फोटं प्रकुर्वीत ऊर्ध्वसंस्थानयोगतः ।। 76 ।।

76. The lower draw is useful in long-range shooting. The parallel draw is useful in hitting targets firmly. The higher draw is useful in hitting strong targets.

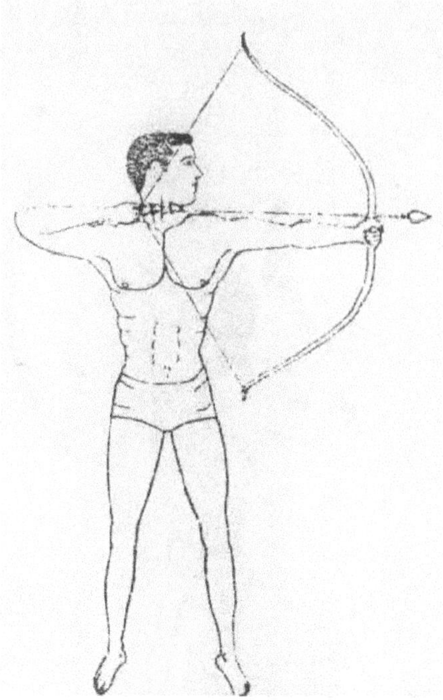

Samasandhāna (Parallel Draw)

अथ धनुर्व्यायाः

Drawing of the Bowstring

कैशिकः केशमूले चेच्छरः शृंगे च सात्त्विकः।
श्रवणे वत्सकर्णश्च ग्रीवायां भरतो भवेत्।। 77।।

77. If the bowstring is drawn up to the tip of the hair, the draw is known as *Kaiśika*, if drawn till the lock of hair, it is known as '*Sāttvika*'. If drawn till the ears, it is known by the name '*Vatsakarṇa*', and if drawn till the neck, it is known by the name '*Bharata*'.

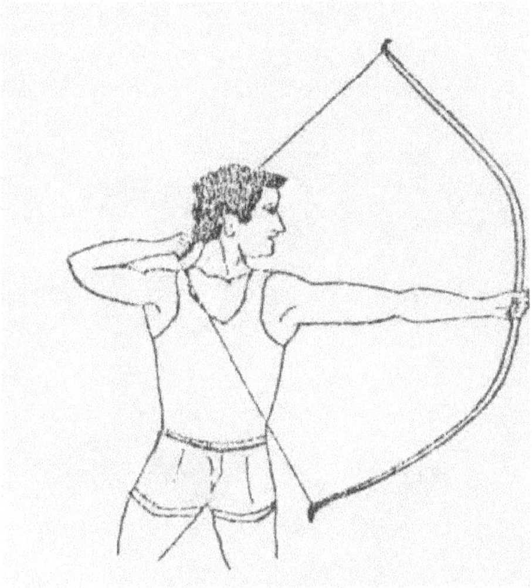

Kaiśika draw

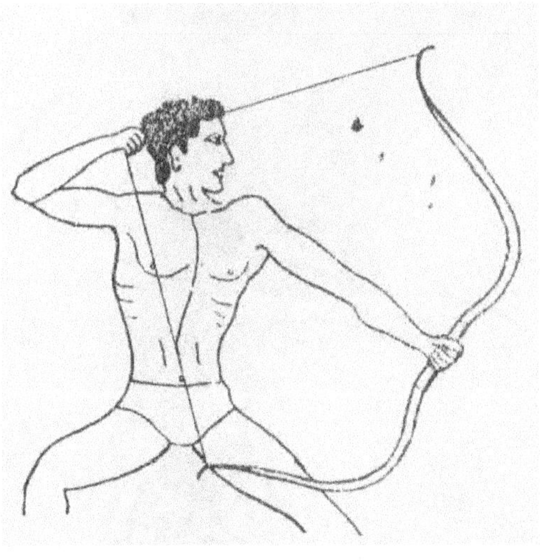

Sāttvika draw

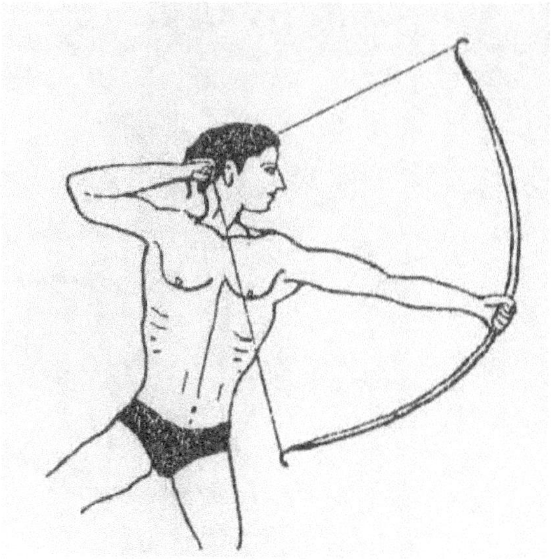

Vatsakarṇa draw

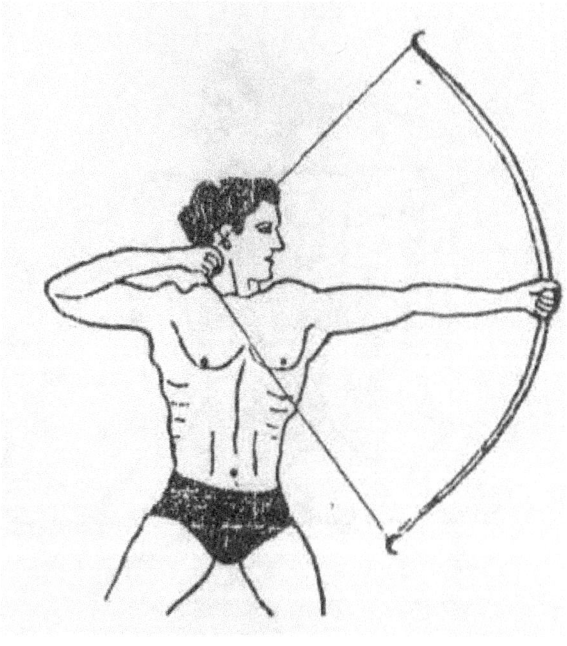

Bharata draw

अंसके स्कन्धनामा च व्यायाः पश्च प्रकीर्त्तिताः।
कैशिकश्चित्रयुद्धेषु अधोलक्ष्येषु सात्त्विकः।। 78।।

78. Bowstring when drawn up to the shoulder, the draw is called as '*Skandha*'. Thus there are five types of draws (*Vyāyas*). *Kaiśika* draw is useful in camouflaged warfares, *Sāttvika* draw is useful to hit targets at low positions.

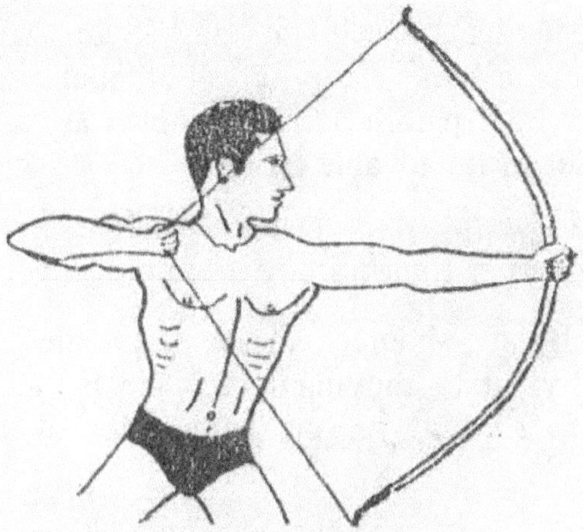

Skandhanāmā draw

वत्सकर्णः स विज्ञेयो भरतो दृढभेदने।
दृढभेदे च दूरे च स्कन्धनामानमुद्दिशेत्।। 79।।

80. *Vatsakarṇa* and *Bharata* are known to hit hard targets, while *Skandha* draw is useful in hitting both hard as well as distant targets.

अथ लक्ष्यम

Types of Targets

लक्ष्यं चतुर्विधं ज्ञेयं स्थिरं चैव चलं तथा।

चलाचलं द्वयचलं वेधनीयं क्रमेण तु।। 80।।

80. There are four types of targets: 1. *Sthira* (immovable, fixed or stationary), 2. *Cala* i.e. moving targets, 3. *Calācala* (a stationary target hit by the moving shooter) (4) *Dvayacala* (a mobile target hit by the moving shooter). One should learn the practice of the targets in the above order.

आत्मानं सुस्थिरं कृत्वा लक्ष्यं चैव स्थिरं बुधः।
वेधयेत्त्रिप्रकारं तु स्थिरवेधी स उच्यते।। 81।।

81. Making himself motionless and steady if a shooter hits all the three types of stationary targets (high, low, and parallel), he is known as '*sthiravedhī*' (the shooter of immovable target).

चलं तु वेधयेद् यस्तु आत्मना स्थिरसंस्थितः।
चललक्ष्यं तु तत्प्रोक्तमाचार्य्येण सुधीमता।। 82।।

82. If a shooter in a motionless position successfully hits a moving target, he is called by the experts as '*cala-lakṣya*' or the shooter of 'a moving target'.

धन्वी तु चलते यत्र स्थिरलक्ष्ये समाहितः।
चलाचलं भवेत्तत्र अप्रमेयनिन्दितम्।। 83।।

83. If a moving shooter hits the steady target, then he will be known as '*calācala*' or 'shooter of stationary target keeping himself in a moving position'.

उभावेव चलौ यत्र लक्ष्यं चापि धनुर्धरः।
तद्विज्ञेय द्वयचल श्रमेणैव हि साध्यते।। 84।।

84. When both the shooter and the target are in a moving stage, then the process of shooting is known as '*dvayacala*' i.e. 'both shooter and target being in moving condition'. This type of shooting efficiency can be achieved through the practice of *śrama* (a practice of shooting to hit a target with the help of many arrows shot by drawing the bowstring till the ears.

Note: According to *Ākāśa bhairava, śrama* means hitting a target with many arrows shot by drawing a bow string till the ears.

पुरतो वर्त्तमानस्य लक्ष्यस्य बहुधा शितैः ।
शरैराकर्णमाकृष्टैर्भेदनं यत् तदद्रिजे श्रम इत्युच्यते।। 85।।

श्रमेणास्खलितं लक्ष्यं दूरं च बहुभेदनम्।
श्रमेण कठिना मुष्टिः शीघ्रसंधानमाप्यते।। 86।।

85-86. If a shooter practises *śrama*, he can unfailingly hit many distant targets. Through the practice of *śrama*, he can achieve firm grip and an ability to hit the target quickly.

श्रमेन चित्रयोधित्वं श्रमेण प्राप्यते जयः।
तस्माद्गुरुसमक्षं हि श्रमः कार्यो विजानता।। 86।।

86. The shooting practice (*śrama*) makes a shooter expert in camouflaged warfare also, and through *śrama* he can achieve victory. Hence, it is advisable that a shooter should always practise shooting (*śrama*) in front of his teacher.

प्रथमं वामहस्तेन यः श्रमं कुरुते नरः।
तस्य चापक्रियासिद्धिरचिरादेव जायते।। 87।।

87. A shooter, who practises shooting first with his left hand, he becomes an expert in the art of shooting quickly.

वामहस्ते तु संसिद्धे पश्चद्दक्षिणमारभेत्।
उभाभ्यां च श्रमं कुर्यान्नाराचैश्च शरैस्तथा।। 88।।

88. Having become proficient with the left hand, one should start practice with the right hand. A shooter should do the practice of shooting arrows as well as rounds with both hands.

वामेनैव श्रमं कुर्यात्सुसिद्धे दक्षिणे करे।
विशाखेनासमेनैव तथा व्याय च कैशिके।। 89।।

89. When proficiency (in shooting) is achieved with the right hand, then again exercise should be started with the left hand. A shooter should practise shooting with *kaiśika* draw (drawing bowstring up to hair tips) standing in *Viśākhā* (keeping the feet parallel and 18 inches apart from each other) and *asampāda* (left leg is placed in front at a distance of 18 inches from the right leg and the body is bent forward) positions.

उदिते भास्करे लक्ष्यं पश्चिमायां निवेशयेत्।
अपराह्णे च कर्त्तव्यं लक्ष्यं पूर्वदिगाश्रितम्।। 90।।

90. At sunrise, the shooting should be practised in the western direction. In the afternoon it should in the eastern direction. Meaning to say that a target for practice should be in the opposite direction of the sun.

उत्तरेण सदा कार्यं प्राणस्य न विरोधकम्।
संग्रामेण विना कार्यं न लक्ष्यं दक्षिणामुखम्।। 91।।

91. One should not aim the target towards the north for the purpose of destroying life. One should not aim towards the south unless it is wartime.

अथ लक्ष्यवेधनम्

Aiming or Shooting of Rounds

षष्टिधन्वन्तरे लक्ष्यं ज्येष्ठलक्ष्यं प्रकीर्त्तितम्।
चत्वारिंशन्मध्यमं च विंशतिश्च कनिष्ठम्।। 92।।

92. A target set at a distance of sixty *dhanus* (360 feet)[1] is regarded as the best one. If the same is set at a

---

[1] One *dhanu* is equal to 4 *hasta*. One *hasta* is equal to 18 inches. As such one dhanu becomes equal to 72 inches or 6 feet.

distance of forty *dhanus* (240 feet), it is regarded as a medium one, whereas a target at a distance of twenty *dhanus* (120 feet) is regarded as the lowest type.

शराणां कथितं ह्येतन्नाराचानामथोच्यते।
चत्वारिंशच्च त्रिंशच्च षोडशैव भवेत्ततः।। 93।।

93. The above distance of the target was described in the case of arrows. Now we shall tell about the distance of targets in case of '*nārācas*'(bullets or rounds). In the case of *Nārācas,* a target set at a distance of forty *dhanus* (240 feet)[1] is regarded as the best one. If the same is set at a distance of thirty *dhanus* (180 feet), it is regarded as a medium one, whereas a target at a distance of sixteen *dhanus* (96 feet) is regarded as the lowest type.

चतुःशतैश्च काण्डानां यो हि लक्ष्यं विसर्जयेत्।
सूर्योदये चास्तमये स ज्येष्ठो धन्विनां भवेत्।। 94।।

94. One who is able to shoot four hundred shots (*kāṇḍa*) at the time of sunrise and the sunset, is considered as the best among shooters.

त्रिशतैर्मध्यमश्चैव द्विशताभ्यां कनिष्ठकः।
लक्ष्यं च पुरुषोन्मानं कुर्याच्चन्द्रकसंयुतम्।। 95।।

95. If the number of arrows shot is three hundred, the shooter is known as 'mediocre'; but if the number is just two hundred, then the shooter is known to be '*kaniṣṭhaka*'; i.e. of the lowest category or standard. Archers' targets should be of a man length (6 feet) and fitted with a *chandraka* (an eye of a peacock tail).

ऊर्ध्ववेधी भवेज्ज्येष्ठो नाभिवेधी च मध्यमः।

---

[1] One *dhanu* is equal to 4 hasta. One *hasta* is equal to 18 inches. As such one dhanu becomes equal to 72 inches or 6 feet.

यः पादवेधी लक्ष्यस्य स कनिष्ठो मतो मया।। 96।।

96. One who shoots the top portion of the eye is known to be the superior one, while one who shoots the middle portion is known as a mediocre one, and the one who hits the lowest portion of the eye is known as an inferior shooter.

अथानाध्यायः

Intermissions (*Anādhyaya*) in shooting

अष्टमी च अमावास्या वर्जनीया चतुर्दशी।
पूर्णिमार्धदिनं यावन्निषिद्धा सर्वकर्मसु।। 97।।

97. As all activities are prohibited on the eighth and the fourteenth day of both bright and dark halves of the moon and also on the day of the new-moon and half of the day of the full moon, shooting practice should also be discontinued on those days.

Note: *Taittirīa Āraṇyaka*, *Śatapatha Brāhmaṇa*, *Āpastamba Dharmasūtra*, and *Yājñavalkya Smṛti* also refers to a suspension of Vedic studies on these days.

अकाले गर्जिते देवे दुर्दिनं वाथवा भवेत्।
पूर्वकाण्डहतं लक्ष्यमनध्यायं प्रचक्षते।। 98।।

98. Practice shooting should be stopped if clouds thunder untimely, or there is rain or if the target is broken or destroyed by the arrows or rounds shot earlier.

श्रमं च कुर्वतस्तत्र भुजंगो यदि दृश्यते।
अथवा भज्यते चापं यदैव श्रमकर्मणि।। 99।।

99. The practice of shooting should be abandoned if a serpent is seen at the place of practice, or if the bow is broken at the time of practice.

त्रुट्यते वा गुणो यत्र प्रथमे बाणमोक्षणे।

श्रमं तत्र न कुर्वीत शस्त्रे मतिमतां वरः।। 100।।

100. If the bowstring snaps at the very first shot, then the practice should be abandoned.

अथ श्रमक्रिया

Shooting Practice

क्रियाकलापान्वक्ष्यामि श्रमसाध्यांशुचिष्मताम्।
येषां विज्ञानमात्रेण सिद्धिर्भवति नान्यथा।। 101।।

101. The process that is involved in the shooting is narrated hereunder for pure-hearted shooters. Only by knowing this process, one can achieve success in shooting and not otherwise.

प्रथमं चापमारोप्य चुलिकां बन्धयेत्ततः।
स्थानकं तु ततः कृत्वा बाणोपरि करं न्यसेत्।। 102।।

103. Firstly the bowstring should be tightened to the nocks (notch at either end of a bow for holding string), and only after taking his position, a shooter should handle the arrow.

तुलनं धनुषश्चैव कर्त्तव्यं वामपाणिना।
आदानं च ततः कृत्वा संधानं च ततः परम्।। 103।।

103. The bow should be picked up with the left hand at first and then the arrow should be mounted on the bowstring by picking up the bow with the right hand.

सकृदाकृष्टचापेन भूमिवेधं तु कारयेत्।
नमस्कुर्याच्छिवं विघ्नराजं गुरुधनुः शरान्।। 104।।

104. The shooter should draw the bow and with one attempt and pierce the earth, then he should salute the Almighty God, the destroyer of hindrances, his teacher/preceptor, bow, and arrows.

अथ प्राणायामाभ्यासः
Breath control in shooting

याचितव्या गुरोराज्ञा बाणस्याकर्षणं प्रति।
प्राणवायुं प्रयत्नेन बाणेन सह पूरयेत्।। 105।।

105. The permission for drawing a bow should be taken from the teacher or preceptor, the breath should also be inhaled (to fill up the lungs) carefully.

कुम्भकेन स्थिरं कृत्वा हुंकारेण विसर्जयेत्।
इत्यभ्यासक्रिया कार्या धन्विना सिद्धिमिच्छता।। 106।।

106. Afterward, *kumbhaka* should be performed (the breath should be held for a short time), thereafter, the breath should be released with the sound of 'hum'. An archer who desires success in his art should practise such breathing exercises (*Prāṇāyāma*).

षण्मासात्सिद्ध्यते मुष्टिः शराः संवत्सरेण तु।
नाराचास्तस्य सिद्धयन्ति यस्य तुष्टो महेश्वरः।। 107।।

107. The *muṣṭi* (the technique of holding bowstrings or grips) can be learnt within six months, and shooting arrows can be learnt within one year. However, the shooting of '*nārācas*', or projectiles can be learnt only with the grace of Almighty.

पुष्पवद्धारयेद्बाणं सर्पवत्पीडयेद्धनुः।
धनवच्चिन्तयेल्लक्ष्यं यदीच्छेत्सिद्धिमात्मनः।। 108।।

108. If a shooter wants to achieve success in shooting, he must hold/handle his weapons very gently and carefully, like a flower, and pull the bow with the same might as if thrashing a snake. The shooter should brood over his target in the same way as if a common man hankers after money.

क्रियामिच्छन्ति आचार्याः दूरमिच्छन्ति भार्गवाः।

राजानो दृष्टिमिच्छन्ति लक्ष्यमिच्छन्ति चेतरे।। 109।।

109. A preceptor expects that his disciple's shooting will be effective and efficient. The descendants of the Bhṛgu (like Paraśurāma) desire, that the arrow of the disciple should hit the target at a great distance. A king desires farsightedness, while others (common men) want to redeem their targets.

जनानां रंजनं येन लक्ष्यघातात्प्रजायते।
हीनेनापीषुणा तस्मात्प्रशस्तं लक्ष्यवेधनम्।। 110।।

110. If the shooting of even the small arrow or round makes the viewer delighted, then the shooting is considered a praiseworthy action.

अथ लक्ष्यस्खलनविधिः
Perfect Shooting

विशाखस्थानके स्थित्वा समसंधानमाचरेत्।
गोपुच्छमुखबाणेन सिंहकर्ण्या च मुष्टिना।। 111।।

111. Perfect shooting takes place if the shooter stands in the '*viśākha*' position known as (standing with the feet apart), uses '*gopuccha*' arrow, holds the bow-string in a '*siṁhkarṇa*' way and draws the bow in '*samasandhāna*' method.

आकर्षेत्कैशिकव्याये न शिखां चालयेत्ततः।
पूर्वापरौ समौ कार्यौ समांसौ निश्चलौ करौ।। 112।।

112. While performing '*kaiśika vyāya*' or drawing the bow in a '*kaiśika'* (method), the top-knot of an archer should not move. He should keep both his right and left shoulders at par and the hands should not be moved while shooting.

चक्षुषी स्पन्दयेन्नैव दृष्टिं लक्ष्ये नियोजयेत्।
मुष्टिनाच्छादितं लक्ष्यं शरस्याग्रे नियोजयेत्।। 113।।

113. At the time of the shooting, the eyes should not move; rather these should be fixed on the target. The view of the target covered by the fist should be placed in front of the arrow.

मनो दृष्टिगतं ज्ञात्वा ततः काण्डं विसर्जयेत्।
स्खलत्येवं कदाचिन्न लक्ष्ये योधो जितश्रमः।। 114।।

114. Realising that the mind is totally fixed on the target, the weapon ('*kāṇḍa*') should be shot to the target. The shooter who has thus practised the shooting never misses the target.

अथ शीघ्रसन्धानम्

Fast Shooting

आदानं चैव तुणीरात्संधानं कर्षणं तथा।
क्षेपणं च त्वरायुक्तो बाणस्य कुरुते तु यः।
नित्याभ्यासवशात्तस्य शीघ्रसंधानता भवेत्।। 115।।

115. A shooter who can quickly take out arrows from the quiver, load them on to the bowstring, hold the bow-string, aim, and shoot the arrows very quickly becomes a "fast shooter" on account of his constant practice.

अथ भेदनविधिः

Rules for various Shooting Ranges

प्रत्यालीढे कृते स्थाने अधः संधानमाचरेत्।
मुष्टया पताकया बाणं स्त्रीचिह्नं दूरपातनम्।। 116।।

116. When a shooter wants to shoot a distant target (*dūrapātanam*), he should assume the position of '*pratyālīḍha*' and aim a feminine type of arrow downwards, drawing it with the grip known as '*patākāmuṣṭi*'.

दर्दुरक्रममास्थाय ऊर्ध्वसंधानमाचरेत्।

स्कन्धव्यायेन वज्रस्य मुष्टया पुंमार्गणेन च।
अत्यन्तसौष्ठवाद्बाह्वोर्जायते दृढवेधिता।। 117।।

117. If the shooter wants to shoot the strong and tough targets, he should aim a male type of arrow upwards (*ūrdhapātanam*) drawing it with a grip known as '*Vajramuṣṭī*' taking a *dardurkrama* pose and drawing the bow-string in '*skandhavyāya*' method. If he follows this technique, he achieves efficiency in beautifully hitting the tough targets.

अथ हीनगतिसमूहः
Movement of Arrows

सूचीमुखा मीनपुच्छा भ्रमरी च तृतीयका।
शराणां गतयस्तिस्रः प्रशस्ताः कथिता बुधैः।। 118।।

118. Wise men enumerate three types of proper motions of the arrows, viz. (i) '*sucīmukha*' (moving in a straight line like the tip of the needle) (ii) '*mīnapuccha*' (moving in a zigzag pattern like the tail of a fish) and (iii) '*bhramarī*' (moving all over the place like a black bee).

सूचीमुखगतिस्तस्य सायकस्य प्रजायते।
पत्रं विलोमितं यस्य अथवा हीनपत्रकम्।। 119।।

119. The arrow moves in a '*sucīmukha*' motion when it lacks its fletched portion or it has very little fletching.

कर्कशेन तु चापेन तदाकृष्टो हीनमुष्टिना।
मत्स्यपुच्छा गतिस्तस्य सायकस्य प्रकीर्त्तिता।। 120।।

120. If the arrow is released from a bow which is hard and with a loose grip, the arrow follows a zigzag trajectory like the tail of a fish known as '*matsyapuccha*'.

भ्रमरी कथिता ह्येषा विद्वद्भिः श्रमकर्मणि।

ऋजुत्वेन विना याति क्षेप्यमाणस्तु सायकः ।। 121 ।।

121. If the arrow after being shot follows the semicircular path, then its movement is known as '*Bhramarī*' by the experts of shooting.

अथ बाणलक्ष्यस्खलनगतिसमूहः
Missed Targets or Deflection of arrows

वामगा दक्षगा चैव ऊर्ध्वगाऽधोगाः तथा ।
चतस्रो गतयः प्रोक्ता बाणस्खलनहेतवः ।। 122 ।।

122. Depending upon the release of an arrow, it may deflect to four different directions. (i) '*vāmagā*' (deflection to the left) (ii) '*dakṣagā*' (deflection to the right) (iii) '*ūrdhvagā*' (deflection to upward direction) and (iv) '*adhogā*' (deflection to the downward direction). These four deflections may lead to the missed targets.

कम्पते गुणमुष्टिस्तु मार्गणस्य हि पृष्ठतः ।
सम्मुखोस्याद्धनुर्मुष्टिस्तदा वामे गतिर्भवेत् ।। 123 ।।

123. If the grip of the bowstring at the rear portion of the arrow shakes and the bow is drawn in '*samasandhāna*' position (or say if the stave is kept parallel to the body) the arrow will deflect to the left.

ग्रहणं शिथिलं यस्य ऋजुत्वेन विवर्जितम् ।
पार्श्वस्तु दक्षिणं याति सायकस्य न संशयः ।। 124 ।।

124. If an archer does not hold the arrow properly and aim it straight, his arrow will undoubtedly go either to one side or short of the target.

ऊर्ध्वं याति चापमुष्टिर्गुणमुष्टिरधो भवेत् ।
स मुक्तो मार्गणो लक्ष्याद्दूरं याति न संशयः ।। 125 ।।

125. If the bow is drawn in *ūrdhava-sandhāna* mode of shooting (or stave is kept above head), and the bowstring is directed downward, an arrow released from such a position will undoubtedly veer far away from the target.

मोक्षणे चैव बाणस्य चापमुष्टिरधो भवेत्।
गुणमुर्ष्टिभवेदूर्ध्वं तदाधोगामिनी गतिः।। 126।।

126. While shooting an arrow, if the bow is drawn in '*adhaḥsandhāna*' mode (or stave is kept lower to the body) and the bow-string is held at a higher level, then the arrow released from such a position will be deflected downwards.

अथ शुद्धगतयः
The Successful Targets or Correct Trajectory of Arrows

लक्ष्यबाणाग्रदृष्टिनां संगतिस्तु यदा भवेत्।
तदानीमुज्झितो बाणो लक्ष्यान्न स्खलति ध्रुवम्।। 127।।

127. The right time to shoot is when the target, the tip of the arrow, and the gaze of the shooter are in one line. In such a situation the shooter never misses the target.

निर्दोषः शब्दहीनश्च सममुष्टिद्वयोज्झितः।
भिनत्ति दृढवेध्यानि सायको नास्ति संशयः।। 128।।

128. If the target and tip at the arrow and shooter's eye are aligned, then the arrow is bound to shoot the target.

स्वाकृष्टस्तेजितो यश्च सुशुद्धो गाढमुष्टितः।
नरनागाश्वकायेषु न स तिष्ठति मार्गणः।। 129।।

129. An arrow that is sharpened well at the tip and is fitted with feathers of a bird and discharged from a firm grip with force, can pierce through the body of a human being or an elephant or a horse.

अथ श्रेष्ठयोद्धालक्षणानि

Characteristic of the Best Warrior

यस्य तृणसमा बाणा यस्येन्धनसमं धनुः।
यस्य प्राणसमा मौर्वी स धन्वी धन्वीनां वरः।। 130।।

130. A shooter who is able to handle his arrows lightly like grass, whose bow works like burning fuel and the who keeps his bow-string safe from any type of damage like his life, he is considered to be the best warrior.

अथ दृढचतुष्कम्

Four tough targets

अयश्चर्म घटश्चैव मृत्पिण्डं च चतुष्टयम्।
यो भिनत्ति हि तस्येषुर्वज्रेणापि न धार्यते।। 131।।

131. If an archer is able to pierce the following four types of (tough) targets, namely, those made of metal, leather, an earthen pot, and a lump of earth, his arrows cannot be countered even by a thunderbolt.

सार्धागुंलप्रमाणेन लोहपात्राणि कारयेत्।
तानि भित्त्वैकबाणेन दृढघाती भवेन्नरः।। 132।।

132. Iron plates measuring the thickness of half-finger should be prepared (as targets for exercise). A shooter who pierces such plates with a single arrow is known as '*dṛḍhghātī*' a tough marksman (marksman of tough targets).

चर्तुविंशति चर्माणि भिनत्त्येकेषुणा नरः।
तस्य बाणो गजेन्द्रस्य कायं निर्भिद्य गच्छति।। 133।।

133. A warrior who can pierce twenty-four pieces of a leather with a single arrow can pierce even the body of a powerful elephant.

भ्राम्यंचले घटो वेद्धयश्चक्रे मृतपिण्डकं तथा।
भ्रमन्तं वेधयेद्वस्तु दृढभेदी स उच्यते ।। 134 ।।

134. An archer, who can hit an earthen jar in whirling water or a lump of earth which is in a rotating condition in potter's wheel or any other moving object, he is known as '*dṛḍhavedhī* ' meaning 'a tough marksman'.

अयस्तु काकतुण्डेन कर्म आरामुखेन हि।
मृत्पिण्डं च घटं चैव विध्येत्सूचीमुखेन हि।। 135 ।।

135. A target made of metal can be pierced by '*kākatuṇḍa*' (beak of the crow) arrow-head and targets of leather (like shields or armour) can be pierced by '*ārāmukha*' (awl type) serrated arrow-head. An earthen jar or a lump of earth may be hit through '*sūcīmukha*' arrowhead.

अथ चित्रविधिः

Citravidhi (Technical Fight/Camouflaging)

बाणभंगं करावर्तं काष्ठच्छेदनमेव च।
बिन्दुकं गोलकयुगं यो वेत्ति स जयी भवेत्।। 136 ।।

136. One who knows how to counter and cut an arrow by tilting his hands, and one who knows how to pierce a piece of wood, or one who knows how to score points in a shooting range (*binduka* i.e. *chāndamārī*) and one who can pierce two round balls (*golaka-yuga*) at a time, always becomes victorious.

लक्ष्यस्थाने धृतं काण्डं ससुखं छेदयेत्ततः।
किचिन्मुष्टिं विधाय स्वां तिर्यग्द्विफलिकेषुणा।। 137 ।।

137. One can cut an arrow easily placed as a target with the help of a two-bladed arrow or an arrow with a circular tip (like a crescent moon).

संमुखं वा समायान्तं तिर्यक्छायं तमम्बरे।

शरं शरेण यश्छिन्द्याद्वाणच्छेदी स जायते।। 138।।

138. But if an arrow is in front of the shooter in the sky, he should not shoot in a curved way, rather he should combat/cut the arrow approaching towards him by taking a transverse position. If he is successful in doing so he is known as '*Vāṇacchedī*' meaning 'one who combats/cuts an arrow in the air'.

अथ धनुर्धराणां वर्गिकरणम्

Classification of Shooter/Archers

काष्ठेश्वकेशं संयम्य तत्र बद्धवा वराटिकाम्।
हस्तेन भ्राम्यमाणां च यो हन्ति स धनुर्धरः।। 139।।

139. A cowrie is tied with a horse-hair to a piece of wood as a target and the piece of wood is spun. If the archer is able to hit the cowrie tied with horsehair to the spinning piece of wood, he is known as *Dhanurdhara*, meaning 'a real expert archer'.

लक्ष्यस्थाने न्यसेत्काष्ठं सार्द्रं गोपुच्छसन्निभम्।
यश्छिन्द्यात्तं क्षुरप्रेण काष्ठच्छेत्ता स जायते।। 140।।

140. A piece of wet wood shaped like a cow's tail is placed as a target. The person who can pierce this wooden piece from a distance with the help of *kṣurapra* (horseshoe-shaped arrow-head) is known as '*Kāṭ hachettā*' meaning 'a piercer of wood'.

लक्ष्ये बिन्दुं न्यसेच्छुभ्रं शुभ्रबन्धूकपुष्पवत्।
हन्ति तं बिन्दुकं यस्तु चित्रयोधा स जायते।। 141।।

141. If a white point is placed on the target that looks like a white '*Bandhūka*[1] or *Vijayasāra*' flower, an archer who is able to hit that point is called a '*citrayodhā*'.

---

[1] A kind of a flower which bloom at mid-day.

अथ धावल्लक्ष्यम्
Hitting the Moving Targets

काष्ठगोलं युगं क्षिप्तं दूरमूर्ध्वपुरः स्थितैः।
अप्राप्तधारं पृष्ठेन गच्छेत्पुच्छमुखेन हि।। 142।।

यो हन्ति शरयुग्मेन शीघ्रसंधानयोगतः।
स स्याद्धनुर्भृतां श्रेष्ठः पूजितः सर्वपार्थिवैः।। 143।।

142-143. If an archer is able to pierce with the help of two gopuccha arrows, implanted by him immediately on the bow, two wooden balls thrown high in the air by the person standing in front of him before they struck the ground, the archer becomes the best of archers (best marksman of moving targets) and is respected by all kings.

रथस्थेन गजस्थेन हयस्थेन च पत्तिना।
धावता वै श्रमः कार्यो लक्ष्यं हन्तुं सुनिश्चतम्।। 144।।

144. Irrespective of whether a shooter rides on the chariot or an elephant, or on horse's back or moves on foot, he must do practice even while moving, to achieve a sure shot success in his aim.

अथ शब्दवेधित्वम्
Shoot at Sound

लक्ष्यस्थाने न्यसेत्कांस्यपात्रं हस्तद्वयान्तरे।
ताडयेच्छर्कराभिस्तच्छब्दः संजायते यथा।। 145।।

145. Pots made of bell-metal should be kept at a distance of two hands (36 inches) from the target. Another person hit the pot with pebbles (*śarkarā*) so that a sound is produced.

यत्रैवोत्पद्यते शब्दस्तं सम्यक्तत्र चिन्तयेत्।
कर्णेन्द्रियमनोयोगाल्लक्ष्यं निश्चयतां नयेत्।। 146।।

146. An archer has to concentrate on the source of a sound and has to determine the location of the target with the power of audition without looking at it.

पुनः शर्करया तच्च ताडयेच्छब्दहेतवे।
पुनर्निश्चयता नेयं शब्दस्थानानुसारतः।। 147।।

147. The bell metal may be hit again with pebbles for producing a sound and the shooter has to determine the location of the target again following the sound.

ततः किचित्कृतं दूरे नित्यं नित्यं विधानतः।
लक्ष्यं समभ्यसेद्धवान्ते शब्दव्यधनहेतवे।। 148।।

148. When one gets expertise in such shooting, the distance of the target can be increased gradually. The practice should be done during darkness.

ततो बाणेन हन्यात्तदवधानेन तीक्ष्णधीः।
एतच्च दुष्करं कर्म भाग्ये कस्यापि सिद्धयति।। 149।।

149. After ascertaining the target on the basis of sound, an extremely intelligent shooter should hit the target with earnest attention. But this work is rather difficult and very few who are fortunate enough can do it.

अथ प्रत्यागमनम्

Military Exercise

एवं श्रमविधि कुर्याद्यावत्सिद्धिः प्रजायते।
श्रमे सिद्धे च वर्षासु नैव ग्राह्यं धनुः करे।। 150।।

150. Thus thc shooting practice should be continued till success is achieved. When shooting practice is perfected, a shooter may abandon the practice. It is also forbidden to do practice during rainy days.

पूर्वाभ्यासस्य शस्राणामविस्मरणहेतवे।
मासद्वयं श्रमं कुर्यात्प्रतिवर्ष शरदृतौ।। 151।।

151. A shooter is advised to do shooting practice for two full months during autumn, so that he may not forget the art of weapons he acquired earlier. [The months of August and September comprise the season of Autumn in India.]

ततस्तु साधयेन्मन्त्रान्वेदोक्तांश्चागमोदितान्।
अस्त्राणां कर्मसिद्धयर्थं जपहोमविधानतः।। 152।।

152. During the period of intermission, a warrior is advised to achieve perfection in the *mantras* cited in the Vedas as well as *agamas* for achieving success in the art of operation of various weapons operated by *mantras* as per scriptural injunctions.

ब्राह्मं नारायणं शैवमैन्द्रं वायव्यवारुणे।
आग्नेयं चापरास्त्राणि गुरुदत्तानि साधयेत्।। 153।।

153. A warrior should strive to learn the operation of weapons named '*Brāhma*'(invented by Brahmā), '*Nārāyaṇa*' (invented by Nārāyaṇa), '*Śaiva*' (invented by Śiva), '*Aindra*' (invented by Indra), '*Vāyavya*' (invented by Vāyu), '*Vāruṇa*' (invented by Varuṇa), '*Āgneya*' (invented by Agni) and other weapons given by the preceptor.

मनोवाक्कर्मभिर्भाव्यं लब्धास्त्रेण शुचिष्मता।
अपात्रमसमर्थं च घ्नन्त्यस्त्राणि कुपुरुषम्।। 154।।

154. A person who has attained excellence in the operation of divine weapons operated by *mantra* should be fare and pure in his heart, speech, and action. These weapons kill an unworthy, an incapable operator and evildoers.

प्रयोगं चोपसंहारं यो वेत्ति स धनुर्धरः।
सामान्ये कर्मणि प्राज्ञो नैवास्त्राणि प्रयोजयेत्।। 155।।

155. A warrior who knows the operation and

withdrawal of these weapons, is known as a real bowman. A wise warrior or musketeer does not use his arms in day to day affairs.

अथौषधि:

Medication

हस्तार्क लांगलीकन्दं गृहीत्वा तस्य लेपतः ।
शूरस्यापि रणे पुंसो दर्पं हरति सत्वरः ।। 156 ।।

156. By applying a coat of the paste of the root of Lāṅgali (Jalapippalī) collected on the *Hasta Nakṣatra*, even a coward person wins over the mighty fighter.

गृहीतं योगनक्षत्रैरपामार्गस्य मूलकम् ।
लेपमात्रेण वीराणां सर्वशस्त्रनिवारणम् ।। 157 ।।

157. By taking the root of an '*apāmarga*' (Achyranthes Aspera) plant on the *Puṣya Nakṣatra* and anointing its paste all over his body, a warrior gets the power to ward off all weapons of the enemies.

अधःपुष्पी शंखपुष्पी लज्जालुर्गिरिकर्णिका ।
नलिनी सहदेवी च पुत्रमार्जारिका तथा ।। 158 ।।
विश्णुक्रान्ता च सर्वासां जटा ग्राह्या रवेदिने ।
बद्धा भुजे विलेपाद्वा काये शस्त्रौघवारिक ।। 159 ।।

158-159. The roots of the plants *Adhaḥpuṣpī* (Pimpinella), *Saṅkhapuṣpī* (Canscora Decussata), *Lajjālu* (Mmosa), '*Girikarṇikā*' (a variety of Acyranthes with white blossoms), '*Nalinī*', '*Sahadevī*' (Centratherum anthelmaricum), '*Putramārjārikā*', and '*Viṣṇukrāntā*' protect from weapons when tied on the arms or applied over the body.

गृहीतं हस्तनक्षत्रे चूर्णं छुच्छुन्दरीभवम् ।
तत्प्रभावाद्गजः पुंसः संमुखो नैति निश्चितम् ।। 160 ।।

160. By the influence of the powder obtained from

'*chuchundarī*' (Leguminosae) plant on the '*Hasta nakṣatra*' day, even an elephant does not dare to come in front of the warrior.

छुच्छुन्दरी श्रीफलपुष्पचूर्णरालिप्तगात्रस्य नरस्य दूरात्।
आघाय गन्ध द्विरदातिमत्ता मद त्यजत्कशरिणा यथागम।। 161 ।।

161. If the powder of '*chuchundarī*' plant and '*vilva*' tree (wood apple) are anointed on the body of a warrior, then the odour produced is sure to calm down even a mad elephant and a lion.

श्वेताद्रिकर्णिकामूलं पाणिस्थं वारयेद्रजम्।
श्वेतकण्टारिकामूलं व्याघ्रादीनां भयं हरेत्।। 162 ।।

162. The root of the white *adri karṇikā* tree (creeper of clitoria genus) if worn in hands can prevent the advent of an elephant, and the root of white *kaṇṭ ārikā* (Solanum Jacquini) prevents the approach of a tiger.

पुष्यार्कोत्पाटिते मूले पाठाया मुखसंस्थिते।
देहे स्फुटति नो तीक्ष्णं मण्डलाग्रं रणे नृणाम्।। 163 ।।

163. The root of Pāṭhā (aloe plant) uprooted on *Puṣya Nakṣatra* day, if retained in the mouth in *Mūla* constellation, the warrior cannot have fear even from fighters equipped with a sharp and devastating weapon.

गन्धार्या उत्तरं मूलं मुखस्थं संमुखागतम्।
शस्त्रौघं वारयेत्येव पुष्यार्के विधिना धृतम्।। 164 ।।

164. If the end of the root of the '*gandhārī*' (a kind of a decorative tree) is collected on *Puṣya* constellation, and put in the mouth, increases the immunity of the warrior i.e. the wounds caused by the weapons heal up soon.

शुभ्रायाः शरपुंखाया जटानीली जटाथवा।
भुजे शिरसि वक्षे वा स्थिता शस्त्रनिवारिका।

भूपाहिचौरभीतिघ्नी गृहीता पुष्पभास्करे।। 165।।

165. In the *Puṣya* constellation, if '*śubhra*' '*śarapuṅkhā*' or '*jaṭānilī*' or '*Jaṭāmasī*' (Indian spikenard) is taken and applied on arms, head and face, it heals the wounds of the weapons and ward off the fear of the king, thieves, and serpents.

अथाक्षौहिणी सेना

Count of Akṣauhiṇī Army

खं तथा स्वरवस्विन्दुनेत्रैरक्षौहिणी मता।
अक्षौहिन्यां संप्रदिष्टा रथानां वर्मधारिणाम्।
संख्यागणित तत्त्वज्ञैः सहस्राण्येकविंशति।। 166।।

166. The charioteers wearing shields should number 21,870 (by computing the legends) *kha* (sky) (0), *svara* (Tunes) (7), *vasu* (8), *Indu* (moon) (1), and *netra* (eyes) (2). [As per the law of counting in Sanskrit- *aṅkānāṁ vāmato gatiḥ* - The digits are counted from right to left hence 21,870]. According to scholars who are well-versed in Mathematics, the number of chariots and charioteers putting an armour in an '*akṣauhiṇī*' amount to twenty-one thousand eight hundred; the kings are seventy in number added to this make the figure (21800 + 70 = 21870).

उपर्यष्टौ शतान्याहुस्तथा भूयश्च सप्ततिः।
गजानां तु परिमाणमेतदेव विनिर्दिशेत्।। 167।।

167. The number of warriors on an elephant is also the same as told above in connection with the charioteers- that is (21870) twenty-one thousand eight hundred seventy in an '*akṣauhiṇī*' army.

ज्ञेयं लक्षं पदातीनां सहस्राणि तथा नव।
शतानि त्रीणि पंचाशच्छूराणां शस्त्रधारिणाम्।। 168।।

168. The number of infantry soldiers is one Lakh,

nine thousand, three hundred and fifty (19,350) in an '*akṣauhiṇī*' army (all of them are equipped with weapons).

पंचषष्टि सहस्राणि तथाश्वानां शतानि च।
दशोत्तराणि षट् प्राहुः संख्यातत्त्वविदो जनाः।। 169।।

169. The number of cavalry soldiers remains sixty-five thousand six hundred and ten (65,610) as stated by scholars who are well versed in mathematical countings.

खद्वयं निधिवेदाक्षिचन्द्राक्ष्यग्निहिमांशुभिः।
महाक्षौहिणीका प्रोक्ता संख्या गणितकोविदैः।। 170।।

170. The mathematicians said the number of soldiers in a troop called '*mahākṣauhiṇī*' *an* army as two *kha* (00), *nidhi* (9), *veda* (4), *akṣi* (2) *chandra* (1), *akṣi* (3) *agni* (1), *himañśu* (1), i.e. 13,21,24,900 (13 crore 21 lakh 24 thousand 9 hundred).

कोटयस्त्रयोदश प्रोक्ता लक्षणामेकविंशतिः।
चर्तुविंशत्सहस्राणि तथा नवशतानि च।। 171।।

171. In '*mahākṣauhiṇī*' army the number of soldiers are thirteen crore twenty-one lacs, twenty-four thousand and nine hundred, i.e. 13,21,24,900.

महाक्षौहिणिकां प्राहुरिमां तत्वविदो जनाः।
महाक्षौहिणिकायां तु रथाः कोटिमिताः स्मृताः।
सप्तत्रिंशच्च लक्षाणि गीयन्ते तत्वभेदिभिः।। 172।।

172. The numbers of chariots in a '*mahākṣauhiṇī*' troop is stated to be one crore and thirty-seven lakh by the experts. (1,37,00,000).

द्वादशैव सहस्राणि चत्वार्यैव शतानि च।
प्रोक्तानि नवतिस्तद्वदेवमेव मतं गजाः।। 173।।

173. In such a troop the number of elephants is said to be twelve thousand four hundred and ninety.

(12,490).

अश्वाश्चतुष्कोटिमिता लक्षाण्येकादशैव च।
सप्तत्रिंशत्सहस्राणि तथा शतचतुष्टयम्।। 174।।

174. In such a troop the number of horses (cavalry) should be four crores, eleven lacs, seventy-three thousand and four hundred (4,11,73,400).

सप्ततिश्चैव संख्याताः प्रोच्यन्ते पत्तयस्ततः।
षट्कोटयाऽशीतिलक्षाणि पंचाधिकमितानि च।। 175।।

175. The number of infantry soldiers (*pattya*) in *mahākṣauhiṇī* troop is six crores, eighty lakh, and seventy-five (6,80,00,075).

द्विषष्टि च सहस्राणि तथा शतचतुष्टयम्।
पंचाशदिति संख्याता महाक्षौहिणिका बुधैः।। 176।।

176. Sixty-two thousand four hundred and fifty (62,450) is the number of formation known by the scholars as '*mahaksauhinika*'.

ततो व्यूहादिभिर्युद्धकथनम्
Battle Formations

मुखे रथा गजाः पृष्ठे तत्पृष्ठे च पदातयः।
पार्श्वयोश्च हयाः कार्या व्यूहस्यायं विधिः स्मृतः।। 177।।

177. The technique of making a formation (*vyūha*) in a battle is as follows - the charioteers should be placed in front, followed by the elephants followed by the infantry and the cavalry should be placed on both sides.

अर्धचन्द्रं चक्रंच शकटं मकरं तथा।
कमलं श्रेणिकां गुल्मं व्यूहानेवं प्रकल्पयेत्।। 178।।

178. The battle array may also be formed in the shape of an *Ardhacandra* (half-moon), or as a *Chakra* (circle) or a *Śakaṭa* (car), *Makara* (a fish), *Kamala* (a lotus), (*Śreṇikā*) (simply by making rows) or in the shape of a *Gulma* (bush).

ये राजपुत्राः सामन्ताः आप्ताः सेवकजातयः।
तान्सर्वानात्मनः पार्श्वे रक्षायै स्थापयेन्नृपः।। 179।।

179. The King should keep around him for his protection all princes, feudal lords, or subordinate kings and all loyal soldiers.

यस्मिन्कुले यः पुरुषः प्रधानः। तस्मिन्विनष्टे किल सारभूते।
स सर्वयत्नेन हि रक्षणीयः। न नाभिभंगेह्यरका वहन्ति।।
180।।

180. The main or most important person of a family must be protected by all means at all costs. When the chief of a family perishes, the whole of the dynasty is lost. Just as spokes fail to bear the burden of the wheel when the axle is broken.

क्षत्रसारभृतं शूरं शस्त्रज्ञमनुरागी चेत्।
अपि स्वल्पं श्रिये सैन्यं वृथेयं मुण्डमण्डली।। 181।।

181. If a *kṣatriya* (soldier) is imbued with traits of heroism, and a warrior is well trained in arms and loyal to the king. Even a small number of such soldiers in the army serve the purpose and is better than a crowd of people (*muṇḍamaṇḍalī*) without loyalty, courage, and determination to win the war.

अपि पंचशतं शूरा मृद्नन्ति महतीं चमूम्।
अथवा पंच षट् सप्त विजयन्तऽनिवर्त्तिनः।। 182।।

182. Even five hundred determined and well-trained soldiers can defeat a large army. Sometimes even five, six, or seven such heroes who do not withdraw and fight bravely may emerge victorious.

धनुः संगतिसंशुद्धा वाजिनो मुखदुर्बलाः।
आकर्णपलिता योधाः संग्रामे जयवादिनः।। 183।।

183. War veterans who have arms as their means of livelihood can bring victory even if the forward line of the king with their horses is not very strong.

परस्परानुरक्ता ये योधाः शार्ंग धनुर्धराः।
युद्धज्ञास्तुरगारूढास्ते जयन्ति रणे रिपून्।। 184।।

184. The Warriors even armed with a *Śārṅga* bow (made of horn) who co-operate with each other and know battle-craft, may beat enemies fighting them on horseback.

एकः कापुरुषो दीर्णो दारयेन्महतीं चमूम्।
तं दीर्णमनु दीर्यन्ते योधाः शूरतमा अति।। 185।।

185. But a single coward soldier who breaks ranks can destroy the power of a large army. Even the most heroic and greatest fighters will suffer a breakdown of morale (they will desert with such a coward in their midst and face defeat).

दुर्निवारतरा चैव प्रभग्ना महती चमूः।
अपामिव महावेगत्रस्ता मृगगणा इव।। 186।।

186. A strong and insuperable battalion may run away and court defeat, just like animals who are afraid of surging floodwater (if a coward breaks ranks.)

यस्तु भग्नेषु सैन्येषु विद्रुतेषु निवर्त्तते।
पदे पदे अश्वमेधस्य लभते फलमक्षयम्।। 187।।

187. A hero who can regroup fleeing soldiers, return to combat and rout the enemy will receive the eternal reward for performing the *Aśvamedha yajña* (protecting the nation from enemies).

द्वाविमौ पुरुषौ लोके सूर्य्यमण्डलभेदिनौ।
परिव्राड् योगयुक्तश्च रणे चाभिमुखो हतः।। 188।।

189. There are only two types of persons in this world who can penetrate even the orb of the Sun: One is the ascetic who is a high profile Yogī and another is a hero who dies fighting in the battle.

यत्र यत्र हतः शूरः शत्रुभिः परिवेष्टितः।
अक्षयं लभते लोकं यदि क्लीबं न भाषते।। 190।।

190. If a hero dies surrounded by his enemies, it is sure that he will attain eternal fame, due to his bravery, but the eunuch is never talked about.

अथ युद्धधर्मः
War Ethics

मूर्च्छितं नैव विकलं नाशस्त्रं नान्ययोधिनम्।
पलायमानं शरणं गतं चैव न हिंसयेत्।। 191।।

191. One should not kill the enemy who is lying unconscious or the one who is wounded, or who is devoid of weapons, or who is fighting with another warrior, or who has withdrawn or who has come for refuge.

भीरुः पलायमानाऽपि नान्वेष्टव्यो बलीयसा।
कदाच्छिूरतां याति मरणे कृतनिश्चयः।। 192।।

192. Even a weak fighter who is running away should be chased, sometimes he may also shed the fear of death, become aggressive and brave.

अथ विजयलक्षणनि
Signs of Victory

संभृत्य महतीं सेनां चतुरंगां महीपतिः।
व्यूहयित्वाग्रतः शूरान्स्थापयेज्जयलिप्सया।। 193।।

193. An emperor desirous of victory should organize his army comprising four divisions ('*caturaṅga*', i.e. the charioteers, soldiers mounted on an elephant, cavalry and infantry) into a formation or battle array (*vyūha*) to encircle the enemy deploying valiant heroes in front of it.

अल्पायां वा महत्यां वा सेनायामिति निश्चयः।
हर्षो योधगणस्यैको जयलक्षणमुच्यते।। 194।।

194. The happiness and morale of the troops are the factors that contribute to the victory, irrespective of the size of the army, small or large.

अन्वेतं वायवो यान्ति पृष्ठे भानुर्वयांसि च।
अनुप्लवन्ते मेघाश्च यस्य तस्य रणे जयः।। 195।।

195. If the wind blows or the Sun shines behind and also if the birds and the floating clouds fly behind the back of the soldier, then he surely becomes victorious.

अपूर्णे नैव मर्तव्यं संपूर्णे नैव जीवति।
तस्माद्धैर्यं विधातव्यं हन्तव्या परवाहिनी।। 196।।

196. One should not die prematurely; nor can one live after one's time is up. Hence one should exercise patience and kill the enemies.

जिते लक्ष्मीर्मृते स्वर्गः कीर्तिश्च धरणीतले।
तस्माद्धैर्यं विधातव्यं हन्तव्या परवाहिनी।। 197।।

197. In war, if one becomes victorious, he gains wealth, If one dies, he is immortalised and earns name and fame in this world. Hence one should exercise patience and kill one's enemies..

एतं शिवधनुर्वेदस्य भगवतो व्यासस्य च। 198।।

198. This is the teaching of Vyāsa, the compiler and the *Dhanurveda* revealed to Śiva.

Appendix - 2

महर्षि वसिष्ठविरचिता धनुर्वेदसंहिता

(Text of Vasiṣṭha's Dhanurveda)

(Note: Vasiṣṭha's Dhanurveda is borrowed from the Sadāśiva Dhanurveda)

अथैकदा विजिगीषुर्विश्वामित्रो राजर्षिर्गुरुवसिष्ठमभ्युपेत्य प्रणम्योवाच। ब्रूहि भगवन्! धनुर्विद्यां श्रोत्रियाय दृढचेतसे शिष्याय दुष्टशत्रुविनाशाय च। तमुवाच महर्षिब्रह्मर्षिप्रवरो वसिष्ठः शृणु भो राजन विश्वामित्र! यां सरहस्यधनुर्विद्यां भगवान सदाशिवः परशुरामायोवाच तामेव सरहस्यां वच्मि ते हिताय गोब्राह्मणसाधुवेदसंरक्षणाय च यजुर्वेदाथर्वसम्मितां संहिताम्।

Once Viśvāmitra desiring victory, he visited the royal sage Vasiṣṭha and requested him thus: O reverend Lord! Kindly teach me the science of warfare for eliminating the enemy. Vasiṣṭha, the best among Brahmarṣis and Maharṣis said to him, 'Listen to me, O King Viśvāmitra! I am going to narrate to you the mysteries of the science of Dhanurveda, which were earlier told by Sadāśiva to Paraśurāma for the protection of cows, scholars, saints, and Vedas. This science is based upon *Yajurveda* and *Atharveda.*

अथोवाच महादेवो भार्गवाय च धीमते।
तत्तेऽहं संप्रवक्ष्यामि यथातथ्येन संशृणु ।।1।।

1. Whatever was told by Mahādeva (Śiva) to Paraśurāma, the son of Bhṛgu, the same will be briefly narrated by me to you.

तत्र चतुष्टयपादात्मको धनुर्वेदः । यस्य प्रथमे पादे

दीक्षाप्रकारः। द्वितीये संग्रहः तृतीये सिद्धप्रयोगाः चतुर्थे
प्रयोगविधयः।। 2।।

2. *Dhanurveda* has four parts. The first part deals with the instructions on principles, the second part contains rules for the collection of war weapons, the third part describes the application of various weapons and the fourth part is dedicated to the technique of operating various types of weapons.

अथ कस्य धनुर्वेदाधिकार इत्यपेक्षायामाह

(Rights of teaching and learning Dhanurveda)

धनुर्वेदे गुरुर्विप्रः प्रोक्तो वर्णद्वयस्य च।
युद्धाधिकारः शूद्रस्य स्वयं व्यापादि शिक्षया।। 3।।

3. In respect of *Dhanurveda*, the people of *Brāhmaṇa* nature deserve to be the teachers. The people of *Kṣatriya* and *Vaiśya* nature have the right to learn *Dhanurveda* (the science of warfare) for fighting wars. The people of *Śudra* nature can also learn *Dhanurveda* if they want to do so for self-protection.

चतविधमायधम । मक्तममक्त मक्तामक्त यन्त्रमक्त चति।। 4।।

4. The weapons are of four types- *Mukta*, *Amukta*, *Muktāmukta* and *Yantramukta*.

दुष्टदस्युचोरादिभ्य साधुसंरक्षणं धर्म्मतः।
प्रजापालनं धनुर्वेदस्य प्रयोजनम्।। 5।।

5. The purpose of *Dhanurveda* is to protect the people from evil persons, robbers, thieves and also to protect saints and people.

एकाऽपि यत्र नगरे प्रसिद्धः स्याद्धनुर्द्धरः।
ततो यान्त्यरयो दूरान्मृगाः सिंहगृहादिव।। 6।।

6. If just one famous warrior lives in a city, then the enemies will prefer distance, just as animals maintain distance from the den of a lion.

अथ धनुर्दानविधिः
Selection for Military Training

आचार्य्येण धनुर्देयं ब्राह्मणेन परीक्षिते।
लुब्धे धूर्त्ते कृतघ्ने च मन्दबुद्धौ न दापयेत्।। 7।।

7. A preceptor should give the training of military science or select a person for military services after properly examining him. The person should not be greedy, cunning, ungrateful, or foolish.

ब्राह्मणाय धनुर्देयं खंगं वै क्षत्रियाय च।
वैश्याय दापयेत् कुन्तं गदां शूद्राय दापयेत्।। 8।।

8. A person of *Brāhmaṇa* personality should be selected for the training of weapons of mass destruction like missiles etc. A person of *Kṣatriya* personality should be selected for the training of weapons of the class of sword and falchion, etc. A person of *Vaiśya* personality is perfect for the training of weapon of the category of lance or spear. *Śudra* personality types of persons are fit to be trained into operations of weapon like (*Gadā*) mace, etc.

अथ युद्धप्रकाराः
Types of Fighting

धनुष्चक्रंच कुन्तंच खड्गंच्च छुरिका गदा।
सप्तमं बाहुयुद्धं स्यादेवं युद्धानि सप्तधा।। 9।।

9. The fighting has been divided into seven types. The first type of fighting is carried out with the help of missiles, bows and arrows. The second type of fighting is carried out with *chakras* or weapons of the class of circular missiles. The third type of fighting is carried out with the help of weapons of the class of lance or spear (*kunta*). The fourth type of fighting is carried out with the help of weapons of the class of sword (*khadga*). The fifth type of fighting is carried out with the help of weapons of the class of bayonet type (*churikā*). The sixth type of fighting is carried out with the help of weapons of the class of mace (gadā) and lastly, the seventh type of fighting is carried out with hand to hand.

अथाचार्यलक्षणम्

Classification of Preceptors (Trainers)

आचार्य्यः सप्तयुद्धः स्याच्चतुर्भिर्भार्गव : स्मृतः।
द्वाभ्यांचैव भवेद्योद्धा एकेन गणको भवेत्।। 10।।

10. *Dhanurveda* classifies trainers or preceptors into four types according to the types of fighting. A preceptor excelling in different types of fighting has been designated differently. For instance, if a preceptor excels in all sevens types of fighting, he is called as *Saptayodhā*; he is called as a '*Bhārgava*' if he is well-versed in four types of fighting. An expert in two forms of fighting is known as '*yodhā*' and if one is versed in only one type of fighting, he is known as '*Gaṇaka*'

हस्तः पुनर्व्वसुः पुष्यो रोहिणी चोत्तरात्रयम्।
अनुराधाश्विनी चैव रेवती दशमी तथा।। 11।।

11. A person born on Moon's sojourn in a particular constellation was considered to be fit for recruiting in the military. For instance, if a person is born on Moon's sojourn in the constellation of *Hasta*, *Punarvasu*, *Puṣya*, *Rohiṇī*, three *Uttaras* (i.e. *Uttaraṣāḍhā*, *Uttaraphālguni*, and *Uttarabhādrapada*), *Anurādhā*, *Aśvinī*, *Revatī* and also on the tenth lunar day i.e. *Daśamī tithi* are fit for recruiting in the military.

जन्मस्थे च तृतीये च षष्ठे वै सप्तमे तथा।
दशमैकादशे चन्द्रे सर्व्वकार्य्याणि कारयेत्।। 12।।

12. On the other hand, people born in the third, sixth, seventh, tenth or eleventh day of the lunar fortnight was supposed to be fit for conducting all types of work.

तृतीया पंचमी चैव सप्तमी दशमी तथा।
त्रयोदशी द्वादशी च तिथयस्तु शुभा मताः।। 13।।

13. The third, fifth, seventh, tenth, twelfth, and thirteenth day of the lunar fortnight is accepted to be auspicious for military training.

रविवारः शुक्रवारो गुरूवारस्तथैव च।
एतद् वारत्रयं धन्यं प्रारम्भे शस्त्रकर्म्मणाम्।। 14।।

14. Sundays, Fridays, and Thursdays are taken to be very suitable for commencing any work relating to military training or weapon training.

एभिर्दिनैश्च शिष्याय गुरूः शस्त्राणि दापयेत्।
सन्तर्प्यदानहोमाभ्यां सुरान् स्वाहा विधानतः।। 15।।

15. On these days the preceptor should give training and hand over weapons to his disciples after paying due respect to the scholars through donations and performing *homa* according to injunctions of *Śāstras*.

शिष्याय मानुषं चापं धनुर्मन्त्राभिमन्त्रितम्।
काण्डात् काण्डातिति मन्त्रेण दद्याद्वेदविधानतः।। 16।

16. The preceptor should hand over after proper training a *Mānuṣa* bow to his disciple with the chanting of *Dhanurveda mantra* '*kāṇḍāt kāṇḍāt prarohanti...*'[1] as per the procedure of *Yajurveda* (13.20).

अथ वेधविधि

[1] *kāṇḍāt kāṇḍāt prarohantī paruṣaspari*
evā no dūrve pra tanu sahasreṇa śatena.

Shooting Techniques

प्रथमं पुष्पवेधंच फलहीनेन पत्रिणा।
ततः फलयुतेनैव मत्स्यवेधंच कारयेत्।। 17।।

17. The above verse deals with the method of shooting a target. Accordingly, a trainee should be allowed to practice from blunter to sharper arrowheads. First of all, a trainee should pierce a flower with an arrow without any arrowhead, and then he should pierce a fish like pointed object with an arrow equipped with a sharpened arrowhead. By this method, a trainee will be able to hit the target exactly.

मांस वेधन्ततः कुर्य्यादेवं वेधो भवेत्त्रिधा।
एतैर्वेधैः कृतैः पुंसां शराः स्युः सर्वसाधकाः।। 18।।

18. Afterwards, the disciple is made to pierce the upper skin of an animal, etc. (*mānsavedha*) without harming the lower skin or bones. These are the three types of piercing. By practising shooting of arrows gradually at targets in such manner, the soldier will achieve the skill to shoot his targets more effectively and efficiently.

एवं वेधत्रयं कुर्याच्छंखदुन्दुभिनिस्वनैः।
ततः प्रणम्य गुरवे धनुर्बाणान्निवेदयेत्।। 19।।

19. The above mentioned three types of shooting should be done accompanied by the sound of a conch-shell and drum, and then the trainee should entrust his bow and arrow to his preceptor by bowing down to him and offering his obeisance.

अथ चापप्रमाणम्

The Type and Size of a Bow

प्रथमं यौगिकं चापं युद्धचापं द्वितीयकम्।
निजबाहुबलोन्मानात् किंचदूनं शुभं धनुः।। 20।।

20. The first form of the bow is a composite bow made of horn, wood, and sinew (mainly used for practice). The second one is a bow that is used in fighting (battle). A bow that is inferior to the warrior as compared to his physical power and weight is regarded as the best one.

वरं प्राणाधिको धन्वी न तु प्राणाधिकं धनुः।
धनुषा पीड्यमानस्तु धन्वी लक्ष्यं न पश्यति।। 21।।

21. The life of a warrior is more precious than that of a bow. A warrior, who is overburdened by his weapon, never hits the target.

अतोनिजबलोन्मानं चापं स्याच्छुभकारकम्।
देवानामुत्तमं चापं ततोन्यूनंच मानवम्।। 22।।

22. So a bow which is compatible with the physical power and weight of a warrior is considered to be the best one. The *Deva* type of bow is said to be the best one followed by a *Mānuṣa* bow.

अर्द्धपंचमहस्तन्तु श्रेष्ठं चापं प्रकीर्त्तितम्।
तद्विज्ञेयं धनुर्दिव्यं शंकरेण धृतं पुरा।। 23।।

23. A bow measuring five hands[1] and a half (99 inches) is considered to be the best one and that type is called a '*Divya* bow', held by Saṅkara in ancient days.

चर्तुविंशागुंलो हस्तश्चतुर्हस्तं धनुः स्मृतम्।

---

[1] **Note** : The length of one hand is equal to the length of 24 fingers or 18 inches)

तद्भवेन्मानवं चापं सर्वलक्षणसंयुतम्।। 24।।

24. The length of a hand is equal to the length of twenty-four fingers of the hand i.e. 18 inches, and a bow that measures four hands (72 inches) in length is called as *Mānava* or *Mānuṣa* bow attributed with all qualities.

त्रिपर्वं पंचपर्वं वा सप्तपर्वं तथा पुनः।
नव पर्वंच कोदण्डं सर्वदा शुभकारकम्।। 25।।

25. A good quality bow either has three, five, seven, or nine joints. A bow with nine joints was called as 'Kodaṇḍa' which was considered squarely the best one.

चतुष्पर्वंच षट्पर्वम् अष्टपर्वं विवर्जयेत् ।
केषाचिच्च भवेच्चापं वितस्तिनव सम्मितम्।। 26।।

26. A bow having four, six, or even eight joints should be discarded. But there are some bows which measure 9 *vitastis*[1] i.e. 81 inches in size.

वर्जितधनुः
Prohibited Bows

अति जीर्णमपक्वंच ज्ञातिधृष्टन्तथैव च।
दग्धं छिद्रं न कर्त्तव्यं बाह्याभ्यन्तरहस्तकम्।। 27।।

27. A bow that is extremely old, or made of unripe materials, or used by one's kinsmen or burnt or perforated, that one should be discarded.

गुणहीनं गुणाक्रान्तं काण्डदोषसमन्वितम्।
गलग्रन्थि न कर्त्तव्यं तलमध्ये तथैव च।। 28।।

---

[1] Note: One *vitasti* is a distance between the long thumb and a little finger or between the wrist and the tip of the finger and is said to be equal to 12 *aṅgulas* or about 9 inches.

28. A bow without a string or a bow overwhelmed by string should be avoided. A bow with a defect in the stem, or a bow having joints at the neck (upper portion) and also at the bottom should not be used.

अपक्वं भंगमायाति ह्यतिजीर्णन्तु कर्कशम्।
ज्ञातिधृष्टन्तु सोद्वेगं कलहो बान्धवैः सह।। 29।।

29. A bow made of unripe material may break up easily. An old or a bow made of a very old material loses its elasticity. A bow already used by one's kinsmen may always be an object of anxiety or dispute among friends and relatives.

दग्धेन दह्यते वैश्म छिद्रं युद्धविनाशकम्।
बाह्ये लक्ष्यं न लभ्येत तथैवाभ्यन्तरऽपि च।। 30।।

30. A burnt or perforated bow may cause a fire and bring defeat and destruction in war. Such a bow does not reach the target, external or internal.

हीने तु सन्धिते बाणे संग्रामे भंगकारकम्।
आक्रान्ते तु पुनः क्वापि लक्ष्यं न प्राप्यते दृढम्।। 31।।

31. If an inferior type of bow is fixed with an arrow, it may break up in war. A perfect shooting is not possible if the bow is overwhelmed by a string.

गलग्रन्थि तलग्रन्थि धनहानिकरं धनुः।
एभिर्द्दोषैर्विनिर्मुक्तं सर्वकार्य्यकरं स्मृतम्।। 32।।

32. A bow with a knot or joint at the neck or bottom may lead to the loss of wealth. A bow devoid of all such flaws is considered to be good for all purposes.

शार्ंगं पुनर्धनुर्दिव्यं विष्णोः परमायुधम्।
वितस्तिसप्तमं मानं निर्म्मितं विश्वकर्मणा।। 33।।

33. The *Divya* (*mantra* operated) *Sāraṅga* bow is the great weapon of Viṣṇu. It was made by Viśvakarmā and measured seven *vitastis* (63 inches)

न स्वर्गे न च पाताले न भूमौ कस्यचित् करे।
तद्धनुर्नवशमायाति मुक्तैकं पुरूषोत्तमम्।। 34।।

34. That bow could not be handled by anybody on the poles (north and south poles: North pole is called as *Svarga*, south pole is called as *Pātāla*) and the equator (equatorial regions are called as *bhūmi loka*) except Viṣṇu.

पौरुषेयन्तु यच्छांर्ग बहुवत्सरशोभितम्।
वितस्तिभिसार्धषड्भिर्निम्मितं चार्थसाधनम् ।। 35।।

35. Gradually, over many years, Viśvakarmā invented a bow which could be operated manually. It measured seven *vitastis* (i.e. 59 inches). The bow serves all purposes.

प्रायो योज्यं धनुः शांर्ग गजारोहाश्वसादिनाम्।
रथिनांच पदातीनां वांशं चापं प्रकीर्त्तितम्।। 36।।

36. A *Sārṅga*-bow (made of horns) is usually used by the soldiers on an elephant back and the cavalry. However, a *Vāñśa* bow (made of Bamboo) is more useful for charioteers and infantry.

धनुर्द्रव्याणि

The Material for Bow-making

विश्वामित्र शृण्वाथ धनुर्द्रव्यत्रयं क्रमात्।
लोहं शृंगंच काष्ठंच गदितं शम्भुना पुरा।। 37।।

37. Listen O' Viśvāmitra! The bows are made up of three materials: metal, horns and wood.

लोहानि स्वर्णरजतताम्रकृष्णयसानि।
शृंगाणि महिषशरभरोहितानाम्।।

शरभाऽष्टपाद् चतुरुर्ध्वपादो महाविषाण–
उष्ट्रमितो वनस्थः काश्मीरदेशप्रसिद्धो मृगाख्यः।।

दारूणि चन्दनवेत्रधन्वनशालशाल्मलि
साककककुभ.वंशांजनानाम् । ।38 । ।

38. Gold, silver, copper, and steel are the metals that are useful for making metallic bows. The *Śārṅga* bow is made of the horns of a buffalo, Śarabha. Śarabha is an antelope found in Kashmir. It is an octopod that possesses big horns and almost looks like a camel. (Now this species has become extinct). The woods useful in making bow are - sandal, cane, *śāla* (vatica robusta- a valuable timber tree), *dhanvana* (a kind of hedyserum), *kakubha* (pentaptera arjuna), *śālmali* (silk cotton plant), *segaun* (teak wood), bamboo and *añjana* tree.

अथ गुणलक्षणानि

The characteristics of a bowstring

गुणानां लक्षणं वक्ष्ये यादृशं कारयेद्गुणम् ।
धनुः प्रमाणो निःसन्धिः शुद्धैस्त्रिगुणतन्तुभिः । । 39 । ।

39. I shall narrate the characteristics of the bowstring, and these are to be applied while making a string. The length of the string should be equal to that of the bow. It should be without joints and made of twisting three strings.

वर्त्तितः स्याद्गुणः श्लक्ष्णः सर्वकर्मसहो युधि ।
पट्टसूत्रो गुणः कार्य्यः कनिष्ठामानसम्मितः । । 40 । ।

40. The strings should be made of silken strings thinner than that of the wick of the earthen lamp. It should be twisted in the thickness of the little finger. A string thus made withstand all strains during the war.

अभावे पट्टसूत्रस्य हरिणी स्नायुरिष्यते ।
गुणार्थमपि च ग्राह्या स्नायवो महिषी भवाः । । 41 । ।

41. For the want of silk thread, the string can be

made with sinews of a deer or a buffalo or a cow.

तत्कालहत छागस्य तन्तुना वा गुणाः शुभाः।
निर्लोमतन्तुसूत्रेण कुर्य्याद्वा गुणमुत्तमम्।। 42।।

42. Fine strings are to be made with the skin of a goat died recently. The hair on the skin should be removed thoroughly.

पक्ववंशत्वचः कार्य्यो गुणस्तु स्थविरो दृढ।
पट्टसूत्रेण संन्नद्धः सर्वकर्म्मसहो युधि।। 43।।

43. The bowstrings made of bark (skin) of ripe bamboo and twisted around with silken thread are very strong and durable. They can withstand all types of stress and strain in the war.

प्राप्ते भाद्रपदे मासि त्वगर्कस्य प्रशस्यते।
तस्यास्तत्र गुणः कार्य्योः न वित्तः स्थावरो दृढः।। 44।।

44. At the advent of the month of *Bhādrapada* (September) the bark of the *Arka* (Sun Plant) becomes commendable for making fine bowstrings and hence strings made only with it are best and strong and not made with the bark of a popular tree.

अथ शरलक्षणानि

Qualities of Arrow

अतः प्रवक्ष्यामि शराणां लक्षणं शुभम्।
स्थूलं नाति सूक्ष्मंच नाऽपक्वं न कुभूमिजम्।। 45।।

45. Now I shall relate the good symptoms of arrows. An arrow should neither be made out of unripe material and also not be the product of vile land.

हीनग्रन्थिविदीर्णं च वर्जयेदीदृशं शरम्।
पूर्णग्रन्थि सुपक्वं च पाण्डुरं समयाहृतम्।। 46।।

46. An arrow made of weak joints and having cracks should be abandoned. The arrow should have strong welded joints and be made of a ripe material having yellowish shining.

शरवंशा गृहितव्या शरत्काले च गाधिज।
कठिनं वर्त्तुलं काण्डं गृह्णीयात् सुप्रदेशजम्।। 47।।

47. The reed arrows should be made in autumn O' Viśvāmitra! son of Gādhi. The reed which has a round and hard stem and which has grown in a favourable place should be accepted.

द्वौ हस्तौ मुष्टिहीनौ च दैर्घ्ये स्थूले कनिष्ठिका।
विधेयाः शरमानेषु यन्त्रेष्वाकर्षयेत् ततः।। 48।।

48. The arrow should measure two hands without fists (36 inches - 6 inches = 30 inches). In thickness, it should be equal to that of the smallest finger. A curved arrow should be made straight with the help of a machine.

अथ शरपक्षाणि

The Feathers of Arrows

काक–हंसशशादानां मत्स्यादक्रौंचकेकिनाम्।
गृध्राणां कुरराणांच पक्षा एते सुशोभनाः।। 49।।

49. The end of an arrow may be Fletched with the feathers like that of the crow, swan (*Hansa*), *Śaśāda* (a variety of bird which used to eat rabbits), fisher bird (*Matsyāda*), heron (*Krauñca*), *Keki* (peacock) vulture (*Gṛdhra*) and Osprey (*Kurara*).

षडगुंलप्रमाणेन पक्षच्छेदं च कारयेत्।।
दशांगुलमिताः पक्षाः शार्गचापस्य मार्गणे।
योज्या दृढाश्चर्तुसंख्याः सन्नद्धाः स्नायुतन्तुभिः।। 50।।

50. Four feathers are to be attached to each arrow with hard sinews. The gap between the two feathers should be six fingers (five inches). In the bow (*dhaṇu*) named *Sārṅga*, the gap between two feathers should be ten fingers (8 inches).

अथ शराणां वर्णनम्
Types of Arrows

शराश्च त्रिविधा ज्ञेयाः स्त्रीपुंसाश्च नपुंसकः।
अग्रस्थूलो भवेन्नारी पश्चत्स्थूलो भवेत्पुमान्।। 51।।

51. There are three types of arrows - male, female, and impotent. The one heavier towards point is female, the one heavier towards the end is male and

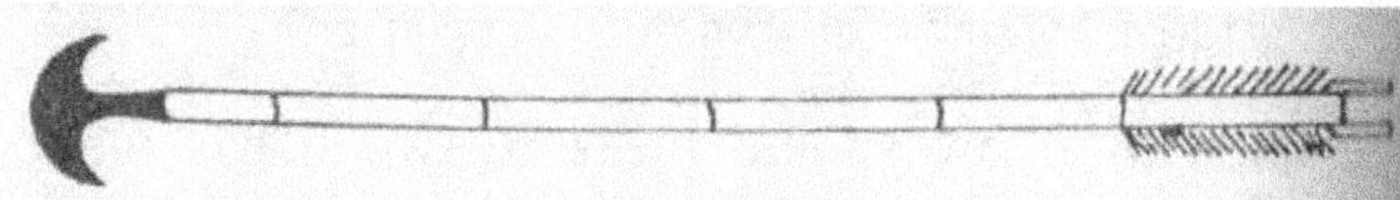

Female Arrow

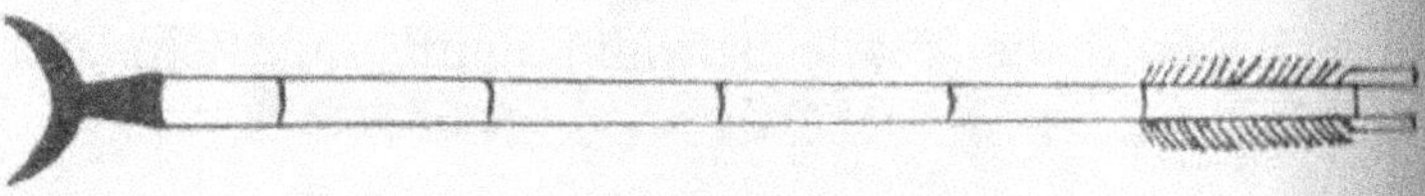

Female Arrow

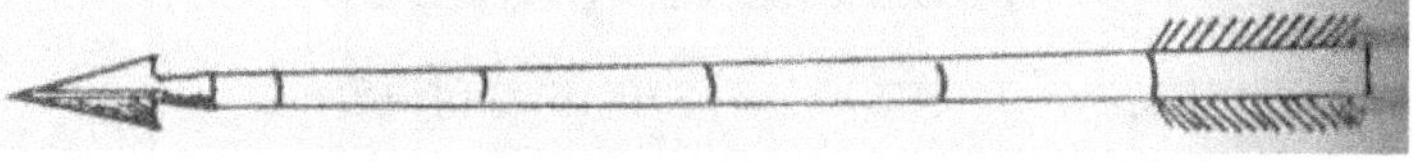

Male Arrow

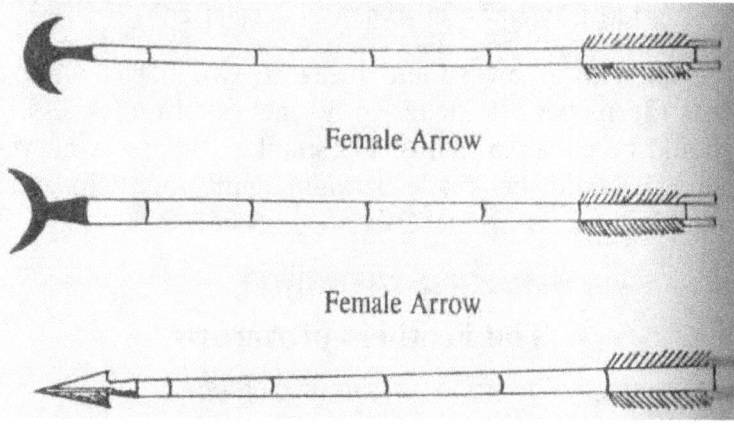

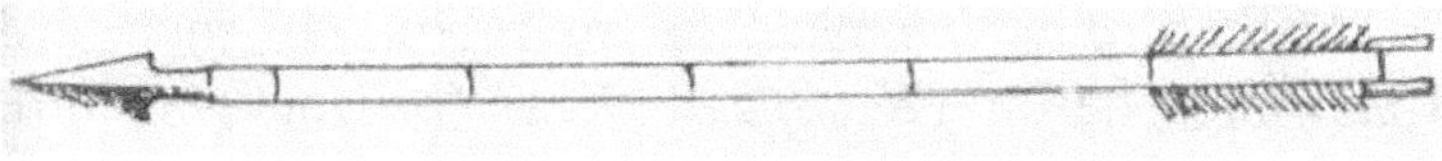

Impotent Arrow

समो नपुंसको ज्ञेयं तल्लक्ष्यार्थं प्रशस्यते।
दूरपातो युवत्या च पुरुषो भेदयेद् दृढम।। 52।।

52. The one equal throughout is termed as impotent. The impotent type is helpful in the practice of archery, the female type is a fast runner and hit targets at a long distance and the male type is able to pierce a strong and tough target.

अथ फललक्षणम्
Arrowhead Types

आरामुखं क्षुरप्रंच गोपुच्छं चार्द्धचन्द्रकम्।
सूचीमुखंच भल्लंच वत्सदन्तं द्विभल्लभम्।। 53।।

53. The arrowheads can be of awl type, razor blade type, like that of a cow's tail, crescent moon shaped, needle-pointed, spear-headed, teeth of calf shaped and a two spear-shaped.

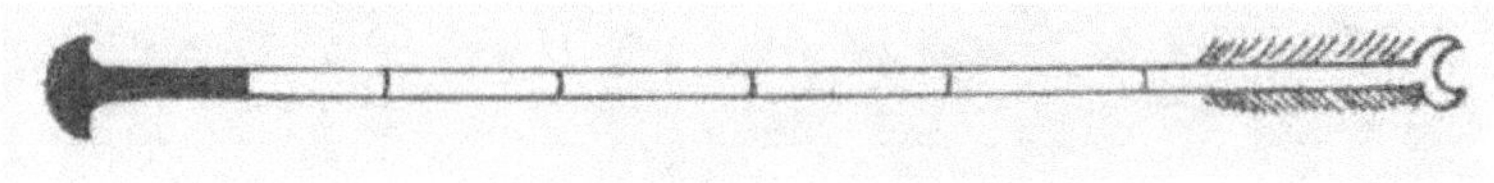

Ārāmukha (Awl type)

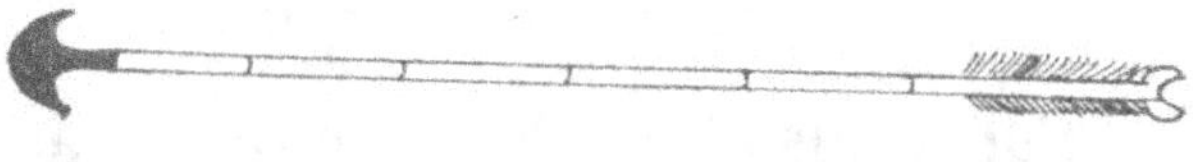

Kṣurapra (Razor Blade type)

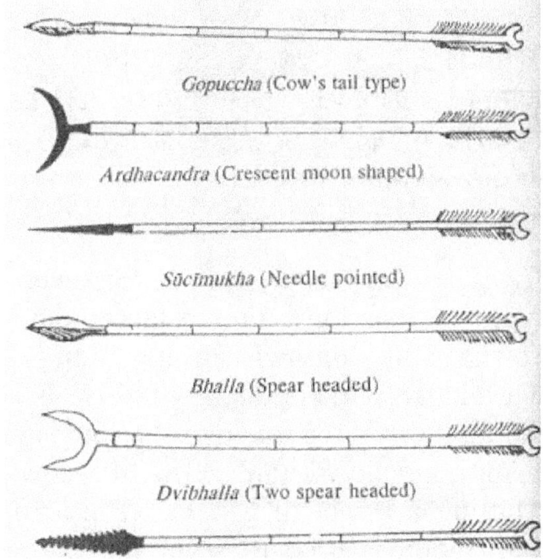

Gopuccha (Cow's tail type)

Ardhacandra (Crescent moon shaped)

Sūcīmukha (Needle pointed)

Bhalla (Spear headed)

Dvibhalla (Two spear headed)

Vatsadanta (Calf's teeth type)

कर्णिकं काकतुण्डंच तथाचान्यान्यप्यनेकशः ।
फलानि देशभेदेन भवन्ति बहुरूपतः ।। 54 ।।

54. The arrowhead may be of petal of flower type, the beak of crow, and many other types. The shape of arrowheads differs from country to country.

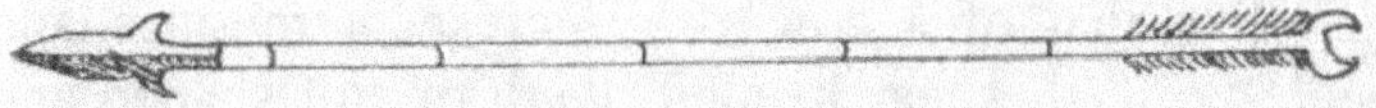

Karṇika (petal of flower type)

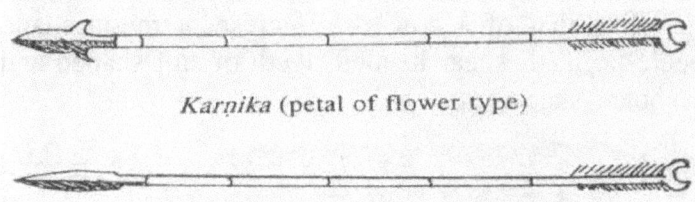

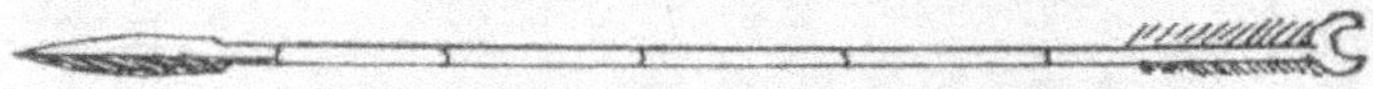

Kākatuṇḍa type (beak of crow type)

अथैतेषां कर्म्माणि

Functions of Various Arrow- heads

आरामुखेन चर्म्मछेदनम् क्षुरप्रेण बाणकर्त्तनम् ।
वा बाहुकर्त्तनम्, गोपुच्छेन लक्ष्यसाधनम् ।। 55 ।।
अर्द्धचन्द्रेण ग्रीवा मस्तकधनुरादीनां छेदनम् ।
सूचीमुखेन कवचभेदनम् भल्लेनहृदयभेदनम् ।। 56 ।।
वत्सदन्तेन गुणचर्वणम्, द्विभल्लेन बाणवरोधनम् ।
कर्णिकेन लोहमयबाणानां छेदनम्,
काकतुण्डेन वेध्यानां वेधं कुर्य्यात् ।। 57 ।।

55-57. The various types of arrowheads have various types of functions. For instance, the *ārāmukha* or an arrowhead like an awl can cut through the skin, the arrowhead like a razor blade (*kṣurapra*) is used to combat the arrows of the enemy or to cut up the hand of the enemy. *Gopuccha* (an arrow-like cow's tail) is good for hitting a target in general. The arrow-shaped like the half-moon is used to sever the enemy's head, neck, and bow. The needle pointed arrows were used to pierce the armour of an enemy. The spearheaded arrow was used to pierce the chest of an enemy, while *vatsadanta* (like the teeth of a calf) is used for cutting up the bow-string. The two-pronged arrowhead is used to combat arrows. *Karṇika* (shaped like a petal of flower) is used for cutting up metal arrows. *Kākatuṇḍa* (crow's beak type) can pierce any pierceable object.

अन्यद्गोपुच्छकं ज्ञेयं शुद्धकाष्ठविनिर्मितम्।
मुखे च लोहकण्टेन विद्धंयंगुलसम्मितम्।। 58।।

58. In addition to the above arrowheads, there is a special *gopuccha* type (shaped like cow's tail) arrowhead which is made of pure wood and has got a metallic nail of three aṅgula length fixed at its tip.

बाणस्य फलस्थाने कण्टकयोजनात् गोपुच्छबाणो भवति।
अनेन शराभ्यासस्तथा लक्ष्याभ्यासो वा कर्त्तव्यः।। 59।।

59. *Gopuccha* arrow is made by adding a nail at the arrow-head. This *gopuccha* arrowhead should be used for practices in aiming for targets and archery.

अथ पायनम्

The Methods of Tempering of Arrow-heads

इषुफले शरवंशामूललेपनाद् भवति तच्चिह्नमेतत्।
यस्मिन् शरवंशसमूहे स्वाति बिन्दुर्निपतति स पीतवर्णो भवति
तस्य मूले विषमुत्पद्यते तन्मूलं ग्राह्यम्। स च सर्वदा
पवनाभावऽपि कम्पते इदमेव तल्लक्ष्मेति।। 60–61।।

60-61. An arrowhead is tempered with the root of the reed plant. When the colour of the white reed plant turns yellow after receiving rainwater on *Svāti Nakṣatra* day, its root becomes poisonous. This root should be procured. The best way to recognise the plant is that it trembles always, even in the absence of wind.

फलस्य पायनं वक्ष्ये दिव्यौषधि विलेपनैः ।
येन दुर्भेद्यवर्म्माणि भेदयेत्तरुपर्णवत् ।। 62 ।।

62. Let me narrate the process of tempering arrowheads by smearing them into the paste of certain medicines. The arrowheads thus tempered were able to pierce even the unbreakable armours just like a leaf of a tree.

पिप्पली सैन्धवं कुष्ठं गोमुत्रे तु सुपेषयेत् ।
अनेन लेपयेच्छस्रं लिप्तं चाग्नौ प्रतापयेत् ।। 63 ।।
शिखिग्रीवानुवर्णाभं तप्तपीतं तथौषधम् ।
ततस्तु विमलं तोयं पाययेच्छस्रमुत्तमम् ।। 64 ।।

63-64. Long pepper (*pippali*), *saindhava* (rock-salt), *kuṣṭha* (medical plant named Costus Speciosus or arabicus used as a remedy for the disease called *takman*, in Hindi this plant is called as *Kūṭha*) should be ground and pounded in the urine of a cow to prepare a paste. That paste should be smeared over the arrow-head or a weapon and then it should be heated on fire till it becomes blue like peacock's neck. When it absorbs the entire paste, it must be quenched in water. Such weapons will become the best weapons.

अथ नाराच–नालिकशतघ्नीनां वर्णनम्

Types of rounds

सर्वलोहास्तु ये बाणा नाराचास्ते प्रकीर्त्तिताः ।
पंचभिः पृथुलैः पक्षैर्युक्ता सिद्धयन्ति कस्यचित् ।। 65 ।।

65. The missiles made completely of metals were called as *nārāca*. Some *nārācas* had five broad wings and they were able to make anybody successful in hitting his target.

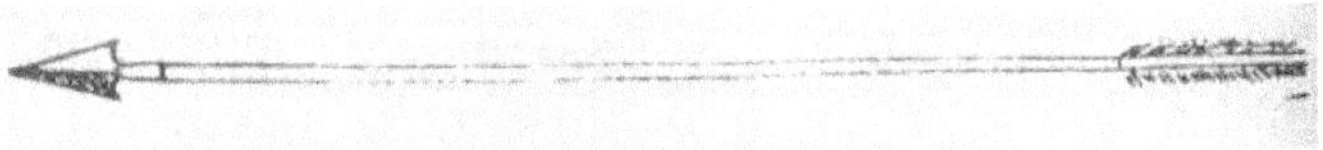

Nārāca Arrow

नालीका लघवो बाणा नलयन्त्रेण नोदिताः।
अत्युच्चदूरपातेषु दुर्गयुद्धेषु ते मताः।। 66।।

66. Gun-shots or bullets were known as small arrows or *Nālikā.* They were fired by a machine fitted with a barrel (just like a modern-day gun). Those small arrows or bullets were useful in shooting a target seated at the very high place or in war taking place in a fortress. Thus in ancient times, guns were also used in fighting.

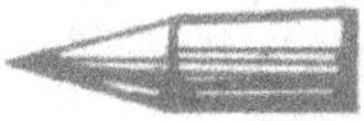

Nālika Arrow (Bullets)

सिंहासनस्य रक्षार्थं शतघ्नं स्थापयेत् गढे।
रंजकबहुलं तत्र स्थाप्यं वटयो धीमता।। 67।।

67. To protect the throne, *Śataghnī* should be stationed on the fort. A lot of gun powder should also be stored there by the wise persons.

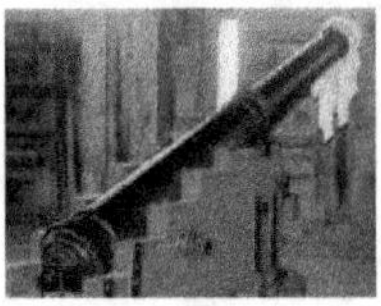

Śataghnī (Cannon)

अथ स्थानमुष्ट्याकर्षणलक्षणानि

Shooter's Positions, Grips and Modes of Shooting

स्थानान्यष्टौ विधेयानि योजने भिन्नकर्म्मणाम्।
मुष्टयः पंचसमाख्याता व्यायाः पंच प्रकीर्त्तिताः।। 68।।

68. '*Sthāna*' (the position to be taken by a warrior while shooting) is of eight types for performing different types of shooting. '*Muṣṭi*' holding the string or 'grips of string' are of five types, while the position of drawing the string is also said to be of five types.

अग्रतो वामपादश्च दक्षिणं चानुकुचितम्।
प्रत्यालीढं प्रकर्त्तव्यं हस्तद्वयसविस्तरम्।। 69।।

69. If during the time of the shooting, the left leg of a shooter is stretched out and the right leg remains contracted at the knee, the distance between both the legs being two hand units (36 inches) apart (of the concerned shooter, such posture of a shooter is known by the term '*Pratyālīḍha*'. (See fig. next page).

आलीढे तु प्रकर्त्तव्यं सव्यं चेवानुकुचितम्।
दक्षिणन्तु पुरस्ताद्वा दूरपाते विशिष्यते।। 70।।

70. If during the time of the shooting, the right leg of a shooter is stretched out and the left leg is contracted at the knee, this position is called as *Ālīḍha*' (see fig. next page). It is extremely useful in hitting distant targets.

पादौ सविस्तरौ कार्य्यौ समौ हस्तप्रमाणतः।
विशाखस्थानकं ज्ञेयं कूटलक्ष्यस्य वेधने।। 71।।

71. If the shooter extends his legs equally and their distance is one hand (18 inches) apart, this position is known as '*viśākhasthāna*' and useful to hit the complex or invisible targets (see fig. next page).

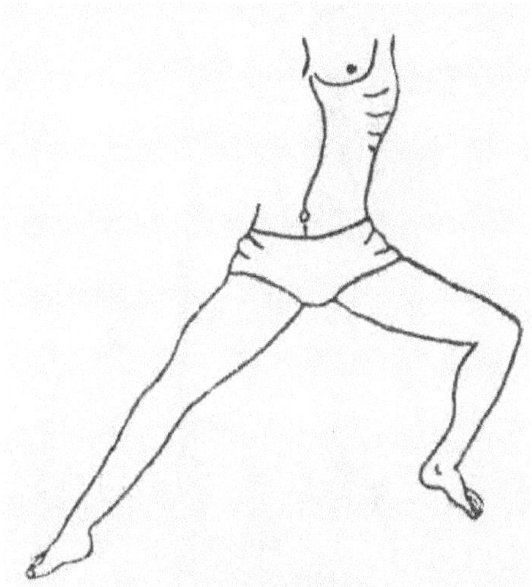

Pratyālīḍha

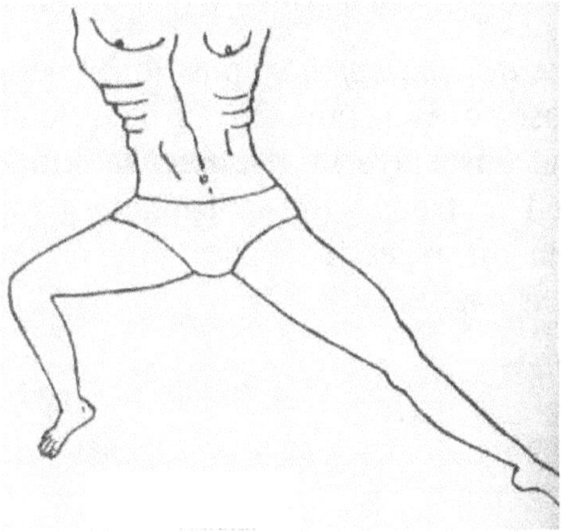

Ālīḍha

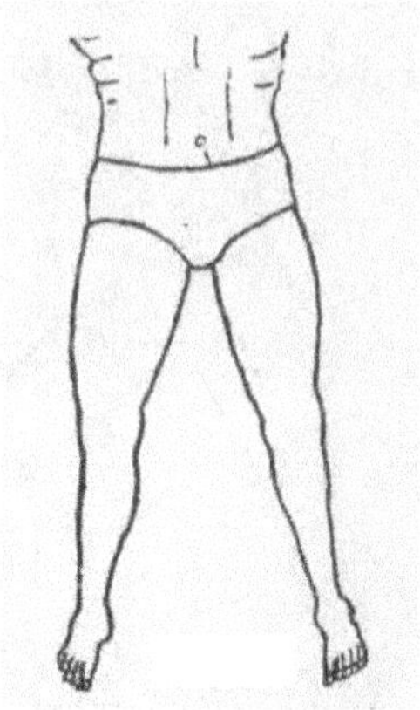

Viśākha

समपादे समौ पादौ निष्कम्पौ च सुसंगतौ।
असमे च पुरो वामो हस्तमात्रेण तं वपुः।। 72।।

72. In the *Samapāda* position, both legs are together close to each other at an equal distance, steps are firm and unsteady. In *Asamapāda* position, the left leg is placed in front with a distance of one hand (18 inches) from the right leg. The body is bent forward. (See fig. next page)

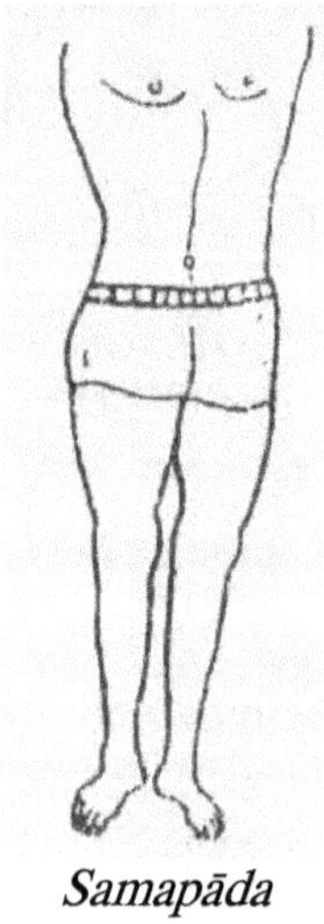

Samapāda

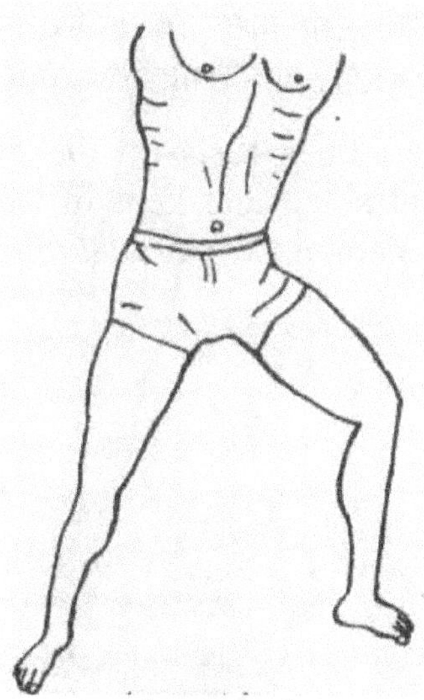

Asamapāda

आकुचितोरू द्वौ यत्र जानुभ्यां धरणिगतौ।
दर्दुरक्रममित्याहुः स्थानकं दृढभेदने।। 73।।

73. If the shooter kneels down and his thighs are contracted, his position is known by the name '*Dardurakrama*', (literally meaning 'the movement of the frog'). This position is useful for hitting a strong or difficult target.

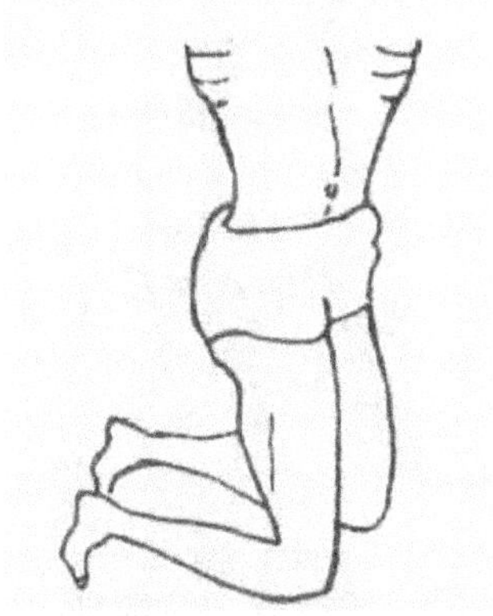

Dardurkrama

सव्यं जानुगतौ भूमौ दक्षिणं च सकुचितम्।
अग्रतो यत्र दातव्यं तद्विद्याद्गरुडक्रमम्।। 74।।

74. If the left knee rests on the ground while the right knee is contracted and kept in front, the position of the shooter is known as '*Garuḍakrama*'.

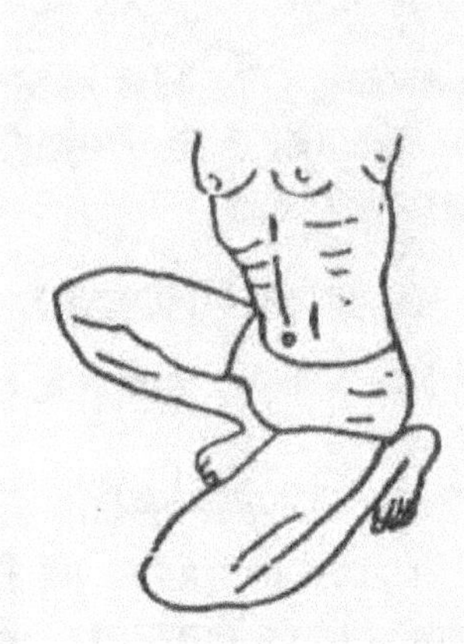

Garuḍakrama

पद्मासनं प्रसिद्धन्तु ह्युपविश्य यथाक्रमम्।
धन्विनां तत्तुविज्ञेयं स्थानकं शुभलक्षणम्।। 75।।

75. A shooter should sit in *Padmāsana* which is a well-known posture of sitting (cross-legged). It is a very good pose for shooters also.

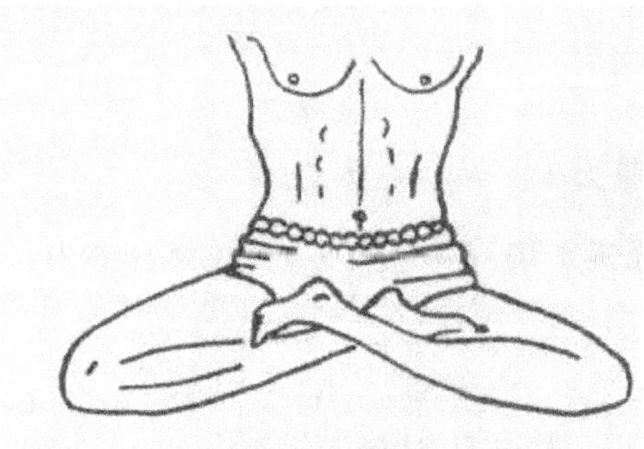

Padmāsana

अथ गुणमुष्टिः

Grips or Position of Release

पताका वज्रमुष्टिश्च सिंहकर्णस्तथैव च।
मत्सरी काकतुण्डी च योजनीया यथाक्रमम्।। 76।।

76. There are various types of grips while triggering or shooting such as *'patākā'*, *'vajramuṣṭi'*, *'Simhakarṇī'*, *'Matsarī'* and *'Kākatuṇḍī'* etc.

दीर्घा तु तर्ज्जनी यत्र ह्याश्रितागुंष्ठमूलकम्।
पताका सा च विज्ञेया नालिका दूरमोक्षणैः।। 77।।

77. If the forefinger is extended and brought under the root of the thumb, the position of the grip is known by the name '*Patākā*'. This form of the grip is applied by a shooter for shooting *nālikās* (gun-shots /rounds/small arrows) at a distant target.

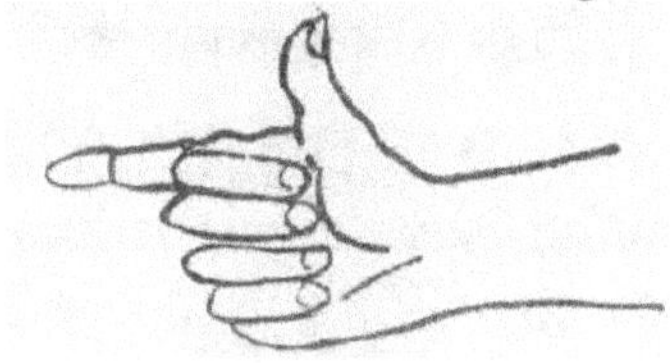

Patākā

तर्ज्जनी मध्यमा मध्यमगुंष्ठो विशते यदि।
वज्रमुष्टिस्तु सा ज्ञेया स्थूले नाराचमोक्षणैः।। 78।।

78. If the thumb enters the gap between the middle finger and the forefinger then such a grip is called *'Vajramuṣṭī'*. Such a grip is used in releasing *nārācās* (missiles/metallic arrows) at distant targets.

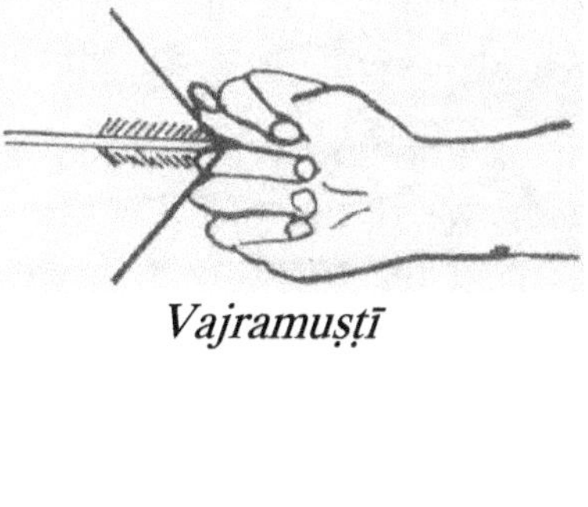

Vajramuṣṭī

अगुंष्ठमध्यदेशन्तु तर्ज्जन्यग्रं शुभं स्थितम्।
सिंहकर्णः स विज्ञेयो दृढलक्ष्यस्य वेधने।। 79।।

79. When the string is held by placing the thumb at the middle part of the forefinger, it is called *Siṅhakarṇa muṣṭi.* It is used in hitting strong targets.

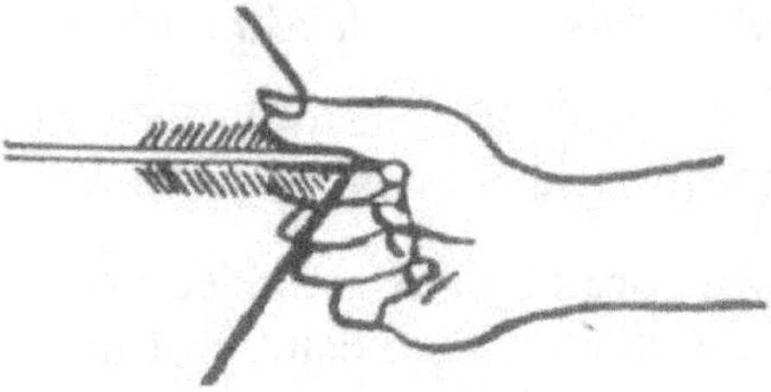

Siṅhakarṇa

अगुंष्ठ नखमूले तू तर्ज्जन्यग्रं च संस्थितम्।
मत्सरी सा च विज्ञेया चित्रलक्ष्यस्य वेधने।। 80।।

80. If the tip of the forefinger is placed squarely on the nail of the thumb, such a grip is known by the name *'Matsari'*. This grip is used in hitting chitra (camouflaged) targets.

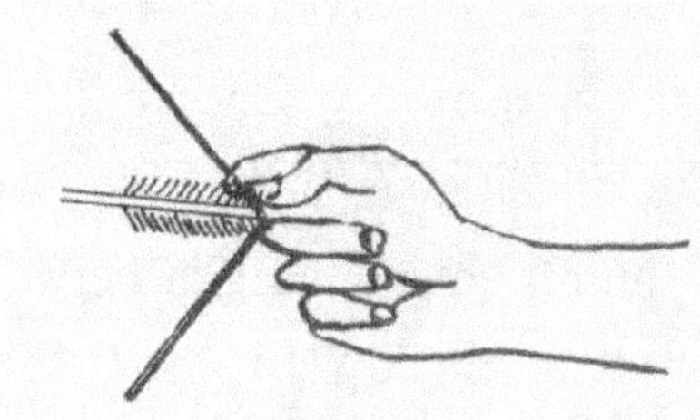

Matsarī

अगुंष्ठाग्रे तु तर्ज्जन्यां मुखं यत्र निवेशितम्।
काकतुण्डी च विज्ञेया सूक्ष्मलक्ष्येषु योजिता।। 81।।

81. A grip is known by the name '*Kākatuṇḍī*' (like the beak of a crow) if the top portion of the thumb is placed on the tip of the forefinger. Such a grip is useful to hit the minute target.

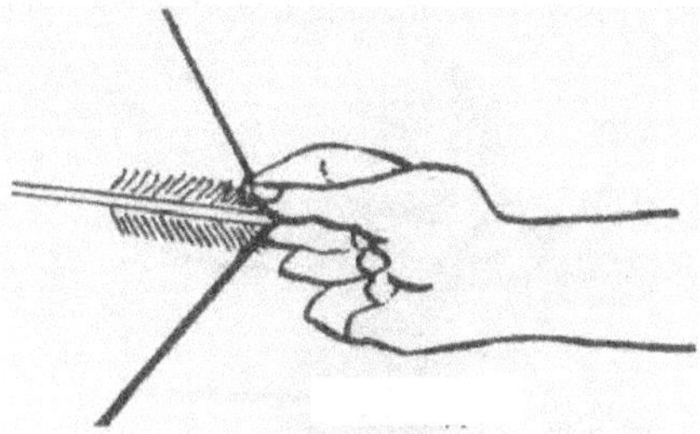

Kākatuṇḍī

अथ धनुर्मुष्टिसन्धानम्

Methods of Drawing the Bow

संधानं त्रिविधं प्रोक्तमधमूर्ध्वं समं तथा।
योजयेत्त्रिप्रकारं हि कार्येष्वपि यथाक्रमम्।। 82।।

82. There are three methods of drawing the bow, namely (i) lower; (ii) higher, and (iii) parallel.

i. In the lower draw, a stave is kept lower to the body.

ii. In the higher draw, the stave is kept higher than the body.

iii. In the parallel draw, the stave is kept parallel to the body.

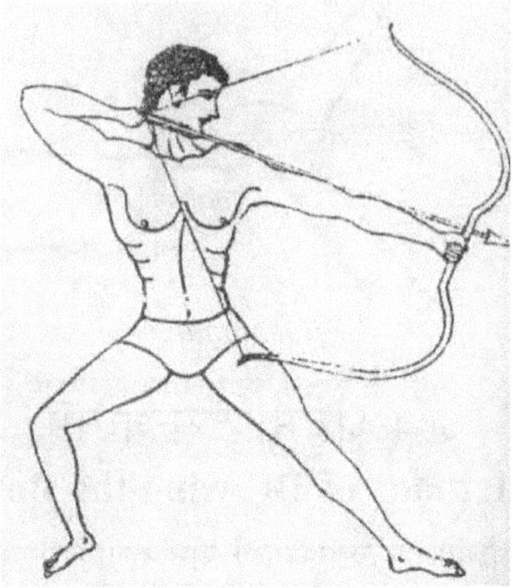

Adhaḥsandhāna (Lower Draw)

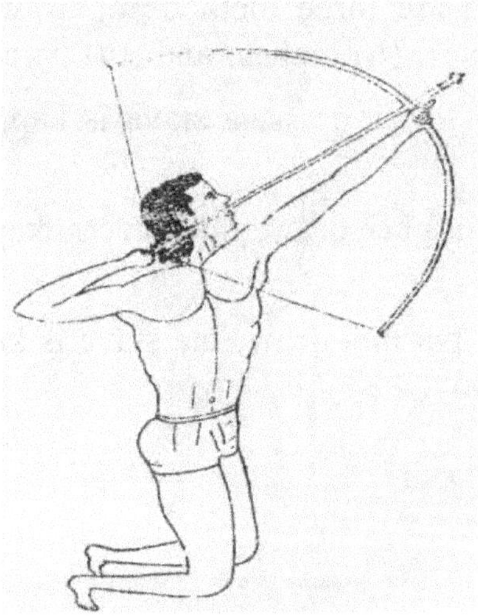

Ūrdhvasandhāna (Higher Draw)

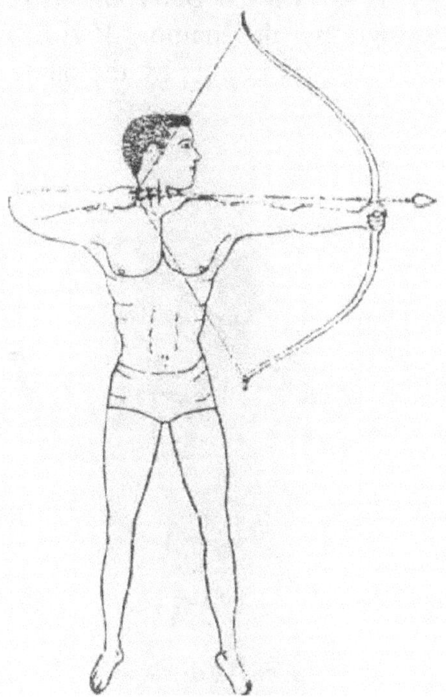

Samasandhāna (Paralel Draw)

अधश्च दूरपातित्वे समे लक्ष्येषु निश्चले।
दृढस्फोटं प्रकुर्वीत् ऊर्ध्वसंधानयोगतः।। 83।।

83. The lower draw is useful in long-range shooting. The parallel draw is useful in hitting targets firmly. The higher draw is useful in hitting strong targets.

अथ धनुर्व्यायाः

Drawing of the Bowstring

कैशिकः केशमूले वै शरः शृंगे च सात्त्विकः।
श्रवणे वत्सकर्णश्च ग्रीवायां भरतो भवेत्।। 84।।

84. If the bowstring is drawn up to the tip of the hair, the draw is known as *Kaiśika*, if drawn till the lock of hair, it is known as '*Sāttvika*'. If drawn till the ears, it is known by the name '*Vatsakarṇa*', and if drawn till the neck, it is known by the name '*Bharata*'.

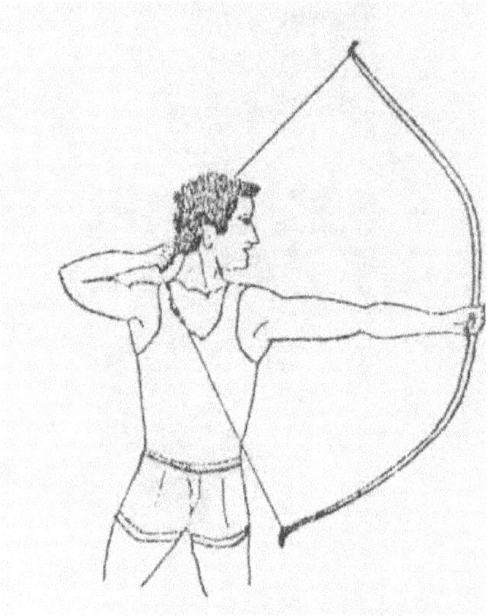

Kaiśika draw

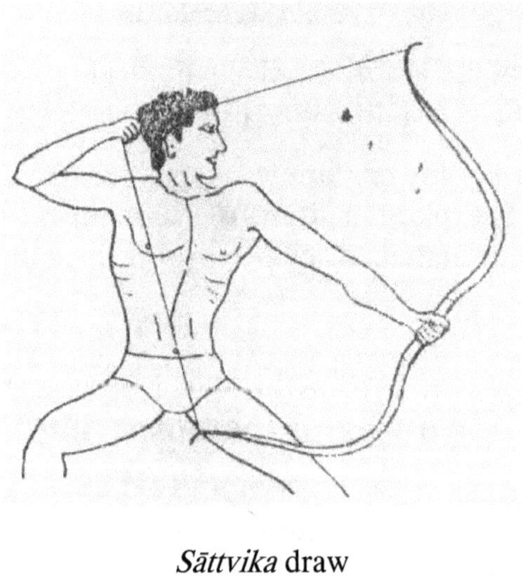

Sāttvika draw

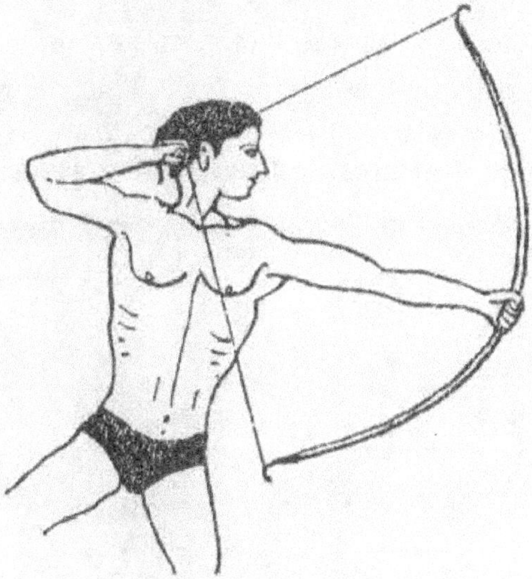

Vatsakarṇa draw

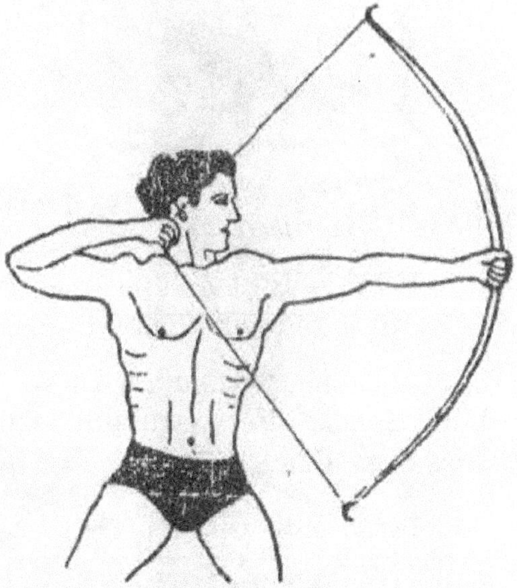

Bharata draw

अंसके स्कन्धनामा च व्यायाः पश्च प्रकीर्त्तिताः।

कैशिकश्चित्रयुद्धेषु ह्यधोलक्ष्येषु सात्त्विकः ।। 85 ।।

85. When the bow-string is drawn up to shoulder, the draw is called as '*Skandha*'. Thus there are five types of draws (*Vyāyas*). *Kaiśika* draw is useful in camouflaged warfares, *Sāttvika* draw is useful to hit targets at low positions.

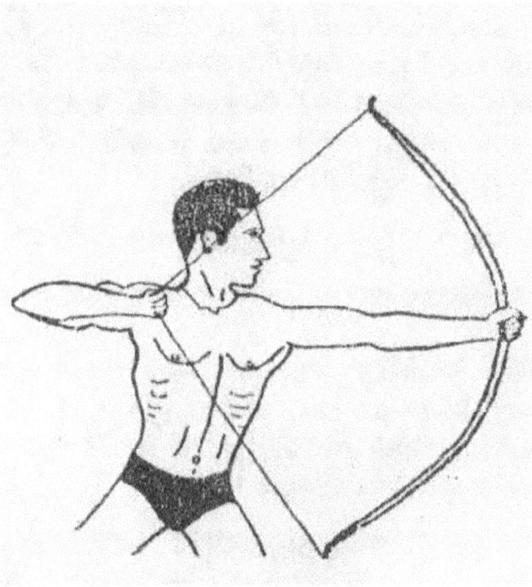

Skandhanāmā draw

वत्सकर्णः सदाज्ञेयो भरतो दृढभेदने।
दृढभेदे च दूरे च स्कन्धनामानमुद्दिशेत् ।। 86 ।।

86. *Vatsakarṇa* and *Bharata* are known to hit hard targets, while *Skandha* draw is useful in hitting both hard as well as distant targets.

अथ लक्ष्यम्

Types of Targets

लक्ष्यं चतुर्विधं ज्ञेयं स्थिरं चैव चलन्तथा।
चलाचलं द्वयचलं वेधनीयं क्रमेण तु ।। 87 ।।

87. There are four types of targets: 1. *Sthira* (immovable, fixed or stationary), 2. *Cala* i.e. moving targets, 3. *Calācala* (a stationary target hit by the moving shooter), 4. *Dvayacala* (a mobile target hit by the moving shooter). One should learn the practice of the targets in the above described order.

आत्मानं सुस्थिरं कृत्वा लक्ष्यं चैव स्थिरं बुधः।
वेधयेत्त्रिप्रकारं तु स्थिरवेधी स उच्यते।। 88।।

88. Making himself motionless and steady, if a shooter hits all the three types of stationary targets (high, low, and parallel), he is known as '*Sthiravedhī*' (shooter of immovable target).

चलं तु वेधयेद् यस्तु आत्मस्थानेषु संस्थितः।
चलं लक्ष्यं तु तत्प्रोक्तमाचार्य्येण शिवेन वै।। 89।।

89. If a shooter in a motionless position successfully hits a moving target, he is called by the experts as '*chala-lakṣya*' or the shooter of 'a moving target'.

धन्वीतः चलते यत्र स्थिरलक्षे समाहितः।
चलाचलं भवेत्तत्र ह्यप्रमेयमाचिन्ततम्।। 90।।

90. If a moving shooter hits the steady target, then he will be known as '*chalācala*' or 'shooter of stationary target keeping himself in a moving position'.

उभावपि चलौ यत्र लक्ष्यं चापि धनुर्धरः।
तद्विज्ञेयं द्वयचलं श्रमेण बहु साध्यते।। 91।।

91. When both the shooter and the target are in a moving stage, then the process of shooting is known as '*dvayacala*' i.e. 'both shooter and target being in a moving condition'. This type of shooting efficiency can be achieved through the practice of *śrama* (a practice of shooting to hit a target with the help of many arrows, shot by drawing the bowstring till ears.

Note: According to *Ākāśa bhairava, śrama* means hitting a target with many arrows, shot by drawing a bowstring till ears.

पुरतो वर्त्तमानस्य लक्ष्यस्य बहुधा शितैः ।
शरैराकर्णमाकृष्टैर्भेदनं यत् तदद्रिजे श्रम इत्युच्यते।।

श्रमेणास्खलितादृष्टिः लक्ष्यं दूरं च बहुभेदनम्।
श्रमेण कठिना मुष्टिः शीघ्र संधानमाप्यते।। 92।।

92. If a shooter practises *śrama*, he can unfailingly hit many distant targets. Through the practice of *śrama*, he can achieve firm grip and an ability to hit the target quickly.

श्रमेन चित्रयोधित्वं श्रमेण प्राप्यते जयः।
तस्माद्गुरूसमक्षं हि श्रमः कार्यो विजानता।। 93।।

93. The shooting practice (*śrama*) makes a shooter an expert in camouflaged warfare also, and through śrama he can achieve victory. Hence, it is advisable that a shooter should always practise shooting (*śrama*) in front of his teacher.

अथ लक्ष्याभ्यासस्वरूपाणि

Target Practice

प्रथमं वामहस्तेन यः श्रमं कुरुते नरः।
तस्य चापक्रियासिद्धिरचिरादेव जायते।। 94।।

94. A shooter, who practises shooting first with his left hand, he becomes an expert in the art of shooting quickly.

वामहस्ते सुसंसिद्धे पश्चाद्दक्षिणमारभेत्।
उभाभ्यां च श्रमं कुर्यान्नाराचैश्च शरैस्तथा।। 95।।

95. Having become proficient with the left hand, one should start practice with the right hand. A shooter should do the practice of shooting arrows as well as rounds with both the hands.

वामेनैव श्रमं कुर्यात्सुसिद्धिर्दक्षिणे करे।
विशाखेनासमेनैव रथी व्याये च कैशिके।। 96।।

96. When proficiency (in shooting) is achieved with the right hand, then again exercise should be started with the left hand. A shooter in a chariot should practise shooting with the *kaiśika* draw (drawing bowstring up to hair tips) standing in *Viśākhā* position (keeping the feet parallel and 18 inches apart from each other) and *asampāda* position (left leg is placed in front at a distance of 18 inches from the right leg and the body is bent forward positions.

उदिते भास्करे लक्ष्यं पश्चिमायां निवेशयेत्।
अपराह्ने च कर्त्तव्यं लक्ष्यं पूर्वदिगाश्रितम्।। 97।।

97. At sunrise, the shooting should be practised in the western direction. In the afternoon it should be in the eastern direction. Meaning to say, that a target for practice should be in the opposite direction of the sun.

उत्तरेण सदा कार्यं अवश्यमवरोधिकम्।
संग्रामेण विना कार्यं न लक्ष्यं दक्षिणामुखम्।। 98।।

98. One should not aim the target towards the north for the purpose of destroying life. One should not aim towards the south unless it is wartime.

अथ लक्ष्यवेधनम्

Aiming or Shooting of Rounds

षष्टिधन्वन्तरे लक्ष्यं ज्येष्ठलक्ष्यं प्रकीर्त्तितम्।
चत्वारिंशन्मध्यमं च विंशतिश्च कनिष्ठकम्।। 99।।

99. A target set at a distance of sixty *dhanus* (360 feet)[1] is regarded as the best one. If the same is set at a

---

[1] One *dhanu* is equal to 4 *hasta.* One *hasta* is equal to 18

distance of forty *dhanus* (240 feet), it is regarded as a medium one, whereas a target at a distance of twenty *dhanus* (120 feet) is regarded as the lowest type.

शराणां कथितं ह्येतन्नाराचानामथोच्यते ।
चत्वारिंशच्च त्रिंशच्च षोडशैव भवेत्ततः ।। 100 ।।

100. The above distance of the target was described in the case of arrows. Now we shall tell about the distance of targets in case of '*nārācas*'(bullets or rounds). In the case of *Nārācas,* a target set at a distance of forty *dhanus* (240 feet)[1] is regarded as the best one. If the same is set at a distance of thirty *dhanus* (180 feet), it is regarded as a medium one, whereas a target at a distance of sixteen *dhanus* (96 feet) is regarded as the lowest type.

चतुःशतैश्च काण्डानां यो हि लक्ष्यं विसर्जयेत् ।
सूर्योदये चास्तमने स ज्येष्ठो धन्विनां भवेत् ।। 101 ।।

101. One who is able to shoot four hundred shots (*kāṇḍa*) at the time from sunrise and the sunset, is considered as the best among shooters.

त्रिशतैर्मध्यमश्चैव द्विशताभ्यां कनिष्ठकः ।
लक्ष्यं च पुरुषोन्मानं कुर्याच्चन्द्रकसंयुतम् ।। 102 ।।

102. If the number of arrows shot is three hundred, the shooter is known as 'mediocre'; but if the number is just two hundred, then the shooter is known to be '*kaniṣṭhaka*'; i.e. of the lowest category or standard. Shooters' targets should be of a man length (6 feet) and fitted with a *chandraka* (an eye of a peacock tail).

---

inches. As such one *dhanu* becomes equal to 72 inches or 6 feet.

[1] One *dhanu* is equal to 4 *hasta.* One *hasta* is equal to 18 inches. As such one *dhanu* becomes equal to 72 inches or 6 feet.

ऊर्ध्वभेदी भवेज्येष्ठो नाभिभेदी च मध्यमः।
पादभेदी तु लक्ष्यस्य स कनिष्ठो मतो भृगोः।। 103।।

103. One who shoots with the top portion of the eye is known to be the superior one, while one who shoots with the middle portion is known as a mediocre one, and the one who hits the lowest portion of the eye is known as an inferior shooter by the Bhṛgu, one of the experts of *Dhanurveda*.

अथानाध्यायः

Intermissions in shooting

अष्टमी च ह्यमावास्या वर्जनीया चतुर्दशी।
पूर्णिमार्धदिनं यावन्निषिद्धं सर्वकर्म्मसु।। 104।।

104. As all activities are prohibited on the eighth and the fourteenth day of both bright and dark halves of the moon and also on the day of the new-moon and half of the day of the full moon, shooting practice should also be discontinued on those days.

Note: *Taittirīya Āraṇyaka*, *Śatapatha Brāhmaṇa*, *Āpastamba Dharmasūtra*, and *Yājñavalkya Smṛti* also refer to a suspension of Vedic studies on these days.

अकाले गर्जिते दैवे दुर्दिनं चाथवा भवेत्।
पूर्वकाण्डहतं लक्ष्यमनध्याये प्रचक्षते।। 105।।

105. The practice of shooting should be stopped if clouds thunder untimely, or there is rain or if the target is broken or destroyed by the arrows or rounds shot earlier.

अनुराधर्क्षमारभ्य षोडशर्क्षे दिवाकरः।
यावच्चरति तं कालमकालं हि प्रचक्षते।। 106।।

106. The practice of shooting should be abandoned if the sun is anyway between the *Anurādhā* (17th star) and *Mṛgśirā* (16th star).

अरुणोदयः वेलायां वारिदो यदि गर्जति।
तद्दिने स्यादनध्यायस्तमकालं प्रचक्षते।। 107।।

107. If it thunders at dawn, then the time is not suitable for practice. One should abstain from learning at that time.

श्रमं च कुर्वतस्तत्र भुजंगो दृश्यते यदि।
अथवा भज्यते चापं यदैव श्रमकर्मणि।। 108।।

108. The practice of shooting should be abandoned if a serpent is seen at the place of practice, or if the bow is broken at the time of practice.

त्रुट्यते वा गुणो यत्र प्रथमे बाणमोक्षणे।
श्रमं तत्र न कुर्वीत शस्त्रे मतिमतां वरः।। 109।।

109. If the bowstring snaps at the very first shot, then the practice should be abandoned.

अथ श्रमक्रिया

Shooting Practice

क्रियाकलापान्वक्ष्यामि श्रमसाध्यांशुचिष्मताम्।
येषां विज्ञानमात्रेण सिर्द्धिभवति नान्यथा।। 110।।

110. The process that is involved in the shooting is narrated hereunder for pure-hearted shooters. Only by knowing this process, one can achieve success in shooting and not otherwise.

प्रथमं चापमारोप्य चुलिकां बन्धयेत्ततः।
स्थानकं तु ततः कृत्वा बाणोपरि करं न्यसेत्।। 111।।

111. Firstly, a bowstring should be tightened to the nocks (notch at either end of the bow for holding the string), and only after taking his position, a shooter should handle the arrow.

तोलनं धनुषश्चैव कर्त्तव्यं वामपाणिना।

आदानं च ततः कृत्वा संधानं च ततः परम् ।। 112 ।।

112. The bow should be picked up with the left hand at first and then the arrow should be mounted on the bowstring by picking up the bow with the right hand.

सकृदाकृष्टचापेन भूमिवेधं तु कारयेत् ।
नमस्कुर्याच्चं विघ्नराजं गुरुं धनुः शरान् ।। 113 ।।

113. The shooter should draw the bow and with one attempt pierce the earth, then he should salute Almighty God, the destroyer of hindrances, his teacher/preceptor, the bows, and arrows.

अथ प्राणायामाभ्यासः

Breath control in shooting

याचितव्या गुरोराज्ञा बाणस्याकर्षणं प्रति ।
प्राणवायुं प्रयत्नेन प्राणेन सह पूरयेत् ।। 114 ।।

114. The permission for drawing a bow should be taken from the teacher or preceptor, the breath should also be inhaled (to fill up the lungs) carefully.

कुम्भकेन स्थिरं कृत्वा हुंकारेण विसर्जयेत् ।
इत्यभ्यासक्रिया कार्या धन्विना सिद्धिमिच्छता ।। 115 ।।

115. Afterwards, *kumbhaka* should be performed (breath should be held for a short time), thereafter, the breath should be released with the sound of 'hum'. A shooter who desires success in his art should practise such breathing exercises (*Prāṇāyāma*).

षण्मासात्सिद्ध्यते मुष्टिः शराः संवत्सरेण तु ।
नाराचास्तस्य सिद्धयन्ति यस्य तुष्टो महेश्वरः ।। 116 ।।

116. The *muṣṭi* (a technique of holding bowstrings or grips) can be learnt within six months, and shooting arrows can be learnt within one year. However, the shooting of '*nārācas*', or projectiles can be learnt only with the grace of Almighty.

पुष्पवद्धारयेद्बाणं सर्पवत्पीडयेद्धनुः ।
धनवच्चिन्तयेल्लक्ष्यं यदीच्छेत्सिद्धिमात्मनः ।। 117 ।।

117. If a shooter wants to achieve success in shooting, he must hold/handle his weapons very gently and carefully, like a flower, and pull the bow with the same might as if thrashing a snake. The shooter should brood over his target in the same way as if a common man hankers after money.

क्रियामिच्छन्ति चाचार्याः दूरमिच्छन्ति भार्गवाः ।
राजानो दृढमिच्छन्ति लक्ष्यमिच्छन्ति चेतरे ।। 118 ।।

118. A preceptor expects that his disciple's shooting will be effective and efficient. The descendants of the Bhṛgu (like Paraśurāma) desire that the arrow of the disciple should hit the target at a great distance. A king desires farsightedness, while others (common men) want to redeem their targets.

जनानां रंजनं येन लक्ष्यपातात्प्रजायते ।
हीनेनापीषुणा तस्मात्प्रशस्तं लक्ष्यवेधनम् ।। 119 ।।

119. If the shooting of even the small arrow or round makes the viewer delighted, then the shooting is considered as a praiseworthy action.

अथ लक्ष्यस्खलनविधिः

Perfect Shooting

विशाखस्थानकं हित्वा समसंधानमाचरेत् ।
गोपुच्छमुखबाणेन सिंहकर्णेन मुष्टिना ।। 120 ।।

120. Perfect shooting takes place if the shooter stands in the '*viśākha*' position - standing with the feet apart, uses the '*gopuccha*' arrow, holds the bow-string in a '*siṅhkarṇa*' way and draws the bow in '*samasandhāna*' method.

आकर्षेत्कैशिकव्याये न शिखां चालयेत्ततः।
पूर्वापरौ समं कार्यौ समांसौ निश्चलौ करौ।। 121 ।।

121. While performing '*kaiśika vyāya*' or drawing the bow in a '*kaiśika*' (method), the top-knot of an archer should not move. He should keep both his right and left shoulders at par and the hands should not be moved while shooting.

चक्षुषी स्पन्दयेन्नैव दृष्टिं लक्ष्ये नियोजयेत्।
मुष्टिनाच्छादितं लक्ष्यं शरस्याग्रे नियोजयेत्।। 122 ।।

122. At the time of the shooting, the eyes should not move; rather these should be fixed on the target. The view of the target covered by the fist should be placed in front of the arrow.

मनो दृष्टिगतं ज्ञात्वा ततः काण्डं विसर्जयेत्।
स्खलत्येव कदाचिन्न लक्ष्ये योधो जितश्रमः।। 123 ।।

123. Realising that the mind is totally fixed on the target, the weapon ('*kāṇḍa*') should be shot to the target. The shooter who has thus practised the shooting never misses the target.

अथ शीघ्रसन्धानम्

Fast Shooting

आदानं चैव तुणीरात्संधानं कर्षणं तथा।
क्षेपणं च त्वरायुक्तो बाणस्य कुरुते तु यः।
नित्याभ्यासवशात्तस्य शीघ्रसंधानता भवेत्।। 124 ।।

124. A shooter who can quickly take out arrows from the quiver, load them on to the bowstring, hold the bow-string, aim, and shoot the arrows very quickly, becomes a "fast shooter" on account of his constant practice.

अथ भेदनविधिः
Rules for various Shooting Ranges

प्रत्यालीढे कृते स्थाने ह्यधः संधानमाचरेत्।
मुष्ट्या पताकया बाणं स्त्रीचिह्नं दूरपातनम्।। 125।।

125. When a shooter wants to shoot a distant target (*dūrapātanam*), he should assume the position of '*pratyālīḍha*' and aim a feminine type of arrow downwards, drawing it with the grip known as '*patākāmuṣṭi*'.

दर्दुरस्थानमास्थाय ह्यूर्ध्वधारणमाचरेत्।
स्कन्धव्यायेन वज्रस्य मुष्ट्या पुमार्गणेन च।
अत्यन्तसौष्ठवं बाह्वोर्जायते दृढभेदिता।।126।।

126. If the shooter wants to shoot the strong and tough targets, he should aim a male type of arrow upwards (*ūrdhapātanam*) drawing it with a grip known as '*Vajramuṣṭi*' taking a *dardurkrama* pose and drawing the bow-string in '*skandhavyāya*' method. If he follows this technique, he achieves efficiency in beautifully hitting the tough targets.

अथ हीनगतिसमूहः
Movement of Arrows

सूचीमुखा मीनपुच्छा भ्रमरी च तृतीयका।
शराणां गतयस्तिस्रः प्रशस्ता कथिता बुधैः।। 127।।

127. Wise men enumerate three types of proper motions of the arrows, viz. (i) '*sucīmukha*' (moving in a straight line like the tip of the needle) (ii) '*mīnapuccha*' (moving in a zigzag pattern like the tail of a fish) and (iii) '*bhramarī*' (moving all over the place like a black bee).

सूचीमुखा गतिस्तस्य सायकस्य प्रजायते।

पत्रं विलोकितं यस्य ह्यथवा हीनपत्रकम् ।। 128 ।।

128. The arrow moves in a '*sucīmukha*' motion when it lacks its fletched portion or it has very little fletching.

कर्कशस्तंतु चापेन याकृष्टो हीनमुष्टिना ।
मत्स्यपुच्छा गतिस्तस्य सायकस्य प्रकीर्त्तिता ।। 129 ।।

129. If the arrow is released from a bow which is hard and with a loose grip, the arrow follows a zigzag trajectory like the tail of a fish known as '*matsyapuccha*'.

भ्रमरी कथिता ह्येषा शिवेन श्रमकर्मणि ।
ऋजुत्वेन विना याति क्षेप्यमाणस्तु सायकः ।। 130 ।।

130. If the arrow after being shot follows the semicircular path, then its movement is known as '*Bhramarī*' by Sadāśiva, author of the *Śiva Danurveda Saṅhitā*.

अथ बाणलक्ष्यस्खलनगतिसमूहः

Missed Targets or Deflection of arrows

वामगा दक्षिणा चैव ऊर्ध्वगाधोगमा तथा ।
चतस्रो गतयः प्रोक्ता बाणस्खलनहेतवः ।। 131 ।।

131. Depending upon the release of an arrow, it may deflect to four different directions. (i) '*vāmagā*' (deflection to the left) (ii) '*dakṣagā*' (deflection to the right) (iii) '*ūrdhvagā*' (deflection to upward direction) and (iv) '*adhogā*' (deflection to the downward direction). These four deflections may lead to the missed targets.

कम्पते गुणमुष्टिस्तु मार्गणस्य हि पृष्ठतः ।
सम्मुखोस्याद्धनुर्मुष्टिस्तदा वामे गतिर्भवेत् ।। 132 ।।

132. If the grip of the bowstring at the rear portion

of the arrow shakes and the bow is drawn in '*samasandhāna*' position (or say if the stave is kept parallel to the body) the arrow will deflect to the left.

ग्रहणं शिथिलं यस्य ऋजुत्वेन विवर्जितम्।
पार्श्वन्तु दक्षिणं याति सायकस्य न संशयः।। 133।।

133. If an archer does not hold the arrow properly and aim it straight, his arrow will undoubtedly go either to one side or short of the target.

ऊर्ध्वं भवेत् चापमुष्टिर्गुणमुष्टिरधो भवेत्।
स मुक्तो मार्गणो लक्ष्यादूर्ध्वं याति न संशयः।। 134।।

134. If the bow is drawn in *ūrdhavsandhāna* mode of shooting (or stave is kept above head), and the bowstring is directed downward, an arrow released from such a position will undoubtedly veer far above from the target.

मोक्षणे चैव बाणस्य चापमुष्टिरधो भवेत्।
गुणमुष्टिर्भवेदूर्ध्वं तदाधोगामिनी गतिः।। 135।।

135. While shooting an arrow, if the bow is drawn in '*adhaḥsandhāna*' mode (or stave is kept lower to the body) and the bow-string is held at a higher level, then the arrow released from such a position will be deflected downwards.

अथ शुद्धगतयः

The Successful Targets or Correct Trajectory of Arrows

लक्ष्यवाणाग्रदृष्टिनां संगतिस्तु यदा भवेत्।
तदानीमुज्झितो बाणो लक्ष्यान्न स्खलति ध्रुवम्।। 136।।

136. The right time to shoot is when the target, the tip of the arrow, and the gaze of the shooter are in one line. In such a situation the shooter never misses the target.

निर्दोषः शब्दहीनश्च सममुष्टिद्वयोकिंतः।
भिनत्ति दृढभेद्यानि सायको नास्ति संशयः।। 137।।

137. If the target and tip at the arrow and shooter's eye are aligned, then the arrow is bound to shoot the target.

स्वाकृष्टस्तेजितो यश्च सुशुद्धो गाढमुष्टितः।
नरनागाश्वकायेषु न स तिष्ठति मार्गणः।। 138।।

138. An arrow that is sharpened well at the tip and is fitted with feathers of a bird and discharged from a firm grip with force, can pierce through the body of a human being or an elephant or a horse.

अथ श्रेष्ठयोद्धा लक्षणानि

Characteristic of the Best Warrior

यस्य तृणसमा बाणा यस्येन्धनसमं धनुः।
यस्य प्राणसमा मौर्वी स धन्वी धन्वीनां वरः।। 139।।

139. A shooter who is able to handle his arrows lightly like grass, whose bow works like burning fuel and the who keeps his bow-string safe from any type of damage like his life, he is considered to be the best warrior.

अथ दृढचतुष्कम्

Four tough Targets

अयश्चर्म घटश्चैव मृत्पिण्डं च चतुष्ट्यम्।
यो भिनत्ति न तस्येषुर्वज्रेणापि विदीर्यते।। 140।।

140. If an archer is able to pierce the following four types of (tough) targets, namely, those made of metal, leather, earthen pot, and a lump of earth, his arrows cannot be countered even by a thunderbolt.

सार्धागुंलप्रमाणेन लोहपात्राणि कारयेत्।

तानि भित्त्वैकबाणेन दृढघाती भवेन्नरः ।। 141 ।।

141. Iron plates measuring the thickness of half-finger should be prepared (as targets for exercise). A shooter who pierces such plates with a single arrow is known as '*dṛḍhaghātī*' a tough marksman (marksman of tough targets).

चर्तुविंशति चर्माणि यो भिनत्तीषुणा नरः ।
तस्य बाणो गजेन्द्रस्य कायं निर्भिद्य गच्छति ।। 142 ।।

142. A warrior who can pierce twenty-four pieces of leather with a single arrow can pierce even the body of a powerful elephant.

भ्राम्यंजले घटो वेध्यश्चक्रे मृतपिण्डकं तथा ।
भ्रमन्ति वेधयेद्यो हि दृढभेदी स उच्यते ।। 143 ।।

143. An archer, who can hit an earthen jar in whirling water or a lump of earth which is in a rotating condition in potter's wheel or any other moving object, he is known as '*dṛḍhabhedhī*' meaning 'a tough marksman'.

अयस्तु काकतुण्डेन चर्म्म चारामुखेन हि ।
मृत्पिण्डं च घटं चैव विध्येत्सूचीमुखेन वै ।। 144 ।।

144. A target made of metal can be pierced by '*kākatuṇḍa*' (beak of the crow) arrow-head and targets of leather (like shields or armour) can be pierced by '*ārāmukha*' (awl type) serrated arrowhead. An earthen jar or a lump of earth may be hit by the '*sūcīmukha*' arrowhead.

अथ चित्रविधिः

Citravidhi (Technical Fight/Coumuflage War)

बाणभंगकरावर्त्तः काष्ठच्छेदनमेव च।
बिन्दुकं गोलकयुग्मं यो वेत्ति स जयी भवेत्।। 145।।

145. One who knows how to counter and cut an arrow by tilting his hands, and one who knows how to pierce a piece of wood, or one who knows how to score points in a shooting range (*Vinduka* i.e. *Chāndmārī*) and one who can pierce two round balls (*golakayuga*) at a time, always becomes victorious.

लक्ष्यस्थाने धृतं काण्डं सम्मुखं छेदयेत्ततः।
किंचिद् मुष्टिं विधाय स्वां तिर्यग्द्विफलकेषुणा।। 146।।

146. One can easily cut an arrow placed as a target with the help of two-bladed arrows with a little curved fist or an arrow with a circular tip (like a crescent moon).

संमुखं बाणमायान्तं तिर्यक्बाणं न संचरेत्।
प्राज्ञः शरेण यश्छिन्द्याद् बाणच्छेदी स उच्यते।। 147।।

147. But if an arrow is rushing in front of the shooter, he should not shoot in a curved way, rather a wise archer should combat/cut the arrow approaching towards him by taking a transverse position. If he is successful in doing so he is known as '*Vāṇacchedī*' meaning 'one who combats/cuts an arrow in the air'.

अथ धनुर्धराणाम् वर्णनम्

Classification of Shooter/Archer

काष्ठऽश्वकेशं संयम्य तत्र बध्वा वराटिकाम्।
हस्तेन भ्राम्यमाणं च यो हन्ति सो धनुर्धरः।। 148।।

148. A cowrie is tied with a horse-hair to a piece of wood as a target and the piece of wood is spun. If the shooter is able to hit the cowrie tied with horsehair to the spinning piece of wood, he is known as *Dhanurdhara*, meaning 'a real expert shooter'.

लक्ष्यस्थाने न्यसेत्काष्ठं सार्द्र गोपुच्छसन्निभम् ।
यश्छिन्द्यात्तत् क्षुरप्रेण काष्ठच्छेदी स जायते ।। 149 ।।

149. A piece of wet wood shaped like a cow's tail is placed as a target. The person who can pierce this wooden piece from a distance with the help of *kṣurapra* (horse-shoe shaped arrow-head) is known as '*Kāṣṭ hachettā*' meaning 'a piercer of wood'.

लक्ष्ये बिन्दुं न्यसेच्छुभ्रं शुभ्रबन्धूकपुष्पवत् ।
हन्ति तं बिन्दुकं यस्तु चित्रयोधा स जायते ।। 150 ।।

150. If a white point is placed on the target that looks like a white '*Bandhuka*[1] or '*Vijayasāra*' flower, a shooter who is able to hit that point is called as '*citrayodhā'*.

अथ धावल्लक्ष्यम्

Hitting the Moving Targets

काष्ठगोलयुगं क्षिप्तं दूरमूर्ध्वं पुरा स्थितैः ।
असम्प्राप्तं शरं पृष्ठे तद् गोपुच्छमुखेन हि ।। 151 ।।

यो हन्ति शरयुग्मेन शीघ्रसंधानयोगतः ।
स स्याद्धनुर्भृतां श्रेष्ठः पूजितः सर्वपार्थिवैः ।। 152 ।।

151-152. If an archer is able to pierce with the help of two *Gopuccha* arrows (implanted by him immediately on the bow) two wooden balls thrown high in the air by the person standing in front of him before they struck the ground, the archer becomes the best of archers (best marksman of moving targets) and is respected by all kings.

[1] A kind of a flower which bloom at mid-day.

रथस्थेन गजस्थेन हयस्थेन च पत्तिना।
धावता वै श्रमः कार्य्यो लक्ष्यं हन्तुं सुनिश्चतम्।। 153।।

153. Irrespective of whether a shooter rides on the chariot or an elephant, or on horse's back or moves on foot, he must do practice even while moving to achieve a sure shot success in his aim.

अथ विधिः

Method of Shooting

वामादायाति यल्लक्ष्यं दक्षिणं हि प्रधावति।
तच्छिन्द्याच्चापमाकृष्य सव्येनैव च पाणिना।। 154।।

154. If the target to be hit is in motion and if it comes from the left side and passes through the right side, then the object should be shot by drawing the bow in the left hand.

तथैव दक्षिणायान्तं विध्येद्बाणाद्धनुर्धरः।
आलीढक्रममारोप्य त्वरा हन्याच्च तं नरः।। 155।।

155. If the target moves from right to left, then the archer should shoot it by drawing the bow in *ālīḍha* way.

वायोरपि बलं दृष्ट्वा वामदक्षिणवाहतः ।
लक्ष्यं संसाधयेदेवं गाधिपुत्र नृपात्मजः।। 156।।

156. O son of the king Gadhī! First, ascertain the strength of the wind that is blowing through north and south and then only fix your aim.

वायुः पृष्ठे दक्षिणे च वहन् सूचयते बलम्।
सम्मुखीनश्च वामश्च भटानां भंगसूचकः।। 157।।

157. If the wind blows either at the right side or at the back of the shooter, then he becomes successful in hitting the target. But he cannot succeed if the wind passes by the left side or through the front portion.

अथ शब्दवेधित्वम्
Shooting at Sound

लक्ष्यस्थाने न्यसेत्कांस्यपात्रं हस्तद्वयान्तरे।
ताडयेच्छर्कराभिस्तच्छब्दः संजायते यथा।। 158।।

158. Pots made of bell-metal should be kept at a distance of two hands (36 inches) from the target. Another person hit the pot with pebbles (*śarkarā*) so that a sound is produced.

यत्र चैवोद्यते शब्दस्तं सम्यक्तत्र चिन्तयेत्।
कर्णेन्द्रियमनोयोगाल्लक्ष्यं निश्चयतां नयेत्।। 159।।

159. An archer has to concentrate on the source of the sound and has to determine the location of the target with the power of audition without looking at it.

पुनः शर्करया तच्च ताडयेच्छब्दहेतवे।
पुनर्निश्चयतां नेयं शब्दस्थानानुसारतः।। 160।।

160. The bell metal may be hit again with pebbles for producing sound and the shooter has to determine the location of the target again following the sound.

ततः किचित्कृतं दूरं नित्यं नित्यं विधानतः।
लक्ष्यं समभ्यसेद् ध्वान्ते शब्दवेधनहेतवे।। 161।।

161. When one gets expertise in such shooting, the distance of the target can be increased gradually. The practice should be done during darkness.

ततो बाणेन हन्यात्तदवधानेन तीक्ष्णधीः।
एतच्च दुष्करं कर्म भाग्ये कस्यापि सिद्ध्यति।। 162।।

162. After ascertaining the target based on sound, an extremely intelligent shooter should hit the target with earnest attention. But this work is rather difficult and very few who are fortunate enough can do it.

अथ प्रत्यागमनम्
Military Exercise

खगं बाणन्तु राजेन्द्र प्रक्षिपेद्वायुसन्मुखे।
रंजकस्य च नालिकाभिरतोह्यागमन् भवेत्।। 163।।

163. O, great King! when khaga (meaning arrow) shot through the *nālikā* (full of gunpowder) in the direction where the wind is blowing, it comes back to the shooter obviously.

एवं श्रमविधि कुर्याद्यावत्सिद्धिः प्रजायते।
श्रमे सिद्धे च वर्षासु नैव ग्राह्यं धनुष्करे।। 164।।

164. Thus the shooting practice should be continued till the time success is achieved. When shooting practice is perfected, an archer may abandon the practice. It is also forbidden to do practice during rainy days.

पूर्वाभ्यासस्य शस्त्राणामविस्मरणहेतवे।
मासद्वयं श्रमं कुर्यात्प्रतिवर्षं शरदृतौ।। 165।।

165. An archer is advised to do shooting practice for two full months during autumn, so that he may not forget the art of weapons he acquired earlier. [The months of August and September comprise the season of Autumn in India.]

ततस्तु साधयेन्मन्त्रान्वेदोक्तान् आगमोदितान्।
अस्त्राणां कर्मसिद्धयर्थं जपहोमविधानतः।। 166।।

166. During the period of intermission, a warrior is advised to achieve perfection in the *mantras* cited in the Vedas as well as *Agamas* for achieving success in the art of operation of various weapons operated by *mantras* as per scriptural injunctions.

ब्राह्मं नारायणं शैवमैन्द्रं वायव्यवारुणे।
आग्नेयं चापरास्त्राणि गुरुदत्तानि साधयेत्।। 167।।

167. A warrior should strive to learn the operation of weapons named '*Brāhma*'(invented by Brahmā), '*Nārāyaṇa*' (invented by Nārāyaṇa), '*Śaiva*' (invented by Śiva), '*Aindra*' (invented by Indra), '*Vāyavya*'(invented by Vāyu), '*Vāruṇa*' (invented by Varuṇa), '*Āgneya*' (invented by Agni) and other weapons given by the preceptor.

मनोवाक्कर्मर्भिभाव्यं लब्धास्त्रेण शुचिष्मता।
अपात्रमसमर्थं च दहन्त्यस्त्राणि पुरुषम्।। 168।।

168. A person who has attained excellence in the operation of divine weapons operated by *mantra* should be fare and pure in his heart, speech, and action. These weapons kill an unworthy and incapable operator.

प्रयोगं चोपसंहारं यो वेत्ति स धनुर्द्धरः।
सामान्ये कर्म्मणि प्राज्ञो नैवास्त्राणि प्रयोजयेत्।। 169।।

169. A warrior who knows the operation and withdrawal of these weapons is known as a real bowman. A wise archer or musketeer does not use his arms in the day to day affairs.

अथास्त्राणि

Missiles

अथास्त्राणि प्रवक्ष्यामि सावधानाऽवधारय।
ब्रह्मास्त्रं प्रथमं प्रोक्तं द्वितीयं ब्रह्मदण्डकम्।। 170।।
ब्रह्मशिरस्तृतीयंच तुर्य्यं पाशुपतं मतम्।
वायव्यं पंचमं प्रोक्तमागेयं षष्ठकं स्मृतम्।। 171।।
नरसिंहं सप्तमंच तेषां भेदाह्यनन्तकाः।
ससंहारं सविज्ञेयं शृणु गाधे यथातथम्।। 172।।

170-172. O son of Gādhi (Viśvāmitra)! let me tell you about the operation and recall of the different types of missiles. Listen carefully. They are 1. *Brahmāstra* (*Brahmāstra* was invented by Brahmā. It was used to kill a particular enemy or make him captive). 2. *Brahmadaṇḍa* (It was a weapon of mass destruction. It was also used to combat *Brahmāstra*). 3. *Brahmaśira* (A powerful missile. It's use was taught by Acharya Droṇa to Arjuna). 4. *Pāśupatāstra* (It was also a weapon of mass destruction. Arjuna learnt its operation from Śiva). 5. *Vāyavya* (It was also a weapon of mass destruction. It used to create storms to kill enemies en mass). 6. *Āganeyāstra* (It was also a weapon of mass destruction. It used to kill enemies en mass by creating fire all around) and 7. *Narsiṁha astra.* These weapons are divided into many sub-types.

वेदमात्रा सर्वशास्त्रं गृह्यते दीप्यतऽथवा।
तत्प्रयोगं शृणु प्राज्ञ ब्रह्मास्त्रं प्रथमं शृणु।। 173।।

173. All *Śāstras* are based upon the Vedas or derive their strength from Vedas. I will speak about the *Brahmāstra* first.

अथास्त्राणां मन्त्रसंस्कारः

Māntrika Operation of Missiles

दादिदान्तांच सावित्रीं विपरीतां जपेत् सुधीः।
जप्त्वा पूर्वां निखर्वंच त्वभिमन्त्रय विधिवच्छरम्।। 174।।
क्षिपेच्छत्रुषु सहसा नश्यन्ति सर्वजातयः।
बाला वृद्धाश्च गर्भस्था ये च योद्धं समागताः।। 175।।
सर्वे ते नाशमायन्ति मम चैव प्रसादतः।
यथातथं दादिदान्तं जपेत् संहारसिद्धये।। 176।।

174-176. A wise warrior should recite *Sāvitrī* (*Gāyatrī*) *mantra* in a reverse order before operating *Brahmāstra.* The weapon thus cast destroys people at mass scale including young, old, the foetus in the womb, and everybody present in the battle-field. Just to achieve perfection in withdrawing the weapon *Gāyatrī mantra* should be recited in its original order.

ब्रह्मदण्डं प्रवक्ष्यामि प्रणवं पूर्वमुच्चरेत्।
ततः प्रचोदयाज्ज्ञेयं ततो नो यो धियः क्रमात्।। 177।।
ततो धीमहि देवस्य ततो भर्गो वरेण्यम्।
सवितुस्तच्च योक्तव्यममुकशत्रुं तथैव च।। 178।।

177-178. For the operation of *Brahmadaṇḍa*, the fighter has to recite *praṇava* (Om) first followed by *Gāyatrī mantra* in reverse order such as - *pracodayāt no yo ghiyo dhimahi devasya bhargo vareṇyaṁ savituḥ tat* - and then the particular enemy's name should also be added.

ततो हन हन हूं फट्' जप्त्वा पूर्वं द्विलक्ष्यकम्।
अभिमन्य शरं तद्वत् प्रक्षिपेच्छत्रुषु स्फुटम्।। 179।।

नश्यन्ति शत्रवः सर्वे यमतुल्या अपि ध्रुवम्।
एतदेव विपर्य्यस्तं जपेत् संहारसिद्धये।। 180।।

179-180. After uttering '*hana hana hūṁ phaṭ'* twice in view of the target, he can operate *Brahmadaṇḍa* missile on the enemy. The enemy even if he equals to Yama will be perished. For withdrawing the same missile he has to utter the *Gāyatrī mantra* in the reverse order (original order).

ब्रह्मशिरः प्रवक्ष्यामि प्रणवं पूर्वमुच्चरेत्।
'धियो यो नः प्रचोदयात्' 'भर्गो देवस्य धीमहि'।
'तत्सवितुर्वरेण्यम्' शत्रून्मे हन हनेति च।। 181।।

'हूं फट्' चैवप्रयोक्तव्यं क्षिपेद् ब्रह्मशिरस्ततः।
पुरश्चर्य्यां पुरस्कृत्वा त्रिलक्ष्यं नियतः शुचिः।। 182।।

नश्यन्ति सर्वे रिपवः सर्वे देवासुरा अपि।
इदमेव प्रयोक्तव्यः विपर्य्यस्तं विकर्षणे।। 183।।

181-183. To operate *Brahmaśira*, the warrior has to utter '*Praṇava'* (*Oṁ*) followed by '*dhiyo yo naḥ pracodayāt'* '*bhargo devasya dhīmahi'* '*tatsaviturvareṇyam*' and lastly '*śatrūn me hana hana'* '*hūṁ phaṭ*' thrice keeping in view the target in mind. It destroys all enemies even the devas (living in North) or asuras (living in the west). For withdrawing this missile, the same *mantra* should be recited in just the reverse way.

पाशुपतास्त्रम्
Pāśupatāstra

अतः परं प्रवक्ष्यामि चास्त्रं पाशुपतन्तव।
यस्य विज्ञानमात्रेण नश्यन्ति सर्वशत्रवः।। 184।।

184. Now I shall let you know about the operation of *Pāśupatāstra*. If one is well versed in the operation of *Pāśupata* missile, he can kill all enemies.

दादिदान्तां च सावित्रीं प्रोच्य प्रणवमेव च।
'श्लीं पशुं हुं फट्' 'अमुकशत्रून् हन हन हुं फट्'।। 185।।

जप्त्वा पूर्व्वं द्विलक्ष्यंच ततः पाशुपतं क्षिपेत्।
पुनस्तदेव व्यस्तं स्यात् संहारे तां नियोजयेत्।
एतत् पाशुपतं चास्त्रं सर्वशत्रुनिवारणम्।। 186।।

185-186. For operating *Pāśupata* missile, a warrior should utter praṇava then recite '*ślīṁ paśuṁ huṁ phaṭ*' '*amuk śatrūn hana hana huṁ phaṭ*' twice keeping in view the enemy in mind. For withdrawing *Pāśupatāstra* one has to recite the above-mentioned phrase in a reverse order.

वच्मि वायव्यमस्त्रं ते येन नश्यन्ति शत्रवः।
ओं वायव्यया या वायव्ययान्योर्वाय या वा तथा।। 187।।
अमुकशत्रूम् हन हन हूं फट् चैव प्रकीर्त्तयेत्।
पूर्व्वमेव तथा जप्त्वा नियुतं द्वितयन्तथा।। 188।।

पुनः संहाररूपेण संहारं च प्रकल्पयेत्।
अस्त्रं वायव्यकं नाम देवानामपि वारणम्।। 189।।

187-189. Now I shall let you know about the

operation of *Vāyavyāstra* which can also bring mass-scale destruction to the enemy. For operation, one has to utter '*Oṁ Vāyavyayā yā vāyavyayā nyorvāya yā vā*' and '*amuka śatrūn* (name the enemy) *hana hana hūṁ phaṭ*' two times. One can also withdraw the same by uttering the above phrase in the reverse order. This *Vāyavyāstra* can defeat even the experts of warfare.

आग्नेयं संप्रवक्ष्यामि यतः परभयं दहेत्।
ओमग्निस्त्यता हृदंच शिवं वनाश्वाविणि च।। 190।।
हगादशरूपनः सद वे ति ततः क्रमात्।
हादति तोयति राम तथा मसो हित्वा वान्।। 191।।

सुसेदवेदया च वदेत् अमुकादीं स्ततो वदेत्।
पूर्वोक्तांश्च कृत्वा शस्त्रेभियोजयेत्।
इमं मन्त्रं पुनर्व्यस्तं संहारे चैव योजयेत्।। 192।।

190-192. Now I shall let you know about the operation of *Āgneyāstra,* which can remove the fear from the enemy. For the operation of *Āgneyāstra*, one has to utter '*Oṁ agnistyatā hṛdañca śivaṁ vanāśvāviṇi hagādaśarūpanaḥ sad ve ti tataḥ hādati, toyati, rāma, tathā maso hitvā vān susedavedayā*' afterwards one should pronounce the name of the enemy. For withdrawing the same the above phrase can be uttered in the reverse order.

'ओं वज्रनखवज्रदंष्टायुधाय महासिंहाय हुं फट्'।
पूर्वं जप्त्वा च लक्षं हि नरसिंहंच योजयेत्।
सिंहरूपास्ततो बाणा पतन्ति शात्रवे वने।। 193।।

193. The seventh missile named as *Narasiṁha* can be operated by uttering '*Oṁ vajra-nakha vajra-daṇṣṭ rāyudhāya mahāsiṅghāya hūṁ phaṭ*' keeping in view the target in mind. When this *Narasiṁha* missile is operated the bullets powerful like a lion are showered upon the crowd of the enemy.

पूर्वोक्तेन प्रकारेण संहारंच प्रकल्पयेत्।
संक्षेपतो महाभाग तवोक्तानि महामते।
भेदास्तेषां शिवेनैव ह्यनन्ताः परिकीर्त्तिताः।। 194।।

194. The withdrawal of *Narasiṁha* missle can also be done by reciting the above-mentioned phrase in reverse order like that of other missiles. I have narrated briefly the operation of some missiles. Śiva, an expert in *Dhanurveda*, has explained numerous types of missiles.

अथौषधिः
Medication

हस्तार्के लांगलीकन्दो गृहीतस्य लेपतः।
शूरस्यापि रणे पुंसो दर्पं हरति कातरः।। 195।।

195. By applying a coat of the paste of the root of *Lāṅgali* (*Jalapippalī*) collected on the *Hasta Nakṣatra*, even a coward person wins over the mighty fighter.

गृहीत्वा योगनक्षत्रैरपामार्गस्य मूलकम्।
लेपमात्रेण वीराणां सर्वशस्त्रनिवारणम्।। 196।।

196. By taking the root of an '*apāmarga*' (Achyranthes Aspera) plant on the *Puṣya Nakṣatra* and anointing its paste all over the body, a warrior gets the power to ward off all weapons of the enemies.

अधःपुष्पी शंखपुष्पी लज्जालुर्गिरिकर्णिका।
नलिनी सहदेवी च पत्रमोंर्जारकयोस्तथा।। 197।।
विश्णुक्रान्ता च सर्वासां जटा ग्राह्या रवेर्दिने।
बद्धा भुजे विलेपाद्वा काये शस्त्रापवारकाः।। 198।।

197-198. The roots of the plants *Adhaḥpuṣpī* (Pimpinella), *Saṅkhapuṣpī* (Canscora Decussata), *Lajjālu* (Mmosa), '*Girikarṇikā*' (a variety of Acyranthes with white blossoms), *'Nalinī'*, *'Sahadevī'* (Centratherum anthelmaricum), *'Mūñja'*, *'Arka'* and

'Viṣṇukrāntā' protect from weapons when tied on the arms or applied over the body.

गृहीतं हस्तनक्षत्रे चूर्णं छुच्छुन्दरीभवम्।
तत्प्रभावाद्गजः पुंसः संमुखो नैति निश्चितम्।। 199।।

199. By the influence of the powder obtained from *'chuchundarī'* (Leguminosae) plant on the *'Hasta nakṣatra'* day, even an elephant does not dare to come in front of the warrior.

छुच्छुन्दरी श्रीफलपुष्पचूर्णरालिप्तगात्रस्य नरस्य दूरात्।
आघाय गन्ध द्विरदाऽतिमत्तामद त्यजत्कसरिणा यथागम।। 200।।

200. If the powder of *'chuchundarī'* plant and *'vilva'* tree (wood apple) are anointed on the body of a warrior, then the odour produced is sure to calm down even a mad elephant and a lion.

श्वेताद्रिकर्णिकामूलं पाणिस्थं वारयेद् गजम्।
श्वेतकण्टारिकामूलं व्याघ्रादीनां भयं हरेत्।। 201।।

201. The root of the white *adri karṇikā* tree (creeper of clitoria genus) if worn in hands can prevent the advent of an elephant, and the root of white *kaṇṭ ārikā* (Solanum Jacquini) prevents the approach of a tiger.

पुष्यार्कोत्पाटिते मूले पाठाया मुखसंस्थिते।
देहं स्फुरति नो तीक्ष्णमण्डलाग्रै रणे नृणाम्।। 202।।

202. The root of *Pāṭhā* (aloe plant) uprooted on (*Puṣya Nakṣatra*) day if retained in the mouth in *Mūla* constellation, the warrior cannot have fear, even from fighters equipped with sharp and devastating weapons.

गन्धार्य्या उत्तरं मूलं मुखस्थं संमुखागतम्।
शस्त्रौघं वारयेत्तत्र पुष्यार्के विधिनोद्धृतम्।। 203।।

203. If the end of the root of the *'gandhārī'* (a kind of a decorative tree) is collected on Pusya constellation, and put in the mouth, it increases the immunity of the warrior i.e. the wounds caused by the weapons heal up soon.

शुभ्रायाः परपुंखाया जटानीली जटाथवा।
भुजे शिरसि वक्त्रे वा स्थिता शस्त्रनिवारिका।
भूपाहिचोरभीतिघ्नी गृहीता पुष्पभास्करे।। 204।।

204. In the Puṣya constellation, if '*śubhra* (white)' '*parapuṅkhā*' or '*jaṭānilī*' or *Jaṭāmasī* (Indian spikenard) is taken and applied on arms, head and face, it heals the wounds of the weapons and ward off the fear of the king, thieves, and serpents.

ततो व्यूहादिभिर्युद्धकथनम्
Battle Formations

ये राजपुत्राः सामन्ताः आप्ताः सेवकजातयः।
तान्सर्वानात्मनः पार्श्वे रक्षायै स्थापयेन्नृपः।। 205।।

205. The King should keep around him for his protection all princes, feudal lords, or subordinate kings and all loyal soldiers.

परस्परानुरक्ता ये योधा शांर्ग धनुर्धराः।
युद्धज्ञास्तुरगारूढास्ते जयन्ति रणे रिपून्।। 206।।

206. The Warriors even armed with Śārṅga bow (made of horn) who co-operate with each other and know battle-craft, may beat enemies while fighting them on horseback.

एकः कापुरूषो दीर्णो दारयेन्महतीं चमूम्।
तं दीर्णानुदीर्यन्ते योधाः शूरतमा अपि।
अतो वै कातरं राजा बले नैव नियोजयेत्।। 207।।

207. But a single coward soldier who breaks ranks can destroy the power of a large army. Even the most heroic and greatest fighters will suffer a breakdown of morale (they will desert with such a coward in their midst and face defeat). So the king should not appoint any such coward in the army.

द्वाविमौ पुरुषौ लोके सूर्य्यमण्डलभेदिनौ।
परिव्राड् योगयुक्तश्च रणे चाभिमुखो हतः।। 208।।

208. There are only two types of persons in this world who can penetrate even the orb of the Sun: one is the ascetic who is a high profile Yogī and the other is a hero who dies fighting in the battle.

यत्र यत्र हतः शूरः शत्रुभिः परिवेष्टितः।
अक्षयं लभते लोकं यदि क्लीवं न भाषते।। 209।।

209. If a hero dies surrounded by his enemies, it is sure that he will attain eternal fame, due to his bravery, but the eunuch is never talked about.

अथ युद्धधर्मः
War Ethics

मूर्च्छितं नैव विकलं नाशस्त्रं नान्ययोधिनम्।
पलायमानं शरणं गतं चैव न हिंसयेत्।। 210।।

210. One should not kill the Enemy who is lying unconscious or the one who is wounded, or who is devoid of weapons, or who is fighting with another warrior, or who has withdrawn or who has come for refuge.

भीरुः पलायमानाऽपि नान्वेष्टव्यो बलीयसा।
कदाच्छिूरतां याति शरणऽकृतनिश्चयः।। 211।।

211. Even a weak fighter who is running away from the war field should neither be chased nor be given asylum. sometimes he may also shed the fear of death and become aggressive and brave.

अथ विजयलक्षणानि

Symptoms of Victory

संभृत्य महतीं सेनां चतुरंगां महीपतिः।
व्यूहयित्वाग्रतः शूरान्स्थापयेज्जयलिप्सया।। 212।।

212. An emperor desirous of victory should organize his army comprising four divisions ('*caturaṅga*', i.e. the charioteers, soldiers mounted on an elephant, cavalry, and infantry) into a formation or battle array (*vyūha*) to encircle the enemy deploying valiant heroes in front of it.

पृष्ठेन वायवो यान्ति पृष्ठे भानुर्वयांसि च।
अनुप्लवते मेघाश्च यस्य तस्य रणे जयः।। 213।।

213. If the wind blows or the Sun shines behind and also if the birds and the floating clouds fly behind the back of the soldier, then he surely becomes victorious.

अपूर्णे नैव मर्त्तव्यं संपूर्णे नैव जीवनम्।
तस्माद्धैर्यं विधायैव हन्तव्या परवाहिनी।। 214।।

214. One should not die prematurely; nor can one live after one's time is up. Hence one should exercise patience and kill the enemies.

जिते लक्ष्मीर्मृते स्वर्गः कीर्त्तिश्च धरणीतले।
तस्माद्धैर्य्यं विधायैव हन्तव्या परवाहिनी।। 215।।
अधर्म्मः क्षत्रियस्यैषः यद् व्याधिं मरणं गृहे।
यदाजौ निधनं याति साऽस्य धर्म्मः सनातनः।। 216।।

215-216. If a warrior wins the war, he will earn a lot of wealth and will attain a delightful life after death. Hence one should exercise patience and kill the enemies in the war. It will be a great virtue for a soldier if he dies fighting in the war. It will be most disgraceful for a soldier if he dies of illness in his house.

अथ व्यूहानाह
Military Arrays

युवास्वरे मध्यसेना युद्धं कुर्य्यादतन्द्रिता।
द्वेसेने पार्श्वयोश्चैका पृष्ठतो रक्षयेत् सदा।
एकां विकटसेनान्तु दूरस्थां भ्रामयेद् युधि।। 217।।

217. If the young soldiers are kept in the middle of the Army, they would fight the war and win. The king should keep two groups of armies on each side and one group at the back. One group of the army should remain far and move here and there (mainly for vigilance).

दण्डव्यूहश्च शकटो वराहो मकरस्तथा।
सूचीव्यूहाऽथ गरुडः पद्मव्यूहादयो मताः।। 218।।

218. There are several types of military formations. These are *Daṇḍa* (staff array), *Śakaṭa* (or car-shaped array), *Varāha* or boar shaped array, *Matsya* or fish-shaped array, *Makara* or crocodile shaped array, *Padma* (lotus) shaped array, *Sūcimukha* or needle-shaped array and *Garuḍa* or eagle-shaped array.

एतान् व्यूहान् परिव्यूह्य सेनापतिर्वसेत् सदा।
बलाध्यक्षादिकान् सर्वान् सर्वदिक्षु नियोजयेत्।। 219।।

219. The Commander-in-chief should always form these arrays. He should deploy army commanders on all sides.

दण्डव्यूहः
Staff Array

सर्वतो भये दण्डव्यूहर रचनाकार्य्या।। 220।।

220. If there is apprehension of danger from all sides, *Daṇḍa vyūha* or staff array should be formed.

शकटव्यूहम्
Car Array

पश्चाद्देशे भये समुत्पन्ने शकटाकारेण व्यूहं रचयेत्।। 221।।

221. If there is apprehension of danger at the back, then *Śakaṭa* or car shaped array should be arranged.

पार्श्वभये वराहव्यूहो गजव्यूहो वा विधेयः।। 222।।

222. If there is the apprehension of danger on sides, then *Varāha* (boar) or *Gaja* (elephant) shaped array is prescribed.

दक्षिणावामपार्श्वयोर्भये उपस्थिते।
वराहव्यूहो गरूडव्यूहो वा कार्य्यः।। 223।।

223. If there is the apprehension of danger on the right and left sides, then *Varāha* (boar) or *Garūḍa* (eagle) shaped array should be created.

पिपीलिकाव्यूहम्
Ant Array

सन्मुखे शत्रुभये जाते पिपीलिका पंक्तिरूपः व्यूहविन्यासः
कार्य्य। स्वल्पा युद्धं कुर्य्यात् बह्वी सेना च सर्वतो भ्रमेत्।
सम भूमौ चाश्ववारा युद्धं कुर्य्युः।
जले करि तुम्बी दृतिं नौकाभिर्युद्धं विधेयम्।
पदातयो भुशुण्डीं गृहीत्वा वा धनूंषिचादाय।
वने वृक्षेष्वन्तर्धाना वारूढा भूत्वा युद्ध्यत।
स्थले चर्म्मखड्गभल्लैर्युद्ध्यत युद्धहंकारिण
स्तुंगा अग्रे स्थाप्याः अन्ये पश्चात् ।। 224।।

224. If there is the apprehension of danger of enemy on the front side, *Pipīlikā* or ant array is prescribed. A few armies should take part in the battle and the major part should move everywhere for vigilance. The cavalry should fight on the plain. For fighting in the water, one may ride on the elephant, boat, or *tumbi* (a particular type of boat made out of the hollow shell of a gourd. The infantry can fight with the help of guns or bows and arrows (missiles) after hiding behind trees or climbing on them. On land, the army can also fight with the help of shields, swords, spear. The warriors who are skilled in war strategy should be kept at the forefront and the rest should be kept behind.

सेनानयः

Commandments to the Army

तत्रादौ व्याकरणशिक्षां वक्ष्यामो राज्ञे।
नृपतिलोट् लकारस्य कुर्य्यात् कण्ठस्थितानि च।। 225।।
रूपाणि कार्य्यं सिद्ध्यर्थं ह्याज्ञैषा मम गाधिज।
मध्यमपुरुषस्यैव प्रयोगान्यो विचिन्तयेत्।। 226।।
सेनानीः प्रतिदिनं सम्यङ् न केनापि स हन्यते।
मध्यममपुरुषोद्भूताः प्रयोगाः सर्वसिद्धिदाः।
तैरेव साधयेद्राज्ञां पुरुषा राजभृत्यकाः।। 227।।

225-227. First of all, we prescribe the education of grammar to the king. The king should learn the use of verbs in the imperative mood by heart, for the sake of attaining success O' Viśvāmitra. A commander who knows how to give commands in the second person, cannot be killed by anybody. The commands given in the second person always yield the desired results. The kings and other officials of Kings should have a proper practice of giving commands in second persons.

पदातिक्रमः

Infantry

समाच्चो द्विपदा ग्राह्या ह्रसमानाः कदाचन।
कूर्द्दने धावने ये वै समास्ते कार्य्यसाधकाः।। 228।।
पश्चाद् गमनं स्थिरीकरणं शयनं धावनं तथा।

चलनं परसेनायां पार्श्वदिक्षु च कारयेत् ।। 229 ।।

228-229. The infantry or the foot soldiers should be of equal height. All of them should be equally experts in jumping and running. They should also be trained in moving backwards, standing still, lying running apace, rushing headlong into the hostile army, and moving in different directions in accordance with signals.

षष्ठ स्थाने ग्रहा येषां क्रूराः पापाः पतन्ति हि।
ते युद्ध्यतां वीरा नान्ये कार्य्यकरा यतः ।। 230 ।।
व भ ध ड छ क वर्ण ह्यादिमायां प्रकल्प्य।
तदनु हि अच वर्ण आदिकाः सर्व्वलेख्याः ।। 231 ।।
उपरिगतभवस्तान् स्थाप्य सर्वान् क्रमेण।
भवति च युवयस्या युद्ध्यतां सा प्रसेना ।। 232 ।।
यथा विवस्वान् भरतः धन्धुमारः डित्थः छत्रपतिः कुक्षिः।
अस्या वस्त्राणि पीतानि ध्वजापीता च तद्वति।
युद्धयूपस्तथा पितश्चतुरस्रांकसंयुतः ।। 233 ।।

230-233. The warriors who have in their birth calendar the inauspicious planets (such as Saturn, Mars, Rahu, and Ketu) in the sixth position should fight. Others will not be successful. The persons whose names starts with *va*, *bha*, *dha*, *ḍa*, *cha*, and *ka* letters should be placed in the forefront of the army, followed by those whose names start with vowels.

For example, soldiers with names like Vivasvān, Bharat, Dhundhumāra, Ḍitha, Chatrapati, Kukṣi, etc. should be placed in the forefront of the army.

The colour of the cloth and that of the flagstaff of the army should be yellow. By fixing up the yellow banners and also the yellow coloured *yūpa*[1] (having a square symbol on it) on the battlefield, one is sure to

---

[1] *Yūpa* is a wooden framwork close to which oblation material is kept.

win.

श्वेतरक्तहरिकृष्णाश्चान्या सेना हित्वादिवत्।
कर्त्तव्यापार्थिवैर्नित्यं जयलाभसुखेच्छुभिः।। 234।।

234. The kings who are desirous to win the battle should arrange the army in five groups named white, red, green, black, and ordinary one.

ब्रह्मा विष्णुश्च रूद्रश्च चन्द्रसूर्यौ यथाक्रमम्।
अधीशाः पंचसेनानां विज्ञेयाः शृणु गाधिज।। 235।।

235. Listen to O Viśvāmitra! that Brahmā, Viṣṇu, Rudra, Candra, and Sūrya are respectively the commander of the five groups of the armies described above.

ब्रह्मा रूद्रबले जीयाद्विष्णुश्चन्द्रबले जयेत्।
रूद्रः सूर्य्यबलं प्राप्य चन्द्रो ब्रह्मबलं युधि।
सूर्य्यो विष्णुबलं लब्ध्वा जयेच्चैव न संशयः।। 236।।

236. Brahmā gains power from Rudra, Viṣṇu wins by the influence of Candra, Śiva wins through the power of Sūrya, and Candra wins the battle through the power of Brahmā. Sūrya gets power from Viṣṇu and wins the battle accordingly.

अ ब्रह्मा विष्णुरिरुद्र उश्चन्द्रस्त्वे च भास्करः।
ओ ज्ञेयो पार्थिवैर्नित्यं अस्त्रशस्त्रविचक्षणैः।। 237।।

237. The kings who excel in the operation of weapons and missiles should know that commander Brahmā is known by 'a', Viṣṇu is known by 'i', Rudra is known by 'u', Candra is known by 'e' and Sūrya by 'o'.

प्राप्य स्वं स्वं बलं सेना पूर्वोक्ता युद्धगा यदि।
क्षणार्द्धेनारीन् सर्वान्मारयन्तीति रुद्रवाक्।। 238।।

238. If the commanders start fighting a war with the help of armies assigned to them, they can destroy enemies in short time.

अथाश्वक्रमः
Training of Horses

मण्डलं चतुरस्रं च गोमूत्रं चार्द्धचन्द्रकम्।
नागपाशक्रमेणैव भ्रामयेत् कटपंचकम्।। 239।।

239. The horses should be trained in the following five movements: circular, square, crescent-shaped, cow's urine's path shaped and snake or zigzag-shaped movement[1].

अथ हस्तिक्रमः
Training of Elephants

गजानां पर्वतारोहणं जलगमनं धावनम् उत्थानम्।
उपवेशनम् अलातचक्रादिभिर्भीतिनिवारणम कार्य्यम्।। 240।।

240. The military training of elephants includes mountaineering, wading through water, running, jumping, rising, sitting, etc. They should also be made fearless from fire by putting up fire circles.

रथक्रमः
Chariots

रथाश्वसाधनन्तु समादिस्थले विधेयम्।। 241।।

241. The horses should be trained to pull the chariots on the plain.

अथ सेनापति करणविधिं वक्ष्यामः
Selection of Commander in Chief

शृणु भो राजर्षे विश्वामित्र आकारविद्याबलयुक्तं

---

[1] Kautalya's *Arthaśāstra* (BK II, Ch. 30) provides us with a detailed account of the various movements employed for the training of horses.

क्षत्रियसेनापतिं विद्ध्यात् । तस्यैते नियमाः समस्तवाहिनीं एकदृष्ट्यावलोकयेत् । अन्यत् सर्व्वान् पदातीन् परिश्रमसदृशमधिकारं दद्यात्। व्यूहरचनायामति निपुणाश्च भवेत् स एव सेनानीर्विधेयः।। 242 ।।

242. Listen to O sage Viśvāmitra! the commander in chief should be physically fit, learned and a powerful person of Kṣatriya personality. He should treat the entire army equally without any favour and fervour. He should also be intelligent enough in arranging the army in an array and also provide such work to the infantry that fits it.

अथ शिक्षा

Training and Education

तत्रादौ पठनपाठनविधिं ब्रूमः।
आदौ क्षात्रकोशव्याकरण सूत्राण्यध्येतव्यानि द्वावध्यायौ।
सप्तमाष्टमौमनोर्मिताक्षराव्यवहाराध्यायश्च जयार्णव।। 243 ।।
विष्णुयामलविजयाख्यस्वरशास्त्राण्यपराणि च।
पठितव्यानि ततः सरहस्यं धनुर्व्वेदमापठेत्।। 244 ।।

243-244. Let us first narrate the method of teaching and learning. The defence personnel should study grammar, military lexicon, *Sūtra* texts, the seventh and eighth chapters of *Manusmṛti*, chapters on *Vyavahāra* on *Mitākṣarā*[1], *Jayārṇava*, *Viṣṇuyāmala*, *Vijayākhya*, *Svaraśāstra* and others. After learning these texts, they can study *Dhanurveda* with all its branches.

हन्ताव्याहन्तव्योपदेशः

[1] *Mitākṣarā* was written during 1070-1100 by Vijñāneśvara. It contains commentaries on *Yajñavalkya Smṛti.* It is considered as the most authoritative exposition on Hindu law of succession as prevailing over whole of India. Britishers referred to this text while framing the Hindu code bill.

The Ethics of the War

सुप्तं प्रसुप्तमुन्मत्तं ह्यकच्छं शस्त्रवर्जितम्।
बालं स्त्रियं दीनवाक्यं धावन्तं नैवघातयेत्।। 245।।

245. The person who is asleep, who is unconscious, who is insane, who is devoid of clothes or weapons, the children, ladies, the helpless praying for mercy, the one who has deserted the battlefield should not be killed.

धर्म्मार्थे यः त्यजेत् प्राणान् किं तीर्थे च जपे च किम्।
मुक्तिभागी भवेत् साऽपि निरयं नाधिगच्छति।। 246।।

246. The soldier who meets death on the battlefield for the sake of protecting *Dharma* deserves salvation. Neither visit of a *Tīrtha*, nor penance yields such fruit as the death on the battlefield. A person dying on the battlefield for the sake of protecting *dharma* never attains hell.

ब्राह्मर्णो गवार्थे वा स्त्रीणां बालवधेषु च।
प्राणत्यागपरो यस्तु स वै मोक्षमवाप्नुयात्।। 247।।

247. The person who lays his life while protecting visionary persons, cows, ladies, or children is sure to attain salvation.

Select Bibliography

Agni Purāṇa: Chawkhamba Sanskrit Series, Varanasi.

Agni Purāṇa: Gita Press Gorakhpur.

Aitareya Brāhmana with Sāyaṇa-Bhaṣya: Edited by Kashinatha Shastri, Poona, 1977.

Aitareya and *Kauṣitaki Brāhmaṇas of Ṛgveda:* Edited by Keith, A.B., Delhi, Motilal, 1971.

Aparājita Pṛcchā: by Bhuvan Deva, Gayakwar Oriental Series, Baroda.

Atharvaveda: Translated into Hindi by Kṣema Karaṇa Trivedī, Dayananda Sansthan, New Delhi.

Atharvaveda: Edited by Raghvir, S. V. Granthamāla, Lahore, 1936.

Auśanasa Dhanurveda Saṅkalanam: Compiled and edited by Rajaram Shastri, DAV College Lahore, Vikrami Saṁvat, 1980.

Bṛhaddevatā: Translated into English by Macdonell, A.A. Harward Oriental Series, 1904.

Garga Saṅhitā: Venkateshwar Press, Mumbai.

Gopatha Brāhmaṇa: Translated in Hindi by Kṣemakaraṇa Trivedi, Prayāga, 1920.

Jaiminīya Brāhmaṇa: Edited by Raghvir, Lokesh Chandra, SVS Nagpur, 1954.

Jāmadagnya Dhanurveda: Rājarājeśvara Paraśurāma.

Kaṭha Saṁhitā: Edited by Shripada Sharma, Aundh, 1942.

Kauṭalya Arthaśāstra: Commentary by Mahamahopadhyaya Ganapati Shastri, Trivendram, 1924.

Kāmandakīya Nītisāra: Compiled and edited by Jayamangala Upadhaya, Anandashrama Sanskrit Series No. 136.

Kāṭhaka Saṅhitā: Edited by Shripada Sharma, Aundh, 1943.

Maitrāyaṇī Saṅhitā: Edited by Shripada Sharma, Aundh, 1943.

Mahābhāratam: Gitapress Gorakhapur.

Mahābhāratam: Bhandarkar Research Institute, Poona.

Max Müller, F.: *Vedas,* Calcutta, Sushil Gupta, 1956.

Max Müller, F.: *Vedic Hymns,* Motilal, Delhi.

Mānasollāsa by Somadeva: Gayakawar Oriental Series No. 20, Baroda.

Nītiprakāśikā of Maharṣi Vaiśampāyana: Edited by T. Chandrashekhara, Govt. Press Madras, 1953.

Raghunandan Sharma: *Vedic Sampatti,* Bombay, 2016.

Ravi Prakash Arya: *Researches into Vedic and Linguistic Studies,* Indian Foundation for Vedic Science, Delhi, 1991.

Ravi Prakash Arya: *Vedic Meteorology,* Indian Foundation for Vedic Science, Delhi, 2006.

Ravi Prakash Arya: *Vedic and Classical Sanskrit: A Contrastive Analysis of Phonological and Morphological Features,* Indian Foundation for Vedic Science, Delhi, 2007.

Ṛgbhāṣya: Dayananda Saraswati , Ajmer.

Ṛgvedādibhāṣvabhūmikā by Dayananda Saraswati: Edited by Yudhisthira Mimansaka, Bahalgarh, Sonepat, 1984.

Ṛgveda Saṅhitā: Commentaries by *Skandha, Udgitha, and Veṅkaṭamādhava,* edited by Vishvabandhu, Hoshiarpur, Punjab.

Sadāśiva Dhanurveda: Edited and Translated into English by Dr. B. Chakravarti, Self Employment Bureau, Kolkata, 2002.

Samrāṅgaṇa Sūtradhāra by Bhoja: Gayakwar Oriental Series

No. 25, Baroda.

Śatapatha Brāhmaṇa: Translated into English by Eggeling, J. Oxford, Clarenden Press.

Śatpatha Brāhmaṇa: *Vijñāna Bhāṣya* by Motilal Sharma, Jaipur.

Śatapatha Brāhmaṇa: Sāmarpaṇa Bhāṣya by Swami Samarpaṇānanda, Prabhat Ashram Meerut.

Satyārthaprakāśa : By Swami Dayananda Sarasvati.

Śāṅkhāyana Araṇyaka: Edited by Swami Shridhara Shastrin, Anandashram, Poona, 1922.

Sāṅkhāyana Gṛhya Sūtra: Edited and translated into English by Oldenberg, H., Oxford, 1886.

Śukranīti: Translated into English by Benoy Kumar Sarkar, edited Dr. Krishan Kumar, J.P. Publishing House, Delhi, 2005.

Taittirīya Brāhmaṇa: With the commentary of Bhaṭṭ abhāskara Miśra edited by Mahavir Sastrin, Mysore, 1908-21.

Trayambaka Dhanurveda: Edited by Rajaram Shastri, DAV College Lahore, Vikrami Saṁvat, 1980.

Vāsiṣṭha Dhanurveda Saṅhitā: Translated into English by Purnima Ray, J.P. Publishing House, Delhi, 2003.

Vṛhat Sāraṅgadhara Paddhati: Sanskrit Pustkalaya, Varanasi.

Vṛhat Vimānaśāstra by MaharṣI Bhārdvāja: Translated into Hindi by Brahma Muni, Srvadeshika Arya Pratinidhi Sabha, Delhi, 1958.

Yajurveda Bhāṣya: Dayananda Saraswati, Ajmer.

Yuktikalpataru by Bhojadeva: Edited by Pt. Ishwar Chandra Shastri, Siddheshwar Press, Kolkata, 1917.

Taittirīya Saṅhitā: Edited by Shripada Sharma, Aundh, 1945.

www.ingramcontent.com/pod-product-compliance
Lightning Source LLC
Chambersburg PA
CBHW050209230526
45470CB00001B/299
9788187710820